RECOGNISING ACHIEVEMENT

Information and Communication Technology for GCSE

D1495024

Denise Walmsley

Brian Sargent

Alun Hinder

Hodder & Stoughton

A MEMBER OF THE HODDER HEADLINE GROUP

004

Orders: please contact Bookpoint Ltd, 130 Milton Park, Abingdon, Oxon OX14 4SB. Telephone: (44) 01235 827720, Fax: (44) 01235 400454. Lines are open from 9.00 – 6.00, Monday to Saturday, with a 24 hour message answering service.
You can order through our website www.hodderheadline.co.uk

British Library Cataloguing in Publication Data
A catalogue record for this title is available from The British Library

ISBN 0 340 800062

First published 2001

Impression number   10 9 8 7 6

Year   2005 2004 2003

Typeset by Pantek Arts Ltd, Maidstone, Kent.

Printed in Italy for Hodder & Stoughton Educational, 338 Euston Road, London NW1 3BH.

Contents

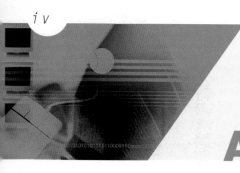

Acknowledgements

Permission to reproduce examination questions has been granted by OCR, and the publishers and authors acknowledgement their cooperation.

The publishers and authors would also like to thank Anne Kelsall for her contribution to the book.

I am very grateful for the time spent by Leana Walmsley reading the early versions of Sections A to C. Support beyond the duties of a daughter!
D.W.

To my wife and daughters for their support
B.S.

Finally, the publishers would like to acknowledge the following picture agencies and photographers for permission to reproduce their images in this book:

Lifefile/Emma Lee: p.7; p.18; p.27; p.49; p.59; p.87 **LifeFile/Dave Thompson** p.33; **Lifefile/Nicola Sutton** p.58 (bottom)

Mike Bull: p.8 (top and bottom); p.10 (bottom left); p.15 (left); p.28; p.32; p.60 (bottom); p.85

Associated Press: p.10 (top)

Safeway: p.10 (bottom right)

Mondex: p.12

Redfern's: p.14

Hewlett Packard: p.16; p.17

Telegraph Colour Library: p.34

Orange: p.38

Corbis: p.47

Nokia: p.58 top

Chubb Electronic Security System: p.60 (top); p.205

Quadrant/Simon Everett: p.63

Science Photo Library/Tek Image: p.65

Wacom: p.66

Still Pictures/Martin Specht: p.200

Introduction

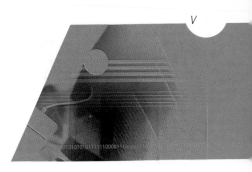

Aims

The aims of this book are:

- to provide the knowledge and understanding you need for the OCR GCSE short course or OCR GCSE full course in Information and Communication Technology (ICT);
- to provide practical support for carrying out coursework on both the short course and full course OCR GCSE Information and Communication Technology;
- to provide hints and tips for the written examination papers;
- and finally, to provide a useful reference text for other ICT GCSEs and ICT Intermediate GNVQ.

Using the book

The text is split into five sections as follows:

Sections A and C cover the background work required for the short course, with Section D covering the coursework element for the short course. For the full course you will additionally need to study Section B for the full course theory paper 2 and Section E for the major coursework task. Section F provides the questions typically found on the examination papers with advice about how to provide answers. Guidance about examination technique is also given in this section.

The text has margin notes which summarise the main points in the text. These notes together with the chapter summary are useful revision aids.

There are also short test questions at the end of each chapter to help with your revision.

Short case studies or descriptions of scenarios appear throughout the book. These are included to help in building skills required to tackle coursework tasks and applications based questions in the examination papers.

At the end of each section there is a short question paper to help you assess your potential examination performance.

Where to start

Your teacher will not necessarily cover topics in the order they appear in the text. There are some aspects of the text for example, that you will need to cover almost immediately in order to start the coursework. However each topic is a self contained unit with cross-referencing to other units for you to 'read around the subject'. Some parts of Section C and D build directly on concepts covered in Section A and B, so there may also be some 'reading ahead' if you wish. Nevertheless Section A, C and E serve as a complete stand-alone reference text for short course. Because each topic is also self-contained you will be able to dip into isolated parts of the book, study the material (possibly in context), test your own knowledge, and then consolidate what you have learned.

Key skills

All the knowledge and practical work needed to achieve a Level 2 key skills in Information Technology is contained in this book.

Section

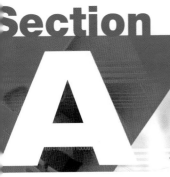

A

Computer systems, communication technology and information management

This section covers all the basic theory that you need to know about computer hardware, software, networks and communications technology. It also covers basic legal, moral and social issues associated with information technology in the workplace and at home.

Throughout the text, reference is made to examples of the use of Information Communication Technologies. The following list of applications is a summary of examples which could be found in the home, at school and general everyday life. It is important that you are able to summarise the main input, process and output of these example applications.

- Newsletters, publicity and corporate image such as business cards/letterhead/flyer/ brochure (see Section C)
- Room layouts, websites and multimedia presentations (see Section B)
- Music scores, cartoons
- Surveys, address lists, tuck shop records, club and society records (see Section C)
- Computer Based Training (CBT) or Computer Aided Learning (CAL)
- Personal Finance
- School reports
- School library
- Scientific experiments, electronic timing, environmental monitoring
- Turtle graphics, control of lights, buzzers and motors (see Section B)
- Automatic washing machines, automatic cookers, toys, central heating controllers, burglar alarms, video recorder/players, microwave ovens and digital watches
- Costing of materials, 3 D modelling and simulation: for example a driving simulator or a flight simulator.

Computer systems:
components and types

Computer systems have two main features: **hardware and software**.

Hardware

The hardware is the part of the computer that you can touch, such as the keyboard, disk drives, monitor (also sometimes called a visual display unit or computer screen), processing unit, mouse, and printer.

Software

The software on the computer is needed to make the computer work. It is the basic step by step instructions which are given to the processing unit to tell it what to do next. Software is also known as 'computer programs'. A typical example of software is a word processor. A word processor allows the person using it to write, edit, save and print letters, memos and many other types of document.

The main difference between hardware and software is that hardware is equipment you can touch whilst software is a set of programs used to carry out tasks.

The main parts of a general purpose computer system

The main hardware components of a computer system are:

- Central Processing Unit (CPU) – this is rather like the 'brain' of the computer. It carries out all the instructions of a computer program. It has a *control unit* which controls the steps taken by the computer and an *arithmetic and logic unit* which carries out all calculations and decisions.
- Internal Memory – this holds the data and instruction that the CPU is currently working with.
- Secondary Storage (Backing Storage) – this storage is additional to the internal memory. It refers to the disks and tapes that are used to store data and programs. It is possible to store large amounts of data and many different programs on backing storage. The items stored on backing storage do not disappear when the computer is turned off. (This means it is non-volatile.)

In addition to these main components we need a way of putting instructions and data into the computer and have a way in which we can obtain output from the computer. For this we need:

- **input devices** (such as the mouse and keyboard) which are used to input data and programs;
- **output devices** (such as the printer and monitor – often called a Visual Display Unit or VDU for short – which are used to output information.

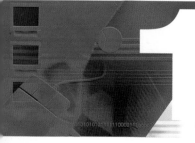

Hardware: equipment you can touch such as the monitor (screen or visual display unit), keyboard, mouse, printer, memory and processor.

Software: programs used on the computer, for example word processors, database and spreadsheet programs.

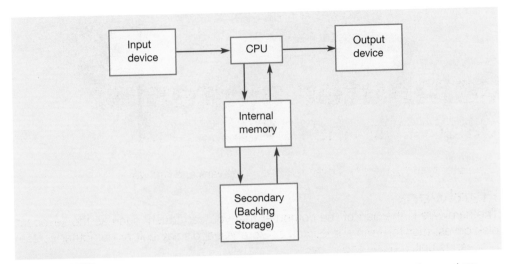

Figure 1.1 Hardware components of a general purpose computer system

Desktop computers and portable computers

Computers come in all shape and sizes. **desktop** computers were the first type of personal computer to be used in offices and by home users. Later desktop computers were designed to be smaller so that they could be carried around and used anywhere, even on trains. These are known as **portable** computers (sometimes we call them **notebook** or **laptop** computers).

Desktop computers are not portable and are not robust enough to be moved around from place to place regularly. The main processing unit may sit on the desk or be constructed as a 'tower unit', which fits under the desk.

Portable computers are more robust and have special, long-life, rechargeable batteries. There are many types of portable computer such as laptop/notebook computers or palm tops. Palmtop computers are smaller than notebook computers and often have very small keyboards, which some people find difficult to use for long periods of time.

The main hardware that makes up a computer: CPU, Internal Memory, Backing Storage together with Input and Output Devices.

A desktop computer is a general purpose machine found in many offices and homes. It is designed to stay in place whilst a notebook (or portable) has the same power and capability but is designed to be carried around.

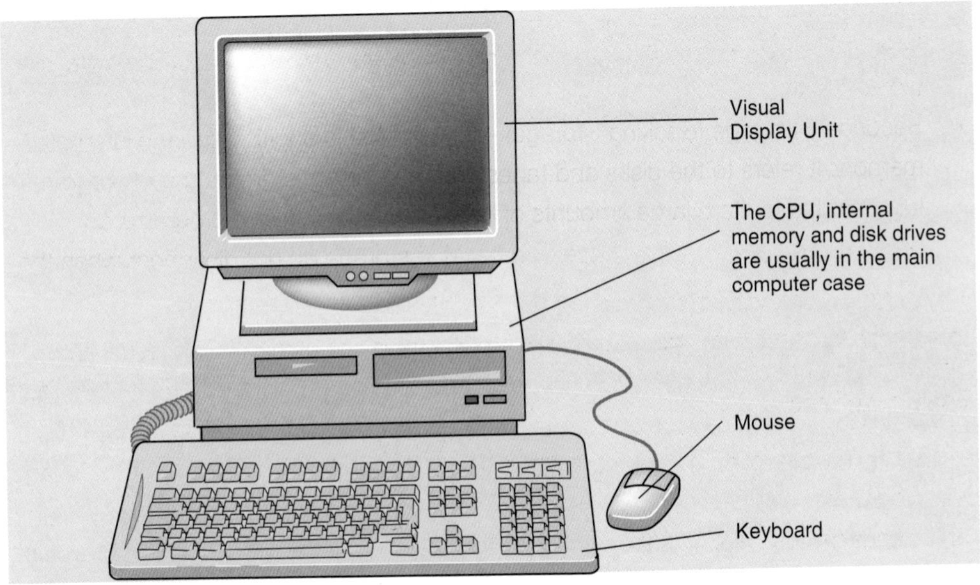

Visual Display Unit

The CPU, internal memory and disk drives are usually in the main computer case

Mouse

Keyboard

Figure 1.2 Desktop computer

Liquid
Crystal
Visual
Display
Unit

Keyboard

Figure 1.3 Notebook computer

Tasks such as word processing can be carried out on palmtops but only a small portion of text can be seen at any one time due to the screen size. Technology is advancing at a rapid rate and portable machines are getting smaller and smaller. Soon portable computers will be as small as a wristwatch. Even today mobile telephones have microprocessors which allow them to be used as calculators or enable users to connect to the Internet.

Computer systems:
components
and types

Summary

 Hardware is the physical parts of a computer e.g. CPU, visual display unit, keyboard, mouse, printer.

CPU: Central Processing Unit – the 'brain' of the computer consisting of the control unit and arithmetic and logic unit, where all the work is done.

Visual Display Unit: the computer screen, also called the monitor.

Software is the program containing the instructions which are followed by the computer, e.g. a word processor.

The main parts of a general-purpose computer are: Central Processing Unit, Internal Memory, Secondary (Backing) Storage, Input Devices and Output Devices.

Internal memory holds the current data and instruction being dealt with by the computer.

Secondary (or backing) storage is the additional memory (e.g disks and tapes), which is used to store data and instructions that we may need to use again and again. Its contents are not lost when the computer is turned off.

The difference between portable (including laptops/notebooks and palmtops) and desktop computers, is that the portable computer is small, light and robust enough to be carried around, while the desktop computer remains in one place in the home or office.

Test and review

1. The 'brains' of the computer is known as the C_____ P_____ U_____.
2. The CPU is a piece of H_____
3. Programs stored in the computer are known as S_____.
4. The main hardware components of a computer are:
   C_____, I_____,
   S_____.
5. State one use for backing storage_____.
6. A computer which is robust and is carried around to be used in different places is known as a P_____, whilst a computer of a similar type which is not designed to be carried around with the computer user is known as a D_____.

Review and thinking tasks

Look on your own computer and identify **three** different pieces of software.

Is your computer a desktop or notebook? Draw and label the main components of your computer including the software you can see on your computer's visual display unit.

2 Input and output devices

Input devices

Input devices are used to put data and instructions into the computer. For example we might enter text or numbers or select items displayed on the screen. There are many different types of input device that are designed for use in different ways. The most common input devices are covered in this chapter. In Section B you will find further notes about voice input and also about other ways we may collect or input data. We will start by looking at the most commonly used input device: the **keyboard**.

Keyboards

Keyboards are found on everyday general-purpose computers like desktops and notebooks. The usual layout of a the keys on a keyboard is rather like the layout of the keys on a typewriter. The top row of letters start with 'QWERTY'. This is why they are called 'Qwerty' keyboards. Keyboards come in many shapes and sizes depending on the design of the computer. In recent years a lot of work has been done to design ergonomic keyboards that are more comfortable to use ('ergonomic' means that they are designed so that they are easier to use). Different designs of keyboard are illustrated in Figures 1.2 and 1.3.

USES

A keyboard is used for a wide range of tasks but is well known for its capability to enter data, which is copied from original paper documents (such as name and address details on a form). Copying data from paper documents is called **transcription**. Keyboards are also used for typing letters, memos, reports and other documents using word processing software.

ADVANTAGES

- Most computers have this device attached to it and a skilled typist can enter data very quickly.

DISADVANTAGES

- It is very easy to make mistakes when typing in data.
- It can be very time consuming to enter data this way, especially if you have not had much practice at typing.
- It is very difficult to enter some data, for example details of diagrams and pictures.

Pointing devices (mouse, touch pad, trackerball and joystick)

Mouse

This is a hand-held input device, which allows the user to communicate with the computer using a pointer on the screen (illustrated in Figure 2.1). A **cursor** is a flashing vertical line indicating the location of the next typed character when a key on the keyboard is pressed. The mouse has buttons that you click to select a new location or item

Input device: an item of hardware a person uses to put data and instructions into the computer.

Keyboard: an input device which looks a bit like a typewriter and is most commonly used for data entry such as typing in text.

Keyboards are very common input devices, but data is not entered quickly, especially if the user is not experienced.

on the computer screen. Some mice have more than one button. Sometimes there are two or even three. Usually, double clicking the leftmost button whilst pointing to an item on the screen usually starts a new process or task such as the word processor. The rightmost button is often used to display a menu of choices you can make about an item on the screen. Underneath the mouse is a moving ball which allows the mouse to be manipulated in such a way that as the ball rolls and the mouse moves, so does the cursor on the screen.

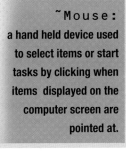

~Mouse: a hand held device used to select items or start tasks by clicking when items displayed on the computer screen are pointed at.

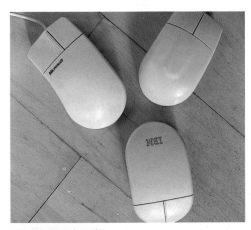

Figure 2.1 A typical mouse input device

USES

The mouse is used to select and move around items displayed on a screen. It is a point and click device and is used as a way of starting tasks by positioning the pointer and selecting items. It can also be used to create simple graphics.

ADVANTAGES

- Some people find it much easier to select items and start tasks by clicking icons or choosing from menus rather than typing in commands.
- It is often a faster method of getting to the tasks you want to start.
- It is quicker to use a mouse to help you move around a document than to use the arrow keys on the keyboard.

DISADVANTAGES

- People new to computers often find it difficult to control the movement of the pointer on the computer screen by moving the mouse around on the desk. They also have difficulty when double clicking the mouse button.
- Mouse balls can become very dirty and stop functioning correctly unless cleaned regularly.

Touch pad

This device is commonly found on notebook computers and by moving your finger across the pad the movement of the cursor is controlled on the screen. The action of double clicking or clicking the mouse button can be copied by tapping on the touch pad with the finger or clicking the button which is positioned next to the touch pad. It has the same uses and advantages as the normal mouse device but does not have a ball and so does not have the problem of the getting dirty. Sometimes it is difficult for new users to get used to using a touch pad when they have used a hand-held mouse.

Touchpads and trackerbals are similar in style to the mouse and are used in a similar manner. They are often found on notebooks.

Figure 2.2 Touchpad device

Tracker Ball

This device is a bit like an upside-down mouse because the ball normally located on the underside of the mouse device is located on top of the tracker ball. The user rolls the ball with the finger to control the cursor movement. Sometimes we see small tracker balls on notebooks. They take up less space than a hand-held mouse device but have the same uses, advantages and disadvantages.

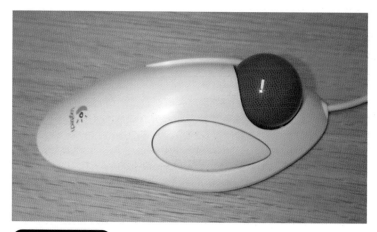

Figure 2.3 Tracker ball device

Joystick

A joystick is similar to a tracker ball in operation except you have a stick which is moved rather then a rolling ball.

USES

Games software often take input from a joystick.

ADVANTAGES

There is an immediate feel of direction due to the movement of the stick.

DISADVANTAGES

* Some people find the joystick difficult to control rather than other point and click devices. This is probably because more arm and wrist movement is required to control the pointer than with a mouse or trackerball.

> **Joysticks** are similar to tracker balls except that control of the pointer is by moving the stick rather than a ball.

- Joysticks are not particularly strong and can break easily when used with games software.

Video digitiser

A 'video-digitiser' captures television pictures from devices such as a TV set, video camera or video recorder and converts them into a format that a computer can use for display, storage or general manipulation. The format a computer can store and use is known as *digital format* because computers store and use digital (number) data. A video digitiser is the ideal tool for capturing images from real-life scenes to incorporate into computer work. It usually fits inside the computer allowing connection to a range of video sources. Taking video pictures or frames is known as 'frame grabbing'.

USES

Converting still or moving images into a digital format for use in a computerised presentation. A video digitiser **may** be required for video conferencing. (If a digital video camera is used there will be no need for a video digitiser.) This is when the video camera captures sound and images which are converted to a computerised format and transmitted over communication lines (see Chapter 4 for a discussion about analogue to digital conversion and transmission of data over communication lines). It can also be used to make television advertisements and pop videos.

ADVANTAGES

- Video digitisers allow us to capture real-life images which are often more appropriate then drawings.
- Captured images can then be transferred to paper.

DISADVANTAGE

- A fast computer with a large memory capacity is required to cope with the large amount of data involved.

Digital camera

Digital cameras look like ordinary cameras but have sufficient memory to store images rather than using film. Each digital picture is made up of thousands of tiny dots, called pixels, and the camera stores data about the colour of each dot. Each image therefore takes up as much memory as is required to store the number of dots which make up the picture. If the picture is made up of a large number of small dots the picture is clear. If the picture is made up of a small number of large dots the picture will not be very clear.

The number of Dots Per Inch (DPI) will give us an idea of how clear we can expect the picture to be. Dots Per Inch (DPI) is called the *resolution* of the image. Because high-**resolution** images have more dots per inch, more computer memory will be needed. Most cameras allow the user to choose the resolution needed for a picture. Storage capacity varies but some cameras store approximately 100 images. Once the photograph is stored in the camera it needs to be transfered to a computer where it can be edited, printed or more permanently stored. Some cameras store images on a floppy disk so that they can be easily transferred. Other cameras are connected to the computer with a lead and special software which is used to transfer the image.

USES

Taking photographs and transferring them to a computer where they can be edited, used in documents and /or printed out.

ADVANTAGES

- There are no expensive developing costs, no film is needed and you can insert images directly into a document on your computer.
- You can also edit, enlarge or enhance the images.

> A 'video-digitiser' captures television pictures from a TV set, video camera or video recorder and converts them into digital data which the computer can store and use.

> Digital cameras look like ordinary cameras but they have memory to store digital data about the images rather than film.

⬤ DISADVANTAGES

- Digital cameras are generally more expensive than ordinary cameras.
- When they are full they can be connected to a computer to download the stored images before they must be used again (or to delete the images). This is not as convenient as simply changing a film. (Some digital cameras overcome this problem by using floppy discs or other storage devices to store images before they are transferred, but floppy discs cannot hold many images and other devices are still expensive.)

Figure 2.4 Digital camera

Scanner

A scanner is another way in which we can capture still images (or even text) to be stored and used on a computer. The scanner shines a light onto the paper and measures the amount of light reflected back from each part of the page. Like a digital camera the page is split into tiny pixels (dots) and a number representing the colour of each dot is sent to the computer. Scanner software usually allows the user to choose between a high resolution (very high quality images taking up a lot of memory) and lower resolutions. Most scanners need a piece of paper to be scanned inside them when they are being used. These are called **flatbed scanners** and usually come in A4 size or larger (such as A3), but there are also some small hand-held ones often used to read text such as bar codes.

> **Scanners** shine light onto an image and the scanning software converts the dots, which make up the image, to digital data.

Figure 2.6 A hand held scanner

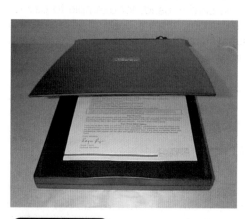

Figure 2.5 A flatbed scanner

USES
Transferring pictures or text from paper into documents stored on the computer. For example a scanner is often required to convert photographs which may be used in a desktop published school magazine.

ADVANTAGES
- Any image can be converted from paper into digital format and later enhanced and used in other computer documents.

DISADVANTAGE
- Images take up a lot of memory space, but it is possible to reduce the size of the data file by reducing the resolution (number of dots per inch) or by using different ways of storing the data (different file formats).

Remote control
Remote control devices are used for transmitting data when the user is some distance from the processor. Items such as video recorders can accept data which is programmed into the system from a remote handset. Special keys for certain tasks or selections are usually found on the handset. An infra-red sensor on the main processing unit picks up the signals sent when the keys are pressed.

USES
To select or enter data from a distance.

ADVANTAGES
- The device provides the user with the convenience of working away from the processing unit.

DISADVANTAGES
- Small remote devices can easily be misplaced.
- The unit and remote need to be quite near to each other and have no other objects between them which may interfere with the signals sent.

Magnetic stripe reader
Magnetic stripes are the dark-looking stripe you see on the back of many plastic cards for example bankcards. The magnetic stripe holds data about the owner of the card, for example a bankcard will contain details such as the bank account number (the card owner's individual account number) and sort code (the code that identifies the branch of the bank where the account is held). When the card is used, for example to pay for goods in a store, the shop assistant inserts the card into the magnetic stripe reader and it is 'swiped' through a slot. The reader looks at the data on the magnetic stripe and money can be taken from the correct account to pay the bill. Note that the money is taken from the bank account, not the card. Data on a magnetic stripe does not change and there is no balance recorded on the card. Bankcards like this are sometimes known as debit cards. There are other types of card issued by banks, called credit cards. When the card is swiped the credit limit (amount the person is allowed to borrow) is checked before the person is allowed to pay for the goods with the card. Note that the card does not contain details of the credit limit.

USES
Magnetic stripe readers are often seen at supermarket tills and in many different types of shops, in fact anywhere where there is a 'point of sale' (somewhere you pay for your purchases). Because the data is read electronically the point of sale is called EPOS (Electronic Point of Sale).

Video digitisers digital cameras and scanners are all devices which are designed to capture images in digital format so that they can be used in computer documents or presentations.

Many devices in the home and office require data input. It is often convenient to do this from a handheld device using infra red to transmit the signals. This is known as a remote control.

Magnetic stripe readers read data found on the magnetic stripe on bank cards at EPOS stations in shops and supermarkets.

ADVANTAGES

- The card can be read many times without damaging the stripe.
- The data is not visible to people because a machine is needed to read the data (although with debit cards the bank details are actually displayed on the card as well).
- Putting magnetic stripes onto cards is not expensive so the cards are quite cheap to produce.
- The data from the stripe is read very quickly so it is much quicker and often more convenient to use cards, which have a magnetic stripe, to pay for goods.

DISADVANTAGES

- Magnetic stripes may get damaged or the magnetic stripe reader could break down.
- The biggest disadvantage of magnetic stripes is that ordinary equipment can read but not change the data. That is why some stores and other organisations have started to use Smart Cards. These are cards containing a small chip (or tiny processor with some memory) instead of a magnetic stripe. The data on the chip may then be changed as the card is used. (Note that the owner of the card must make sure there is enough money on the card to buy goods and be aware that each time goods are bought the balance on the card is decreased.)

Figure 2.7 Magnetic stripe reader and debit card

Sound Sensor – Microphone

It is possible to record sound if you have a sound card in your computer. A sound sensor, which is a microphone, detects sound and inputs it to the computer, and then the sound is converted into digital format. We do this by 'sampling' the sound. We have mentioned that digital format (representing data as numbers) is necessary before we can store the data on the computer. Sound is produced as sound waves not as numbers. Sound waves are in analogue format. To change them to digital format so that the data can be stored in the computer's memory we use a process called *sound sampling*. This process is carried out by software called a sound sampler.

Microphones and sound sampling are used to input sound and convert it to digital format. Sound files of this type take up a lot of storage space, for example one minute of good quality sound takes up approximately 10megabytes of storage space.

The sound sampler measures a sound wave at fixed time intervals (determined by the sound sampling software). Each measurement is given a digital value. Many different kinds of sound can be recorded, including music and speech. This means that a large number of digital values must be stored to represent a sound if a good quality reproduction is required. For example, a one minute good quality recording may take approximately 10 megabytes (equivalent to about 10 million characters) of storage space in the computer.

USES

Microphones are necessary for speech recognition systems, which are now commonly used with word processors. The person using the computer speaks into the microphone. Speech recognition software on the computer converts what the person has said into text. The text is displayed on the screen and can be saved as a word-processed file. (Note that, although speech recognition is getting more reliable it is usually necessary to spend some time 'teaching' the system to recognise the way you speak. However, it still does not always make accurate conversions to text.)

Some users record special sounds, both voice and music, from almost any source. These sounds may be used in computerised presentations for example multimedia teaching software.

ADVANTAGES

- People with a range of disabilities can benefit from the use of microphones and speech recognition, for example those who cannot use a keyboard can create word processed documents by speaking instead of typing and many devices in the home can now be controlled by voice.
- Recording your own sounds means that you can add spoken messages or music to your own presentations or even e-mails.

DISADVANTAGES

- There should be no background noise when recording sound, otherwise it may become distorted. Cutting down the background noise is sometimes difficult and the sound recorded using a microphone is often not very good.
- Sound sampling (converting the analogue sound to digital format using software) often produces very large data files.

Midi instrument

MIDI means Musical Instrument Digital Interface. There are a variety of musical instruments such as keyboards, guitars and drums, which send and receive electronic messages. If a musical keyboard is connected to a computer using a MIDI the musical information such as pitch is converted to digital data which can then be stored on a computer. This stored data can also be sent back to the keyboard to reproduce the signals sent to it. MIDI is also used to allow different instruments, e.g. an electronic piano and a synthesiser to communicate and work together.

USES

The music industry uses MIDI to input music directly into a computer so that it can be edited and developed, often by mixing it with other sounds which are input from a microphone. Some programs allow you to enter a tune from a musical instrument, then convert this into written music, which can be printed out.

> **Musical Instrument Digital Interface (MIDI)** allows signals to be sent and received in digital format from the instrument (such as a music keyboard) directly to the computer. Digital data is stored in files on the computer and are much more compact than sound sampled files.

●ADVANTAGES

- Once the tune has been played on the musical instrument, all the details are held on the computer. These details may then be changed. It is possible to speed up the tune, slow it down or even make it sound like a completely different instrument.
- The data stored is very compact and takes up about 1/20th of the space taken up by even the lowest quality recorded sound samples.

●DISADVANTAGE

- A musician is required to play the instrument to acquire the input, so some musical knowledge is required.
- To take advantage of the digitally recorded sound, knowledge of software and music is required to edit recorded tunes, so the main disadvantage to using MIDI is the fact that it has limited specialist use.

Figure 2.8 Keyboard interfaced to a computer

Output devices

Monitor (Visual Display Unit)

A monitor, which is sometimes called a Visual Display Unit (VDU) or computer screen, is the most common output device used on computer systems. On a typical computer it may measure 15 inches or 17 inches across its display area (the size of the screen measured across the diagonal). In a notebook the display area is often smaller and usually is a Liquid Crystal Display (LCD). These are lighter and more compact than the VDUs seen on a desktop computer. VDUs also have different resolutions (dots per inch) and the higher the resolution the more expensive the VDU. High resolution VDUs are needed for applications where there are lots of graphics to display for example Computer Aided Design (CAD) work.

●USES

VDUs or monitors are used to display output to the user as they carry out tasks. For example when typing text into a word processor at the keyboard, the VDU displays each character (or letter) as the keys on the keyboard are pressed.

> **VDUs or monitors (computer display screens) come in a variety of sizes and resolutions depending on the job they are needed for. They provide immediate visual feedback to the computer user.**

ADVANTAGES

- As each task is processed the results can been displayed immediately on the screen.
- Output can be scrolled backwards and forwards easily, if results are too large to display on one screen. It is also possible, using certain software, to enlarge the display results.

DISADVANTAGES

- The results displayed on the screen will disappear when the computer is switched off.
- Each new screen of information will replace the displayed output from the previous screen.
- Only a limited amount of information can be displayed at any one time.
- Screens are made of glass and can be very fragile.

Figure 2.9 Visual Display Units (VDUs)/Monitors

Printers (laser, ink-jet and dot-matrix)

Because monitors do not give permanent output we often need results printed out on paper. We call this printed output 'hard copy'. Printers provide this hard copy output. There are generally three main types of printer in use today: laser, ink-jet and dot-matrix.

Laser printers

Laser printers produce high quality printed documents at fast speeds (on average at 10 pages per minute). They are very quiet when in operation. Prices have dropped rapidly since laser printers were first developed. It is possible to buy a very good laser printer for very little more than other types of printer. For many years laser printers could only produce black print, but in recent years colour laser printers have become more common even though they are more expensive. Laser printers use cartridges of fine black (or coloured) powder which is transferred to the paper to produce the printed document. This powder is called toner. Toner cartridges are expensive but they last a long time, making a page printed by a laser printer much cheaper than a page printed by an inkjet printer.

> A laser printer provides high quality, fast printed hardcopy for the computer user and although initial purchase costs are becoming much lower, the cost of toner cartridges is high.

●USES

Laser printers were first used in offices where it was important to get high quality print-outs quickly and quietly. Now prices are lower and they are used anywhere where a large amount of printing is done including schools and many businesses.

●ADVANTAGES

- Laser printers are fast and almost silent, producing high quality output.
- A large number of printouts can be done using a single toner cartridge, so frequent purchases of replacements are not necessary.

●DISADVANTAGE

- Laser printers are usually the most expensive to buy.
- Laser printers are also often quite large and are heavier than other types of printer.
- Repairs can be expensive.
- The cost of toner cartridges is much higher than the cost ink cartridges or ink ribbons used in other types of printer.

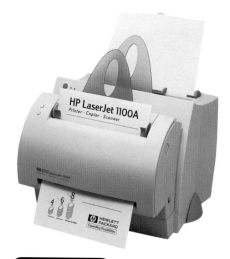

Figure 2.10 Laser printer

Ink-jet printers

Ink-jet printers are very popular because they are relatively cheap to buy and usually offer colour printing. They are also very quiet in their operation. However, they tend to be slower than most laser printers with the better ones producing about 4 pages per minute. Colour ink-jet printers are a popular purchase for the single user with a small amount of printing to do.

These printers also have cartridges but the cartridges contain ink and are quite small. They operate by heating the ink as it flows through a nozzle. The heating process causes a small droplet of ink to form. This is then released as a single dot which forms part of a letter or image. There are many dots so the quality is usually very good but producing each droplet of ink can be slow. Ink-jet printers vary in price with the slowest ones being some of the cheapest printers available and the faster ones costing a similar amount to a small laser printer. The main disadvantage of an ink-jet printer is the cost of buying the cartridges. They are much cheaper to buy than laser toner cartridges but they do not last as long. If you do not need to do a lot of printing, however, an ink-jet printer is probably a better buy than a laser printer, especially if colour printouts are required.

> **Ink-jet printers produce high quality printouts but they tend to be slow. They operate almost silently and are ideal for a single home user, particularly if occasional colour printouts are required. Initial purchase costs are low but frequent replacement of cartridges can be expensive.**

USES

Home users who do not need to do a lot of printing, but occasionally may need to print out in colour, often choose to buy an ink-jet printer.

ADVANTAGES

- Ink-jet printers are relatively inexpensive to buy, especially if colour is needed.
- Ink-jet printers are also lighter in weight than other printers and some are small enough to be carried around in the pocket of a notebook/portable carry case.
- Ink-jet printers are very quiet when they are printing with only a faint hiss and the movement of the paper being heard.

DISADVANTAGES

- Ink-jet printers are slower when they are printing than laser printers.
- If left unused for long periods of time the cartridges can easily dry out.
- Replacing colour cartridges can be a particularly expensive running cost.

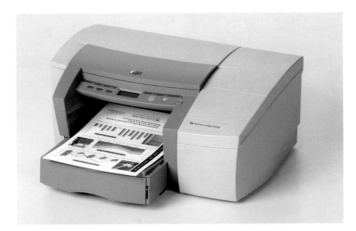

Figure 2.11 Ink-jet printer

Dot-matrix printers

Dot-matrix printers are not used much today. They were the first type of printer to be used extensively in homes and schools and were until quite recently a very cheap alternative to ink-jet and laser printers, with much lower running costs. Dot-matrix printers print by striking tiny pins against a carbon ribbon. The print head contains a grid (or *matrix*) of these pins and different combinations of pins are pushed out to form different characters. This makes them much slower than ink-jet printers and they are very noisy because you can hear the pins hitting the paper. Any printer that works by banging something against the paper in this way is called an *impact* printer. There have been many different types of impact printer and all have been slow and noisy. The quality of print is dependent on the number of pins making up each character. The pins strike an ink ribbon and in order to produce letter quality it is necessary to print a line twice. This means the ink ribbon will wear out more quickly.

USES

Dot-matrix printers are ideal when carbon copies are needed. This is because they are impact printers and the print head bangs on the top copy of paper the carbon paper transfers a copy to the paper beneath the carbon paper. You will often find them in use

> Dot-matrix printers are noisy, impact printers, producing low quality output at slow speeds. They are relatively inexpensive to buy and have low running costs. They are fairly robust and ideal when carbon copies of printouts are required.

in factories and garages where invoices and delivery notes are produced. Often the factory wants to keep a copy and the quality is not important.

ADVANTAGES

- The main advantage of dot-matrix printers now is the ability to produce carbon copies. They provide a cheap, reliable method of getting a second copy of a printout.
- The other advantage is the low cost of printouts, because printers are cheap to buy and running costs are low.

DISADVANTAGES

- Dot-matrix printers are noisy, slow and produce a lower quality output.

Figure 2.12   Dot-matrix print head

Plotter

A plotter (sometimes called a graph plotter) is an output device, which produces high quality line diagrams on paper. Pens are used to draw lines on the paper, which is placed in the plotter. Some plotters have a flat area to put the paper onto, others use a large roll of paper. Usually plotters can use larger paper than printers.

USES

Graph plotters are used for drawing building plans, graphs and three-dimensional drawings. They are often used by architects and by engineers designing machines, bridges etc.

ADVANTAGES

- Drawings are of the same quality as if an expert drew them.
- Larger sizes of paper can be used than would be found on most printers.

DISADVANTAGES

- Plotters are slower than printers, drawing each line separately.
- They are often more expensive to buy than printers.
- Although drawings are completed to the highest quality they are not suitable for text although text can be produced.
- There is a limit to the amount of detail these plotters can produce, although there are plotters which are pen-less and are used for high-density drawings like printed circuit boards.

Plotters may be used to produce high quality line diagrams often using a pen to draw computerised output of items such as building plans.

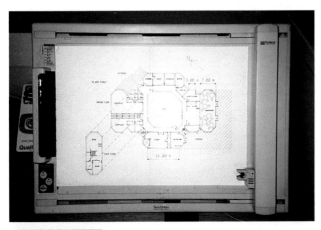

Figure 2.13 A plotter

Speakers

Speakers are used as output devices when they are attached to the part of the computer which has a sound card inside it. Headphones may also be used instead of speakers.

USES

Any program that produces sound needs speakers or headphones for the sound to be heard. Multimedia (when sound, text, graphics and video sequences are put together on computer) teaching software such as programs which teach a foreign language need speakers or headphones to output sound.

ADVANTAGE

- Everyone in the room can hear the sound from a speaker. This is useful if a presentation is being made to an audience.

DISADVANTAGES

- The output from speakers can disturb others trying to work on other tasks.
- High quality external speakers can be expensive.

Control devices (lights, buzzers, robotic arms, motors)

Many other devices may be connected to the computer to produce output. For example lights may be connected to a computer which will respond to electrical signals that tell them to switch on and off. Buzzers may also be sounded because the computer sends an electrical signal to switch them on and off.

Also, a computer can control all sorts of devices which are operated by motors. Robotic arms are an example of a device which has its movement controlled by the computer. When an output device moves something it is called an *actuator*.

USES

Control devices like lights, buzzers and motors are used when the computer is controlling a situation such as traffic lights or car assembly.

ADVANTAGE

- Devices which need controlling, because they use electrical signals from a computer, can be controlled very accurately.
- Using a computer to control devices means that fewer people are required for manual jobs and less money is needed to pay wages.

Speakers and headphones are connected to the part of the computer which has the sound card in it. This means that users can hear the sound from, for example, multimedia presentations and music software.

Control devices like lights, buzzers, robotic arms and motors all respond to electrical signals produced by the computer. Instead of printed instructions to tell a human operator to turn something on or off the signals are sent directly to the devices.

◼DISADVANTAGE

- If the computer or control device goes wrong, the system comes to a halt.

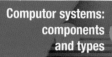
**Computor systems:
components
and types**

Summary

✓ **Keyboard:** an input device which looks a bit like a typewriter and is most commonly used for data entry, such as entering text or numbers.

✓ **Mouse:** a hand-held input device which has buttons and is moved on a flat surface. It moves a pointer on the screen and the user clicks on items using the buttons to select them. It moves along a flat surface and has a ball, which rolls in all directions underneath it.

✓ **Trackerball:** an input device which behaves like an upside down mouse.

✓ **Joystick:** an input device which also moves a pointer on the screen. Moving a stick on the top of the device moves the pointer. It is often used with games software.

✓ **Touchpad:** an input device that is often found on notebook computers. It behaves like a mouse by just using the fingertips over the pad.

✓ **A video digitiser**, **digital camera** and **scanner** are all input devices which capture images.

✓ **Video digitiser:** can capture moving images from a video camera. Images are stored in digital format.

✓ **Digital Camera** is a camera, which does not need film. Instead images are captured and stored immediately in digital format. This data can then be put straight into the computer for display.

✓ **Scanner:** a device which copies images and text and converts them to digital format to be stored in computer memory.

✓ Images take up a lot of space in computer memory because data has to be stored about each dot on a picture. The more dots per inch the higher the resolution and the larger the data file.

✓ Remote control devices input data to computerised systems from a distance using infra-red.

✓ Magnetic stripe readers are input devices, which read data from the magnetic stripes found on plastic cards such as bank cards.

✓ Sounds such as speech or music may be input to the computer using a microphone with sound sampling software. Music may also be input to a computer using a Musical Instrument Digital Interface (MIDI). Sound data files which have been recorded using a microphone and sound sampling software tend to be of lower quality and take up more space than a MIDI data file.

✓ A Visual Display Unit (VDU) or monitor is the computer screen which displays output from the computer so it is an output device. The output on a monitor is not permanent.

✓ Printers are output devices that produce a permanent copy of output on paper. There are laser, ink-jet and dot-matrix printers.

✓ Laser and ink-jet printers are higher quality than dot-matrix printers but are more expensive.

✓ Laser printers print faster than ink-jet printers and dot-matrix printers.

✓ Plotters are output devices, which usually use a pen to produce line diagrams such as building plans, although there are plotters, which are pen-less and are capable of producing more detailed drawings.

✓ Control devices such as lights, buzzers, robotic arms and motors are all output devices that respond to electrical signals produced by the computer.

Test and review

1. The most common method of data entry to a computer is using a K_____.

2. Name two point and click devices. _____

3. Video digitisers are used to capture video and still images. The images are converted to D_____ format.

4. Name two other devices which may be used to capture still images._____.

5. State ONE advantage of using a scanner. _____
_____

6. Give ONE reason why images take up a lot of memory space in the computer. _____
_____

7. Resolution means d_____ per _____.

8. Sound input can be captured using microphone sensors and sound sampling or M_____.

9. MIDI means M_____ I_____ D_____ I_____.

10. VDU means V_____ D_____ U_____.

11. Name TWO different types of printer _____.

12. Which type of printers produce high quality, fast printouts?
_____.

13. Which type of printers produce low quality output?
_____.

14. What types of printout can a plotter produce that ordinary printers have difficulty in producing? _____.

15. Control devices receive electrical signals from the computer. Examples of control devices are: _____
_____.

Review and thinking tasks

Look at your computers in school. What sort of input devices do you use? List them What do they look like? What sort of output devices do you have at school? Get your teacher to show you an ink-jet print cartridge or laser toner cartridge. If possible look at both. Which is bigger? Why do you think ink-jet print cartridges dry out sometimes? Do you think this will happen with your toner cartridges?

Storage devices and media

Difference between internal memory and backing storage

In Chapter 1 the main components of a computer system were introduced and the idea of computer storage (or memory) was discussed.

- Internal storage is the memory that is occupied by the current data and instruction being dealt with by the computer. Its contents are lost when the computer is turned off.

- Secondary or backing storage is the additional memory (often discs), which is used to store data and instructions that we may need to use again and again. Its contents are *not* lost when the computer is turned off.

Internal memory must hold details of the current program or piece of software running on the computer. However, when the current program has finished running, it can be replaced by a new piece of software. For example you may want to run a word processor to write a letter. When you have finished you stop the word processor by 'exiting'. Next you decide to set up a spreadsheet to calculate how to use your spending money for the month. Both these programs are stored on backing storage, usually a hard disc, but during the time you are using them they occupy internal memory (or main memory) in the computer.

Why do we do use internal memory and backing storage like this?

For two reasons:

- Internal/main memory is *volatile* if it is in RAM, which means data is lost when the computer is switched off or when you reset the computer (have you ever lost work when the computer has frozen and has to be reset?);

- internal/main memory is *also too* small to hold details of everything we need to do on computer.

For these two reasons backing storage is used to save the bulk of our data and software. However it is important to note that when items have been put into the main memory, it is much faster to access details stored there and this is why we do not just work from details held in backing store. Main memory or internal memory is referred to as *Immediate Access Store (IAS)* because it operates so quickly.

How do we measure the size of memory?

Storing an individual character such as a letter, number or other character (for example, '£' and '*') like those on your keyboard, requires a set amount of space called a *byte*. So one character needs one byte of storage space.

> The difference between Immediate Access Storage (IAS) and backing storage is that IAS is small, possibly volatile and fast, whilst backing storage is large, non-volatile and not very fast to read from.

To store 1024 characters we need 1024 bytes or *1Kilobyte* (=1Kb). To make life easier we usually take 1 kb as 1000 bytes.

1 million bytes or 1000Kb is called *1 Megabyte* (=1Mb) and 1000Mb is called *1 Gigabyte* (=1 Gb). All these numbers are approximate.

Now we can see clearly that backing storage is much larger than IAS. Many home computers have IAS, which is measured in Megabytes, perhaps 32, 64, 128 or 256Mb, whilst backing storage such as hard disks (see below) are measured in Gigabytes, perhaps on a home computer, 5, 10 or even 15 Gb.

Backing storage media and devices

Hard disks and drives

A hard disk is the *storage media*, which actually holds the stored data. The hard drive is the *device*, which reads and writes to the hard disk. In desktop computers and notebooks there is usually one hard disk and one hard disk drive which accesses the data stored on disk. It comes as one unit and is usually stored inside the main computer unit, although external hard drives may be purchased and plugged into the computer unit to provide extra storage. Hard drives and their disks, in desktop computers, usually have a capacity to store approximately 10 Gigabytes (1000 million bytes/characters) but this is changing all the time as computers get faster and better.

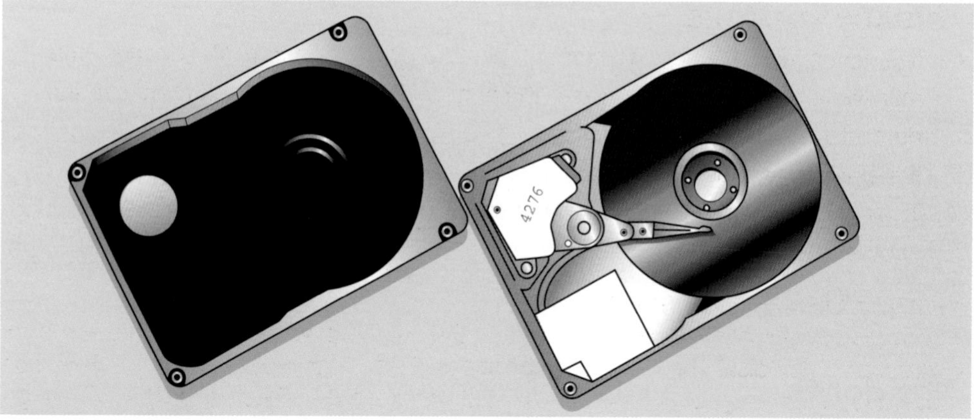

> **Hard disks** have an approximate capacity of 10Gb. They are magnetic and often store all the software and data needed by the user. Read/write heads in the hard disk drive accesses the data.

Figure 3.1 A microcomputer hard disk drive showing the disk inside.

In bigger computers such as those that fill whole rooms and deal with bank transactions (called mainframes), the disk drive may contain many hard disks stacked like a set of plates. There has to be many read-write heads to read the data on this type of device.

The important thing to remember about hard disks is that they are *magnetic* media. Data is stored magnetically onto tracks which are rings on the disk, which obviously get smaller and smaller as you move closer to the centre of disk. The disk rotates at high speed passing underneath the read-write heads. The read-write heads are the part of the disk drive that reads the data into main memory (IAS) to be processed or write data from main memory after it has been dealt with.

●USES

Hard disks are used to store all software necessary to carry out your daily tasks on the computer. When you create new documents or files, it is likely that you will save them to your hard disk.

Figure 3.2 A typical mainframe disk drive with a disk pack inserted

ADVANTAGES

- Hard disks are necessary to support the way your computer works and have the great advantage that they have a large storage capacity.
- Stored items are not lost when you switch off the computer
- Usually they come as a fixed unit inside the computer and so cannot easily get lost.

DISADVANTAGES

- It is not as fast to access items from the hard disk as it is from IAS because the read-write heads have to move to the correct part of the disk and then read the data into IAS.
- If the hard disk crashes the computer will not work.
- The disk is fixed inside the computer and cannot be taken out and re-used in another machine.

Floppy disks and drives

Floppy disk drives usually appear as a slot on the outside of your computer into which you insert your floppy disk, The disk does not appear to be floppy, because it is inside a hard protective outer case. The disks are portable and are $3\frac{1}{2}$ inches square. A HD – high-density disk – could store approximately 2 Megabytes (2 million characters). The disk has a little tab (see Figure 3.3) which, when selected, stops accidental overwriting of data.

Floppy discs have a small capacity (approx. 2Mb), but are portable. They are not strong and can be easily damaged.

Figure 3.3 Floppy disk

All disks must be *formatted* before use. Floppy disks can now be bought already formatted. Formatting simply sets out the way the data is going to stored on the disk. The disk is divided up into section and there is also an empty index. Each time new data (or a program) is stored on the disk there is a new entry put into the index to indicate where the new data is stored. Formatting a disk which has data on it already, will prevent access to that old data so it is important to be sure that you do not accidently format a disk with important data or programs stored on it.

USES

- Floppy disks are often used for data, which is so personal to a user that it must be kept private from anyone else needing to use the machine. They also are often used to keep extra copies of data stored on your hard disk in case the computer crashes (a back-up copy), or when it is necessary to transport data from one machine to another.

ADVANTAGES

- Floppy disk drives have the advantage that very private data can be stored and kept safe from other users because the disk can be taken away.
- Because floppy disks are quite small they can be taken away and it is possible to access the data using a different computer.
- Floppy disks provide additional storage so an extra copy of data can be kept.

DISADVANTAGES

- Floppy disks are not very strong and can easily get damaged or lost.
- Not all machines will read from the same floppy disk.
- The amount of storage space is often too small for some data files, for example if you want to store large images.

Optical disk drives (CD-ROM and DVD)

CD-ROM

CD-ROM means Compact Disk Read Only Memory. This means that data cannot be written to this type of disk. As the name indicates, this type of disk is small (compact) and contains the sort of data and programs that do not need to change (read only), for example encyclopaedias and games software. CD-ROM disks do not store data magnetically like floppy disks and hard disks. Instead, they have data stored digitally and a laser beam in the CD-ROM drive is used to read the data off the disk. This is why they are known as optical storage devices. CD-ROM storage capacity is fairly high at 650 Megabytes.

USES

Encyclopaedias and other reference material, teaching software (See Section B for Computer Aided Learning – CAL), libraries of clipart and games software.

ADVANTAGES

- Data cannot be erased from CD-ROMs.
- CD-ROMs are portable because they are small.
- CD-ROMs have a much larger storage capacity than floppy disks.

DISADVANTAGES

- Because they are portable they can easily get lost.
- It is not possible to save to a CD-ROM.
- A CD-ROM has a smaller storage capacity than a hard disk.
- Accessing items on a CD-ROM is slower than accessing items from a hard disk.

CD-ROM
means Compact Disk Read Only Memory. It is an optical storage device and is able to store approximately 650Mb so it is frequently used for multimedia reference material. It is portable.

Figure 3.4 CD-ROM and drive

Digital Versatile Disks (DVD)

DVDs are a relatively new technological development and are rather similar to CD-ROMS, except that they are capable of storing more data, approximately 5 Gigabytes.

⬤ USES

DVDs can be used to store films, which are notably better in picture quality and sound. So much so that DVD players are available to connect to your television and they are becoming very popular.

⬤ ADVANTAGES

- DVDs have a very large storage capacity.
- Sound and picture quality is excellent.
- There is an increasing availability of products in DVD format.

⬤ DISADVANTAGE

- Because DVD technology is relatively new it still has strong competition from VHS video players and CD-ROM players.

> **DVD** means Digital Versatile Disc. It is also an optical device similar to a CD-ROM but is capable of storing more data. Often films are stored on DVD.

Storage used for making back-ups

Just in case anything goes wrong and data is spoiled in some way, it is useful to have an extra copy of the data. This is called a *back-up* copy. Although copies may be made onto floppy disks from the hard disk, the small amount of data we can store does not make floppy disks a good choice for large volumes of data. Sometime we may choose to back-up our data onto tape. Magnetic tape is ideal for back-ups. However today there are more modern devices such as zip drives and jaz drives (see Section B) but they store only a small amount of data compared to a magnetic tape.

Magnetic tape

This type of storage today looks like a small cassette, rather like an audio-tape cassette. The cassettes can be inserted into the tape drive and data and programs from the hard disk can be transferred (usually overnight) to the tape. In large-scale mainframe computer systems tape come as large spools simply because a large amount of data needs to be transferred at any one time. They are being used less and less as technology advances.

Figure 3.5 Magnetic tape cassette

The importance of back-ups

Because backing storage is not volatile and is always available when we require data and software it seems that nothing can go wrong providing we have everything stored away there. Backing storage usually takes the form of a hard disk and they do have a limited life span. It is very important not to rely on one item of backing store. You must always keep an additional and exact copy of all your work elsewhere. Most people, for small items, will choose to use a floppy disk for this task although for large-scale copying nowadays it is more common to use a zip drive (see Section B). Remember, a copy of your work is known as a *back-up*.

Common reasons for spoilt original copies on backing store.

- A hard disk which has failed. This is sometimes called a hard disk crash and usually means it is unlikely that data stored on the disk can be read.
- A virus infection (see Chapter 6).
- Lost floppy disk (some people keep original copies on floppy disk).
- Computer Network failure, (A network is a set of computers connected together where some people use its main computer's storage to save data – see Chapter 4) which means you cannot get to your data.
- Human error – when someone may delete or change important data by mistake. The old copy before the change or deletion is the correct version of the data and being able to go back to another copy which has not been changed in any way, is particularly important.

> A back-up is an extra copy of data and/or software taken for security reasons. Common storage devices used for back-ups are magnetic tape and zip drives (see Section B) although for small volumes of data, like a single document, a floppy disk may be used.

Computor systems:
components
and types

Summary

✓ Internal memory known as Immediate Access Storage (IAS and stored on RAM) is volatile but secondary (backing) storage is non-volatile.

✓ Hard disks and their drives often provide secondary storage, especially on desktop and note book computers.

✓ Hard disk drives have read/write heads, which move above the surface of the disk locating the address of data you need. The data is stored on the tracks on the disk.

✓ Hard disks have the capability of storing a large amount of data.

✓ In mainframe computers the hard disks come as a stack all together and are known as a disk pack.

✓ Floppy disks are smaller and portable and so they are often used for a user's own private data. A high density (HD) disk stores approximately 2Mb of data. They are $3\frac{1}{2}$ inches square.

✓ Magnetic tape is another type of storage media and today it comes in cassette form. They are frequently used for back-ups because they have a larger storage capacity than floppy disk.

✓ CD-ROMs are capable of storing 650Mb of data, are portable and read only so the are ideal for reference material, such as multimedia encyclopaedias. CD-ROMs are an optical device, where a beam of laser light is used to access the data.

✓ DVDs are similar to CD-ROMs because they are optical devices and are used for storing large multimedia material, particularly films.

✓ A 'back-up' is a copy of your original data or software taken for security reasons.

✓ Magnetic tapes now look like small audiocassettes and are often used for backing-up large volumes of data.

✓ Back-ups may be required when a virus spoils our original copy of data, when the place where we stored our data originally is not accessible, or when data is accidentally spoiled by the human computer user.

Test and review

1. IAS means I_____ A_____ S_____.
2. Backing/Secondary storage is necessary because IAS stored on RAM is v_____.
3. Hard disks are often used secondary storage. What is the most common use of a hard disk on today's small computer systems?_____
4. A floppy disk is useful because it is p_____.
5. State TWO advantages of using CD-ROMS rather than using hard disks for storing multimedia reference material.
6. DVDs and CD-ROMS are o_____ devices.
7. What is a back-up and why do we need it?

Review and thinking tasks

Look at a typical CD-ROM and compare it to a floppy disk. How are they different? Write down three different things about their appearance. Make a back-up copy of a folder you have on the hard disk of your computer. Will it fit? How much more space is there left on your disk? Look around your local shopping centre next time you go out. Can you see any DVD players or DVD films?

4 Introductory communications

Communication links

Computers can carry out a variety of tasks. We have seen that a person can use an individual computer with only a printer, mouse, monitor and keyboard attached to it. Individual computers not connected to anything are known as 'stand-alone' computers.

Sometimes it may be necessary for an individual computer to exchange information with another computer. To do this the two computers must have a connection so that they are linked in some way. Computers that are linked can communicate with one another over a long distance. In order to do this it is necessary to send messages in digital format from one computer to another.

Digital communication lines

Digital communication lines are especially designed to transmit these messages. The lines which allow digital messages to be transferred are known as *Integrated Services Digital Network lines (ISDN)* and large amounts of data may be sent along these lines at any one time, making them a very fast communication link. Most telephone companies provide this type of communication link.

> **Computer** to computer messages can be sent in digital format over ISDN lines.

Using ordinary telephone lines to link computers

Ordinary telephone lines often transmit sound signals because they were originally designed for speech. The signals are in analogue form. To transmit digital data in analogue format it must be converted. Then when the analogue message reaches the end of the telephone line it must be converted back to digital format for the receiving computer to be able to accept it. To make the conversion from analogue format to digital format and back again a *MODEM (MOdulator-DEModulator)* is required.

Digital ←→ Modem ←→ Analogue ←→ Modem ←→ Digital

Figure 4.1 Analogue to digital conversion via modems

Other types of communication link

There are other types of communication links. For example it is possible to communicate via satellite, microwave and radio waves. Wireless communication links which operate without the need for cables are becoming increasingly popular.

Sometimes the location of one computer and the computer we wish to communicate with may only be yards away. It may be just in the next room. In this case we may

> **Computer** to computer messages can be sent over ordinary telephone lines if a MODEM converts digital to analogue for transmission over the line and back to digital again at the other end using another MODEM.

Figure 4.2 MODEM

choose to use a length of cable which is dedicated to carrying data just between these two machines.

Comparing digital and analogue communication links

USES

Digital lines are used for transmitting large volumes of data at a fast rate. Analogue lines are often used by single users with little data to transfer, perhaps for a small amount of e-mail used over a conventional telephone line.

COMPARATIVE ADVANTAGES AND DISADVANTAGES

- Digital lines are more expensive to install than normal telephone lines and the line rental is higher.
- Modems must be purchased for use with normal telephone lines.
- There is a much faster transmission rate typically found on digital lines because they have a higher bandwidth (more data is transmitted in parallel – at the same time) than with an ordinary voice telephone line).

Computer networks

A *network of computers* is when several computers have communication lines linking them. There are many types of computer network. One type of computer network is when we have many individual computers linked so that a message may be sent from one to another. Another type of computer network is when we have one main computer called a *network server*. This controls access to work areas which are usually stored on the network server.

As we have seen an alternative to using networked computers is to use your computer as a *stand-alone* computer. Some computers have software which allows the user to select whether it should operate as a stand-alone computer or as a networked computer.

> **A network**
> is a set of computers connected together to allow communication of data and processes from one machine to another.

> **A stand-alone**
> computer is a computer which is not connected to a network.

USES

A computer network is often used to allow users to share data and software. A typical example of where you will see a network in operation is in a bank or supermarket. Cashiers in banks will have a computer on their desk, which can access the main network server computer so they can see your account. Supermarket assistants sometimes have a small computer known as an Electronic Point Of Sale (EPOS). The EPOS is connected

Figure 4.3 EPOS till

to a main network server computer which stores all the details about the stock. In both these situations the main server computer controls access to shared data.

ADVANTAGES

- When computers are networked together both programs (software), for example a word processor) and data (for example stock data) can be shared.
- It is also possible for all network users to communicate with one another and for them to share other resources like printers.

DISADVANTAGES

- Initial installation costs of a network can be quite high because of the cost of installing communication links.
- There is an extra task involved in making sure the shared resources are safe and secure. To do this extra task a **specially trained person** will also need to be employed. This is why we have to have our own user identification and password to gain access to private data (see below for a full explanation of user identification and passwords).
- If the network fails, users may not be able to look at the work that they need to see.
- If a lot of users are **logged on** together the system may operate very slowly.

User ids and passwords

When using a networked computer, it is important that we can only see the data which belongs to us and other resources which we are allowed to see. We should not be able to see other users' personal data. To achieve this kind of privacy users must 'logon' (sign in) to the system by giving a user identification (user id, sometimes also known as a personal id or network id) and a password to allow them access. The user id gives each user a personal identity, which is recognised by the system. The password attempts to ensure that the person is who they say they are. For security reasons it is important to:

- keep passwords private;
- change passwords frequently;
- log off the network properly.

Sharing resources and communicating are the main advantages network users have over stand-alone computer users.

Disadvantages of using networks are: extra work and special expertise involved in maintaining the network, inaccessibility of shared resources if the network server fails and slow response if too many users are connected at the same time.

User ids and passwords help to ensure privacy for individual users but it is essential to keep passwords private, change them frequently and also for users to log off the network properly.

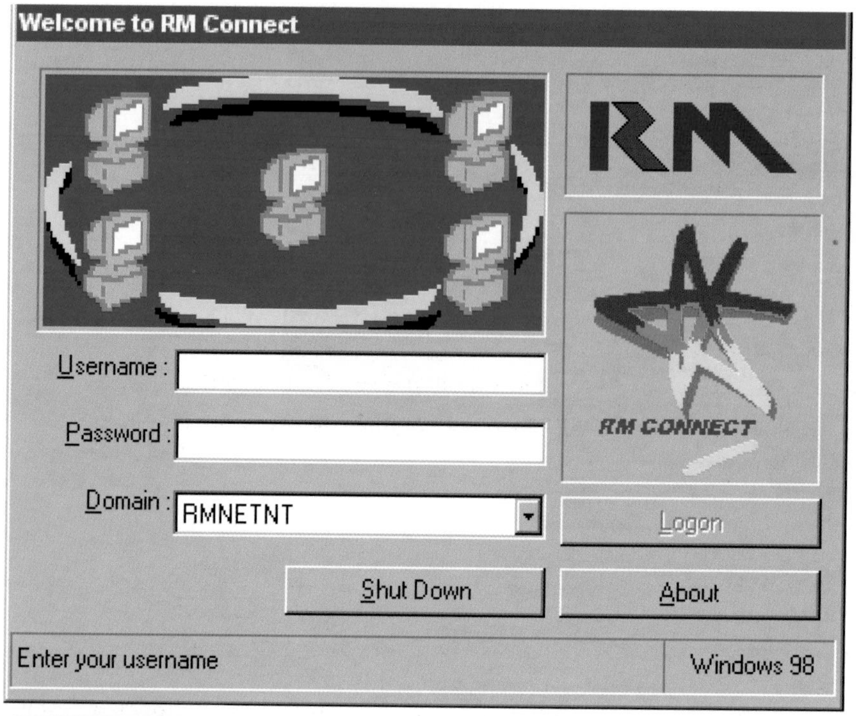

Welcome to RM Connect

Username :

Password :

Domain : RMNETNT ▼

Shut Down   About

Logon

Enter your username   Windows 98

Figure 4.4 LOGON screen

Ways of communicating

There are many different ways of communicating using computers. We are going to look at facsimile, electronic mail, voice mail and tele/videoconferencing in particular.

Facsimile (fax)

It is possible to send a fax using a computer as well as by using a fax machine. A fax is when we send a copy of a document over communication lines. This could be printed out immediately at the other end of the line. A fax is an image of a document. It is sent to a particular fax number and is not necessarily private since it is not to a private address of an individual person. It cannot be transmitted if the fax number is busy.

> A fax machine scans the images and transmits a copy (like a photocopy) over communication lines to be printed out at the other end.

Figure 4.5 Facsimile machine

USES

Fax machines are used to transmit documents which are not of a personal nature. For example solicitors may fax details of their service to a new client.

ADVANTAGE

- Immediate hard copy (printed on paper) is sent to the chosen destination.

DISADVANTAGES

- Only one fax number can be selected each time a message is sent. so it is not possible to broadcast the same document to many different fax machines in one go.
- Fax machines are not suitable for sending private messages or documents because many people in a busy office environment often share fax machines.
- It is not possible to edit a received document and re-print it, or attach other items or files, which cannot be printed out.

Electronic mail (e-mail)

Electronic mail is when a message is sent from one person directly to another using computers which are connected to a network. There is a special computer which receives all mail and sorts it out, deciding which '*mailbox*' it needs to go to. This is called a *mail server* and it acts a bit like a post sorting room. Each user has their own mailbox which is labelled with their own personal e-mail address. This means that this method of communication is very private. All sorts of documents can be attached to the e-mail including pictures, sound, video etc.

> E-mail allows person to person communication via a computer.

To be able to send e-mail, the user will need:

1. a computer processor;
2. a communication link: using analogue or digital telephone lines;
3. software to enable you to read, write, send and retrieve messages. This software may be purchased separately or may come as part of a package with other software;
4. an agreement with a service provider. This means that you agree to certain rules in order to have a mail box set up on the service provider's computer. (Note that service providers are companies which earn money by providing access through their network server to the **Internet**. They are sometimes referred to as Internet Service Providers or ISPs – see below;
5. an e-mail address can be provided by the service provider, for example, A.Jones@myservice.co.uk. (Note that e-mail addresses are usually made up of your e-mail identification for your mail box such as A.Jones, the '@' sign to indicate which place your mail box is set up at such as 'myservice.co.uk'.)

> To use e-mail you must have a communication link, hardware, software and an agreement with a service provider.

When a user's computer is not connected to the service provider's computer (usually known as a mail server), any mail is stored in the mailbox on the mail server. When you dial into your service provider your computer will link to their server and then you will be able to download your messages. You are then able to read your messages 'off-line'. This simply means that now you have your messages on your own computer you can read them at leisure without being connected to your service provider. E-mail is therefore very cost effective to use once it has been set up.

> E-mail users can send, receive, forward and reply to messages. They can also attach documents and send multiple copies of the same message to many recipients.

Basic e-mail facilities:

1. send a message, by simply typing in the address of the person you are sending it to with a message. This may have been checked for spelling.

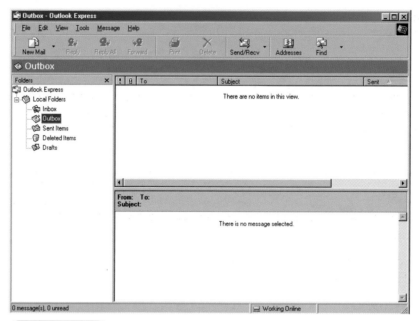

Figure 4.6 E-mail window

2. reply to a message you have received.

3. forward a message you have received to another person.

4. attach a variety of different types of documents, including sound files.

5. send multiple copies to a large number of recipients.

Some e-mail users have permanent access to a computer network and their own server. These users are usually business users. They have high-speed communication lines and their own network regularly downloads mail to user work areas.

●USES

Business and home users use e-mail. Personal messages and greetings are often sent between friends and similarly business colleagues may send information particularly with documents attached. In addition it is possible to join mailing lists. For example many newspapers are now on-line and by joining their mailing lists certain types of news summaries are automatically sent to you by e-mail.

Most schools have an e-mail facility. It allows communication between schools in different countries and schools partnership projects to develop and grow.

●ADVANTAGES

*   E-mail allows person to person communication.
*   Broadcasting the same message to a large number of people very fast.
*   Important documents may be attached.
*   If the person concerned is not currently on-line the mail server will store the message for later retrieval.

●DISADVANTAGES

*   As a single user you may need to subscribe to a service provider to obtain an e-mail address.
*   You need to learn how to use the software and be reasonably computer literate to use e-mail.

Voice mail systems

Voice mail systems are really like digital answering machines that allow people calling to leave messages. Many systems also direct callers to specific telephone extensions connected to a business telephone network. These digital systems play recorded messages so that callers can choose an option to help them find the correct person to speak to within the business. Once the system has helped to direct the caller to the correct telephone extension, it is possible to leave a message. The person receiving a message can then listen to it, delete and/or forward it on to someone else.

USES

Many businesses use voice mail systems to assist callers in finding the correct service they require. Some banks have voice mail systems, which use computer generated voice output messages to provide information to callers. Callers may then leave messages or even make transactions based upon numbers selected and security codes entered.

ADVANTAGES

- Fast routing of callers to the service they require.
- Ability to leave messages in the relevant voice mailbox.

DISADVANTAGES

- Sometimes they can be impersonal and the service required may not be easy to get to by selecting numbers and options.

> **Voice mail** systems are digital message management systems which may allow users to choose from a range of pathways to locate the telephone extension of their choice and then leave messages for absent recipients.

Tele/video conferencing

Teleconferencing allows groups of people in different locations to talk together over communication lines as though they were all sat round a table in a meeting, even though they are far apart. This saves on travelling costs and on travelling time to the meeting. It is very convenient except that it is sometimes difficult to exchange ideas when people are not talking to one another face to face in one another's company.

Videoconferencing is similar to teleconferencing except that people in the meeting can now see one another because video cameras are used. Desktop videoconferencing systems are available which have the correct software, video and sound systems attached to them. Often users can work on the same document.

What is needed for groups of people to tele/videoconference.

1. appropriate hardware. This may be a simple multi-way telephone system for teleconferencing, or a more sophisticated hardware set up for videoconferencing.
2. relevant software.
3. people to be available at the same time.
4. systems which can work together.

> **Tele/ videoconferencing** allow groups of people who may be located a large distance from one another to hold a meeting using sound or pictures.

USES

Business meetings and academic groups will sometimes use tele/videoconferencing rather than setting up a location to meet, particularly if all the people involved are located a large distance away from each other.

As computers are becoming commonplace and software to support teleconferencing has become more readily available, more people are beginning to use this facility, Videoconferencing can be used to allow groups of children to participate in lessons from a distance.

ADVANTAGES

- Tele/videoconferencing saves on travelling costs and on travelling time to the meeting.

⬤DISADVANTAGES

- It sometimes difficult for people to exchange ideas when they are not face to face in one another's company.
- Videoconferencing equipment is expensive.
- Over a distance synchronising sound and vision is technologically challenging.

Note: there are now videophones (telephones which have a screen to display a picture of the person at the other end of the line) which have been developed commercially. This equipment is very expensive when compared with an ordinary telephone facility. As digital communication becomes more commonplace and speed of transmission increases, the sound and vision synchronisation problem will become less problematic.

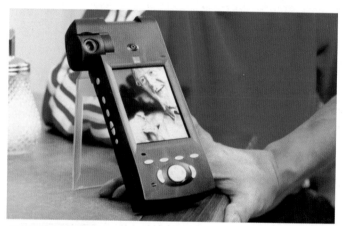

Figure 4.7 A videophone

**Computer systems:
components
and types**

Summary

✔ Computer to computer messages can be sent in digital format over ISDN lines.

✔ **Analogue** means a physical measurement of a continuous nature, for example sound, light and temperature.

✔ **Digital** means a numerical representation, where discrete values are used. In computers we use the values 0 and 1.

✔ Computer to computer messages can be sent over ordinary telephone lines if a MODEM converts digital to analogue signals for transmission over the line. A MODEM is then used at the other end to convert the analogue signal back to digital again.

✔ A network of computers are connected together to allow communication of data and processes from one machine to another.

✔ The advantages of networks is sharing and communicating.

✔ The disadvantages of networks are the initial set up costs, the cost of expertise and time involved in maintaining user security and slow response rate if too many users are connected at the same time.

✓ User ids identify the user to the system and passwords help to ensure that the user is who they say they are. Both help to ensure privacy for individual users.

✓ It is essential to keep passwords private, change them frequently and also for users to log off the network properly.

✓ Fax machines scans images and transmits a copy (like a photocopy) over communication lines.

✓ E-mail allows individual users to communicate with other users over a network of computers.

✓ Voice mail systems are digital message management systems, which may allow users to choose from a range of pathways to locate the telephone extension of their choice. Users will always be able to leave messages for people who are absent.

✓ Tele/videoconferencing allow groups of people who may be located a large distance from one another to hold a meeting using sound (and in the case of videoconferencing, pictures).

Test and review

1. Computer to computer messages can be sent in digital format over I_____lines.

2. ISDN stands for I_____ S_____ D_____ N_____.

3. Computer to computer messages can be sent over ordinary telephone lines if a M_____ converts digital to analogue for transmission over the communication line .

4. Computers are connected together to allow communication of data and processes from one machine to another. This is called a N_____?

5. State TWO advantages of using networks. _____
_____

6. State TWO disadvantages of using a network _____
_____

7. U_____ I_____ and P_____ help to ensure privacy for individual users.

8. It is important for users to L____ O____ the network properly to ensure privacy.

9. State three facilities which are required for a user to be able to use e-mail.
_____
_____

10. Videoconferencing awllow groups of people who may be located a long distance from each other to hold a meeting using S_____ and P_____.

Review and thinking tasks

Look at your school computers. Are they connected in any way? Are you able to send e-mail messages? Do you need to logon to a network? Can you send e-mail from home? Do you change your password regularly? Try and find a situation where there is videoconferencing or transmission of pictures and sound over a computer network. Typical examples may be found on the Internet where you can watch people working in offices or where there are sites which are set up just so that you watch people carrying out everyday activities.

Storing data

Types of data
We know that we can store data in computer memory. Data is commonly stored on backing store. In computer systems there are many different types of data. The most common types are text, numeric and date/time. When we tell the computer that we want certain data items to be a certain type, for example numeric, from that point onwards it will not let us input data of a different data type into that data item.

Text
Text data allows input of any letter, number, space, punctuation mark or special character like £, %, &, etc. Examples of text data are: Forename, Surname such as Angela Jones or Business name such as Partner & PartnerSon. If we store numbers in a text data type, we will not be able to do calculations with them. This is why we must have a separate data type 'numeric'.

Numeric
This data must only be numbers. It can be whole numbers or decimal numbers. It can also be formatted which means it can look a certain way. It can be formatted as pounds and pence for example. An example of an unformatted number is 345.678. An example of a formatted number with two decimal places is: 345.68. An example of a formatted number, which is known as currency on some systems is £345.68.

Date/time
This data must only have days, months, years and time format. Formats can be in different layouts such as the full name of the month followed by the day of the month followed by the year or a simple dd/mm/yy format which will accept for example 05/12/77 as a date.

Boolean
This data can only have two values: TRUE and FALSE. An example of a Boolean could be added to our example of the pupil details on page 42. To indicate whether a pupil is vegetarian or not we may specify a Boolean field named Vegetarian, which can only contain the values True or False.

Groups of data
Individual data items with their own data type are sometimes called *fields*. An example of a field is Date of Birth (note its data type will be DATE).

Groups of these fields, which are related in some way, are known as a *record*. An example of a record is a pupil school record. One field may be date of birth and other related fields may be 'Forename' and 'Surname' (note their data types will be TEXT). This type of record and an example of a stock record is shown overleaf. Note that the pupil record has a pupil registration number. This is a special field called a 'Key Field', which identifies each individual pupil. There cannot be any duplicate values stored in a key field.

> **Different data types are required for different situations, for example text, numeric and date/time. Boolean: these data types may look a certain way because they are formatted.**

> **A field is an individual data item with a certain data type and perhaps a certain format.**

> **A record is a group of related fields. They represent a person, object or thing, for example customer, pupil or stock item.**

PUPIL RECORD

Field name	Data type
Pupil Registration Number	Number
Forename	Text
Surname	Text
Date of Birth	Date
House and street name	Text
Town	Text
County	Text
Postcode	Text

A file contains many records. Note that the way fields are set out for each record is the same, for example a record may contain three fields: forename, surname and date of birth. The records mean that these three items are filled with data for each person with a name and date of birth. The whole set of data becomes the file.

STOCK RECORD

Field name	Data type
Product number	Number
Product Description	Text
Number in stock	Number
Cost per item	Number or Currency
Supplier reference number	Number
Warehouse location	Text

A group of related records are known as a *file*. An example of a file is a group of pupils in a school. It will contain many individual pupil records. For every individual in the school there will be one record. For example if there are 1000 pupils in the school there will be a file of 1000 pupil records. Each pupil record may contain many fields. An example of the pupil data stored in part of a file is given below (note some address fields have been omitted from the example).

PUPIL File

Pupil No	Forename	Surname	Date of Birth	Postcode
23	Alice	Brown	14/12/89	WG12 3BR
29	Molly	Reece	12/09/88	WG12 4XV
54	Brian	Trimble	05/05/90	NE1 34Z
77	Vivien	Jones	07/06/90	NE7 33X
88	Peter	Martinez	08/04/90	NE8 44Q

QUESTIONS

Let's check what we have said by answering some simple questions about the pupil data file above.

1. What data type do we use for date of birth?
2. What data type do we use for postcode?

3. How many fields are there in a pupil record?
4. Which fields make up a pupil record?
5. What is the date of birth of Brian Trimble?
6. How many pupils are in the file?

ANSWERS

1. date
2. test
3. 6
4. pupil no, forename, surname, dob, postcode
5. 05/05/90
6. 6

(answers 1–6 printed upside-down)

Summary

Computor systems: components and types

✓ Different data types are required for different situations, for example text, numeric and date/time. These data types may look a certain way because they are formatted

✓ A field is an individual data item with a certain data type and perhaps a certain format

✓ A record is a group of related fields. They represent a person, object or thing, for example customer, pupil or stock item

✓ A file contains many records. The layout of each record is the same, for example a record may contain three fields: forename, surname and date of birth

Test and review

1. Different data types are required for different situations, for example
   N_____, D_____ or T_____.
2. These data types may look a certain way because they are F_____.
3. A F_____ is an individual data item with a certain data type and perhaps a certain format.
4. A R_____ is a group of related fields, they represent a person, object or thing, for example customer, pupil or stock item
5. A F_____ contains many related records.
6. An example of a file is a _____ file.

7. Consider the stock record on page 42.

a) Name two fields which are numeric _____

b) Why is number in stock a numeric data type? _____

_____

c) Write down an example of the data that you could store in an individual stock record. _____

_____

d) Construct a file of six records using the empty table below, labelling the top row of the table with appropriate field names.

Review and thinking tasks

Think about the data in your school. Sometimes teachers will keep a record about your achievements. What fields would they wish to store data in? What data types could you choose for each of them? How many pupils are there in your class? Do you think that a record will be required for each of them? How many records will be required? Try and draw a list of everyone in your class with an IT test result for each person. Label which items are fields. Draw a circle around the group of fields, which represent a record, and a square around what you think represents the file.

Information management:
legal issues, implications, health and safety

Introduction

In this chapter we will look at some of the problems caused by people who break the law by copying software and spreading viruses. There are also those people who break into computer systems and gain access to information that is private. These people are known as hackers. We will also look at the way information technology affects our lives today and how the use of computers may cause health and safety problems.

Software copyright

It is a criminal offence to steal software or to copy software without the permission of the person who owns the copyright on a piece of software. It is also an offence to run copied software on your computer. The law, which makes this a criminal offence, is *the Copyright, Designs and Patents Act 1989*. To ensure that software copies are legal companies usually issue a licence. Individual licences like this usually come packaged with any software you buy. Sometimes companies also issue a special number to type in when you install your software. Businesses however may buy many licences and only one copy of the software. These are called multiple licences and allow more than one user to use the copy of the software. Multiple licenses are usually available at reduced cost and sometimes rather than specify how many licences are needed it is possible to buy a '*site licence*'. A site licence means that anyone using a computer at a given site (such as a school or any business premises) can legally use a copy of the software. Users cannot take copies of software away from the site. It is only licensed for those machines at the site.

Copying software for your own use without purchasing a licence is known as 'software piracy'. Sometimes people copy the software and pass it on to others, sometimes even selling it. They may even issue a copy of the licence agreement. All of these examples of copying software are against the law. Software costs a lot of money to develop and so illegal copying of software costs software companies lost income.

Copying software illegally is so common that it is estimated that more than half of the software running on computers in the UK is not licensed. It is very tempting for employees using software at work to illegally copy the software and take it home for their own use. It is also possible for employees to distribute illegal copies of software to colleagues. Many people who do this are sometimes unaware that they are breaking the law.

Viruses

A computer virus is a program which:

- attaches itself to another program or a file;
- can cause damage and destroy essential files on your computer system;
- can spread and be passed from file to file and computer to computer.

It is against the law to knowingly distribute or write a virus because viruses are spread with intent to cause unauthorised changes of computer material. There are many different viruses which are often identified by name. Many viruses are spread by e-mail from

> **The Copyright, Designs and Patents Act 1989 is the law which deters people from illegally copying/stealing software or running copied software on their computers.**

> **A virus is a computer program, which intentionally causes damage to computers or data (or at the very least affect the way a computer works) and can spread by copying itself to other files.**

downloading files from the Internet or by using floppy disks in one computer and then in another. Viruses spread very quickly between computers that are connected to a network. Because they can cause so much damage to computer systems and files, it is important to take precautions against being 'infected' by a virus. There are several ways of doing this.

- When opening e-mail, be sure not to open messages from unknown senders. They may have a virus hidden in its attachment or text message.
- Check your computer regularly for viruses using anti-virus software.
- Do not accept free copies of software.
- Always virus check your floppy disk when you have been using a different machine.
- Make sure you regularly back-up your files just in case your anti-virus software does not detect the latest virus.

Anti-virus software can search for and detect viruses. Generally the files containing most viruses that are detected can be 'disinfected' immediately although if the virus is very new the way to disinfect the disk is not a simple matter. Because new viruses are always being made it is important to keep upgrading your anti-virus software.

Hacking

Hacking is when a person gets into a computer system to look at files, which are private and do not belong to him or her. When a person does this it means that they probably have logged onto a computer system as though they are someone else.

Hacking is defined as '*unauthorised access to data held on a computer system*'. Once hackers break into a computer system this way they may:

- look at data;
- copy data;
- change data.

Usually a hacker has worked out the password and user identification of a person who is authorised to use the computer system. Some people have special monitoring software which can obtain your password as you type it on the keyboard of your computer. Even though your password is not displayed on your own computer monitor as you type it in it may still be displayed on the computer monitoring your input. If these people intercept your telephone link to a banking system, it is possible for them to obtain your bank details, password and other security information. Once they have all this information they can make transactions on your bank account by pretending to be you.

To fight against this type of hacking banks have had to take more care. Some banks now have other security procedures as well as user ids and passwords. Sometimes data is coded in a special way so that it is impossible to read it as it is being transmitted.

People who hack into computer systems do not always want to steal money. Sometimes the hacker may be a young computer enthusiast who hacks into a computer system to prove that it can be done.

In order to protect a computer system from unauthorised access it is important to:

- log off correctly every time you leave your machine;
- choose a password which is not obvious;
- keep your password private;
- change your password frequently.

Try to prevent viruses spreading by installing anti-virus software, not using copied or downloaded software and check your hard disk and floppy disks regularly.

Anti-virus software can detect and 'disinfect' your disks but it must be up-to-date or it will not deal with new viruses.

Hacking is the unauthorised access of data held on a computer system.

Social effects of ICT

Computers have affected our lives both in the home and at work.

At work computers have:

- mostly removed the boring repetitive manual tasks in factories because robots are being used more often;
- reduced the long drawn out process of calculating pay because computers are good at doing lots of calculations; this also means they are good in science and engineering applications where many calculations are done;
- reduced the time taken to search for different types of information because, for example, computers are good at finding details of stock or customers, very quickly;
- reduced the time taken to keep records accurate, because generally many computerised files have replaced manual files. For example, because many stock files are computerised, it is possible to automatically keep the amount of stored stock up to date and keep track of sales trends.

The changing patterns of employment include *reduced clerical staff and manual workers* meaning that there has been some *unemployment*. Due to the introduction of computers thousands of office jobs have been lost. Instead of an army of payroll staff or filing clerks we have automated payroll systems. Many of these jobs were lost in the 1960–70s when computers were first used in larger businesses to cope with the ever increasing burden of calculating the pay for a large number of employees. For some of these businesses it was becoming impossible even with a large number of people to make sure all the pay had been calculated and prepared accurately and on time. More recently banking systems have become more automated with more and more Automatic Teller Machines (ATMs) reducing the number of banking staff required.

It also means that those workers left in jobs working with computers now have *different jobs and have to be trained to use computers*. For example, a secretary may need to

> The use of computers has changed the way people work because manual work is carried out by robots and manual records which are often stored on computer are easier search and keep up to date. This has caused some unemployment.

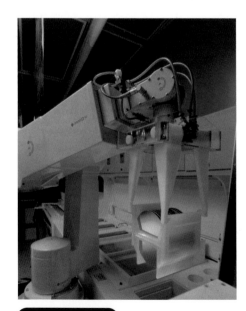

Figure 6.1 Robots on a production line

be trained to use a word processor rather than using a typewriter. In some instances because computers need to be maintained and users need support there has been an *increase in jobs in the computer industry*. For example, computer programmers are needed to continually improve and write software. Computer repair centres and advice lines have provided new jobs. In fact there is a whole new industry related to computer manufacture, maintenance and development.

There are also jobs where people have no need to go to the office as they can work from home. This is called *teleworking or telecommuting*. Because of computer technology and better communications technology, it is also possible for people to meet using video-conferencing (see Chapter 4). Businesses are still a little slow to benefit from employing people to work in this way because they fear that it may be difficult to control the work-force. Some workers also prefer to have daily social contact with colleagues especially if they are working in a team. They are also unable to separate home and work commit-ments and find it difficult to motivate themselves to get the work done. On a more positive note workers save commuting time and costs and have more flexible working hours.

In the home microprocessor-controlled devices like washing machines and dishwash-ers have reduced the time spent on domestic tasks. There is an increase in leisure time and leisure related activities associated with digital devices and computers. For example people play games on their home computers, spend time on the Internet and even bank and buy things over the Internet.

> Some new jobs have been created in the computer industry and also in business because jobs have changed.

Advantages of having this technology at home:

- It is easier to carry out domestic tasks because we are able to use the microprocessor-controlled devices in a flexible way. For example we can choose from many programmes on a washing machine.
- It is easier for people who are ill or disabled to shop for goods from home.
- It provides entertainment in the form of games.

> Advantages of ICT in the home are that it simplifies domestic tasks and provides more leisure time. It is also easier for people to shop and bank from home.

Disadvantages of having this technology at home:

- Some people find the technology complicated. For example there may be many different optional buttons available to programme a machine, such as a video recorder.
- Sometimes digital control devices are costly to repair because an expert is needed to fit the new part.
- People feel there is no need to leave the home and may have less social contact.
- Using the Internet and playing computer games at home can be time consuming and reduce social interaction with other members of the family.
- There are problems when undesirable material is published on the Internet, particularly when younger people in the family are allowed to search the Internet unsupervised. It is possible to buy software which blocks access to undesirable material – these are known as 'network nannies or supervisors' but they are no substitute for properly supervised use of the Internet.
- People can become too reliant on microprocessor controlled equipment in the home. For example, if the washing machine breaks down, it is considered extremely inconvenient to lose the flexibility and automated programmes available and instead wash by hand or go to the launderette.

> The main disadvantage of having ICT in the home is that it can make people reliant upon it and prolonged use of ICT for entertainment can reduce social interaction with others.

Computers also affect our everyday lives.

- Many people use their bank cards and credit cards to shop. They can do this because of the large computers at banks and because of automated communications between shops and banks.
- Many large companies send computerised statements telling people how much they owe, for example electricity bills. This means that customers have detailed information about the current status of their account.
- Government establishments like the Inland Revenue also monitor the tax that people pay using computers. This means that they have more accurate records about us.
- Information such as the availability and cost of items we wish to purchase is often readily available over the Internet. This affects our everyday decisions.

These are just a few examples but there are many more. Even when we shop in a supermarket the computer produces a receipt that tells us exactly what we have bought as well as how much everything costs. An Automatic Teller Machine (ATM) will give us cash if we put our bankcard into it and provide the correct information. Computerised security cameras can monitor public places like shopping precincts to help reduce crime. Car parks have computerised barrier systems.

> Shops, banks, businesses and the government rely on computers so much that any contact we have with these organisations means that we are affected by ICT in everyday.

> Increased use of ICT can have many positive effects such as availability of up-to-date information and the reduction of boring and mundane tasks.

Figure 6.2 An ATM in use

It is important to remember that information and communication technology (ICT) can be used to our advantage but sometimes things can go wrong:

- Photo editing software can be used to change pictures. This may lead to undesirable images being published over the Internet and misleading photographs being published in newspapers.
- Hacking can result in computer fraud, for example stealing money from someone's bank account because they have gained unauthorised access.
- Incorrect and even undesirable data may be stored about people without them knowing what it is.
- Crimes such as software theft (see software copyright notes above) may be committed.
- Staff who are monitored by computer systems at work may begin to resent their employer.

Internet

Information technology is still changing rapidly and this affects us all. Communications technology has also changed and improved. Systems today often combine both of these technologies. The result is that networked systems have increased and the use of the Internet has grown. The Internet is discussed on television, radio, in offices and schools. It is now common knowledge that the Internet provides a convenient way to access a wide range of information.

What is the Internet?

There is a difference between the Internet and the World Wide Web (www). The Internet is an **international network of computers connected by communication lines**. Some of these computers are small personal computers and some are large supercomputers.

The World Wide Web (www) is **a collection of pages (a page capable of being accessed over the Internet) with links to other pages.** For example there may be a page which contains information about today's UK weather. There may be a map on the page which divides the UK into areas. If you click on an area there could be a link containing the address of another page giving more detailed weather information for that area. These links containing addresses, which take you another page, are called '*hyperlinks*'.

There are many hyperlinks connecting many pages. If we tried to map out all the hyper-link pathways on paper the drawing could look like a spider's web. For this reason we call the pages '*web pages*'. A hypertext link could be hidden in a diagram, picture or a sequence of words. Some web pages are kept together in a group and are known as a '*web site*'. Each web site has a start page called the '*home page*'. To be able to access pages you will need a '*web browser*' (software which allows you to look at pages over the Internet). A web page address is known as a URL or Uniform Resource Locator. An example might be: http://www.bbc.co.uk. The http part of the address means that it is a web page which uses 'hypertext transfer protocol' – a set of rules for transferring the content of the pages from one computer to another. Web pages belonging to a particular web site may have links to pages on other web sites on a different computer. Each web site is located on a particular computer which has a Point Of Presence (POP). This simply means other users can locate it over the Internet. The

> **Increased us of ICT may have negative effects and encourage crimes such as computerised fraud and software theft.**

> **The Internet is a network of computers around the world which collectively provides a facility to exchange information. No one person is responsible for the Internet. There are concerns about computer crime over the Internet, undesirable material being transmitted over the Internet and the security of data transfer over the Internet.**

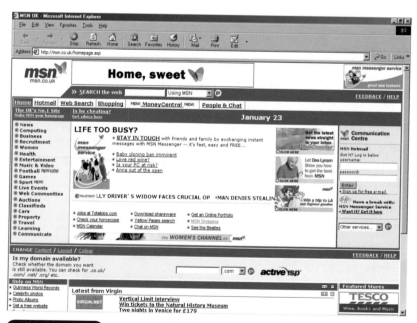

Figure 6.3 A typical web page

confusion between the 'www' and 'Internet' is because web sites are located on computers connected to the Internet.

Web pages have to be written using commands that allow the content to be transferred and displayed in a certain way. The commands belong to a computer language known as HyperText Markup Language (HTML). Sometimes it is possible to convert documents you have created to HTML documents ready for use on a web site.

There is no one responsible for the Internet and no world-wide law governing the Internet. As a result, and due to different laws in different countries, some material may be regarded as legal in one country and illegal in another country. Sometimes information may be unreliable and there are always concerns about the security of data sent over the Internet. Some Internet sites have ways of stopping people hacking and getting data from them. The way they do this is to make their site secure. To let visitors to their site know that it is a secure site, a message could be displayed and a picture of a closed padlock can be displayed on the screen.

Criminals may set up sites to persuade people to buy products which are of no use. For example, to prove how gullible people can be when browsing ('surfing') the Internet a test site was set up called 'Bellilug'. This site displayed details of products for entertaining pets over the Internet. People visiting the site were asked if they would be willing to pay to subscribe to their site. Thousand of users e-mailed to say that they would without realising that 'Belillug' was the word 'gullible' with just the letters mixed up! Sometimes sites are set up claiming to be selling products or services when in fact they just take the customers money and no goods or services are provided.

Health
There are a number of health issues relating to the prolonged use of ICT.

- Repetitive Strain Injury (RSI) is when people suffer from strain of the tendons and ligaments in the arms and shoulders. It can sometimes be recognised as aching and stiffness of the arms and shoulders or may be even a tingling sensation in the fingers. In severe cases users are unable to use the their hands normally whilst mild cases can be helped by purchasing keyboards which have a good design or by providing wrist supports.

- Back problems can be caused by poor posture when using computer equipment. To prevent back problems it is important to have adjustable screens (which will tilt and swivel) and adjustable chairs (which can have the seat height changed and back support changed). Sometimes footrests and backrests may be required.

- A badly positioned screen can strain the user's eyes. Eyestrain can also be caused by glare from the computer screen. Sunlight bouncing from windows or from overhead lighting can cause the glare. Window blinds and light diffusers (something placed over the light to spread it out rather than allow it to shine directly at an object) can help reduce glare. Adjustable chairs and screens can help the user to position themselves more comfortably so that they are not straining their eyes to look at the screen.

- General fatigue and stress such as the examples above can sometimes be caused because of long periods of time sitting in front of the computer. It is important to take breaks away from this type of situation, perhaps by taking a ten-minute break or doing some other task which does not involve the computer.

RSI is strain in the upper limbs. It can be prevented by well designed keyboards and using wrist supports.

Providing adjustable screens and chairs can prevent back problems.

Using diffused lighting, window blinds and adjustable screens or chairs can prevent eyestrain.

Taking breaks away from the computer may prevent health problems.

Employers must obey the Health and Safety law which covers use of visual display units. Free eyesight tests for those using computers on a regular basis should be provided and regular breaks must be taken.

Safety

There is a range of safety issues related to using computers.

- It is important that electrical sockets are not overloaded and that liquids are kept away from electrical equipment.
- Computers generate a lot of heat and there is a risk of fire. It is important that the correct fire extinguishers are available.
- People can easily trip over trailing wires possibly causing serious injury. There should be no trailing wires or other hazards which could cause personal injury.

> Fire extinguishers, good ventilation, safe lighting, sufficient electrical points and no trailing wires should be features of a safe working environment.

Computer systems: components and types

Summary

- A virus is a computer program which has been written to cause damage to computers. Viruses can spread by copying themselves to other files.
- The Copyright, Designs and Patents Act 1989 is the law which deters people from illegally copying/stealing software or running copied software on their computers
- Anti-virus software can detect and remove viruses.
- Hacking is unauthorised access to data held on a computer system. Once hackers break into a computer system, they may look at, copy, change or delete data.
- The use of computers has changed the way people work because robots carry out a lot of manual work and clerical work has been reduced. This has caused some unemployment.
- Some new jobs have been created by increased use of ICT such as computer repairers, user support staff, computer programmers etc.
- Some jobs have changed and it is necessary to train staff to do different tasks on the computer.
- Teleworking is when people have no need to go to the office. They can work from home because of better computer technology and better communications.
- Advantages of ICT in the home are that domestic tasks are simplified and using microprocessors often gives more flexibility. People have more leisure time because domestic tasks are automated and it is also easier for people to shop and bank from home.
- The disadvantages of having ICT in the home is that it can be difficult to learn how to use it properly at first, but eventually it can make people reliant upon it. Cost of repairs can be expensive and prolonged use of ICT for entertainment can reduce social interaction with others.
- Shops, banks, businesses and the government rely on computers so much everyone is affected by ICT in their everyday life.
- Hacking can result in computer fraud, for example stealing from someone's bank account because they have gained unauthorised access.

✓ There are concerns about the people's privacy. Incorrect and even undesirable data may be stored about people without them knowing what it is. Other people may gain unauthorised access to this data.

✓ It is an offence to copy software without obtaining a licence.

✓ There are concerns about computer crime over the Internet, undesirable material being transmitted over the Internet and security of data transferred over the Internet.

✓ Eye strain can be prevented by providing diffused overhead lighting and suitable window blinds.

✓ RSI is strain in the upper limbs. It can be prevented by well designed keyboards and using wrist supports.

✓ Back problems can be prevented by providing adjustable screens and chairs.

✓ All these health problems may be prevented by taking 10 minute breaks away from the computer every 2 hours.

✓ Fire extinguishers, sufficient electrical points and no trailing wires should be features of a safe working environment.

Test and review

1. What is a virus? (Tick which options are correct)
   a) a computer program
   b) a copyright program
   c) bacteria which get into the computer
   d) software which affects the way the computer works
   e) software which causes the computer to shut down
   f) software which can spread by copying itself to other files
   g) bacteria which stick to the surface of a disk but come off when you insert it in the computer.

2. It is legal to copy software but illegal to run copied software. TRUE or FALSE?

3. What would you use to 'disinfect' or 'clean' your disks if it has a virus?

4. A hacker is a person who_____.

5. The use of computers has changed the way people work because manual work is carried out by R_____ .

6. Some new jobs have been created by increased use of ICT such as computer repair, user support, programmers etc. but an example of a job which has been lost is_____

7. An example of a job which has changed due to the increased use of ICT is
   _____.

8. When people have no need to go to the office they can work from home because of better computer technology and better communications. This is called T_____.

9. Computer misuse may lead to crimes such as

_____.

10. There are concerns about computer crime over the Internet because_____

_____

_____

11. Name three health problems caused by prolonged use of computers.

_____

12. Name three features of a safe working environment.

_____

 # **Review** and thinking tasks

Look at your computers in school. Do they have a virus checker? Make sure you use it.

Can you think of any examples of computer misuse that you have read about in newspapers or seen reported on TV? Look on the Internet to see what you can find about hacking and computer misuse. Look around your computer room at school. Is it safe? Are there any trailing wires? Is it free from health hazards, for example do you have adjustable chairs? Think about the difference between health and safety and make a list of all health related hazards and all saftey issues we have discussed in this section.

Section A Test your knowledge

1. The Central Processing Unit is the main piece of hardware in your computer. Name two other important pieces of hardware.
2. Software is also required to make your computer work. What is software?
3. Backing storage is used for storing programs and data. Name two types of backing storage.
4. Portable computers and desktop computers are similar because they can do the same sort of tasks. List three differences between portable and desktop computers.
5. Name two common input devices.
6. Images must be converted to digital format to be edited on the computer or to be used in computer presentations. Name two ways in which images can be captured or converted to digital format.
7. Explain why computer images take up a lot of memory space?
8. Sound input can be captured using two methods. State what they are and explain why one method is more advantageous than the other.
9. A VDU is an output device which gives feedback to the user. Name two other output devices.
10. Which type of printer would you choose to produce high quality, fast printouts?
11. What is a control device? Give one example to illustrate your answer.
12. Explain the difference between IAS and backing storage.
13. Compare hard disks with floppy disks, explaining their relative advantages and disadvantages.
14. Why are CD-ROMs ideal for storing multimedia reference material?
15. What is DVD?
16. Explain why we take backups of our work.
17. Describe what we mean when we refer to a term 'computer network'.
18. List the advantages and disadvantages of using a computer network.
19. Explain why users need a user id and password to logon to a network.
20. E-mail has several advantages over facsimile. State two of these advantages.
21. Describe what we mean when we refer to 'data type'. Give two examples to illustrate your answer.
22. A file is a collection of related records. Explain why each record needs a key field, giving an example of a typical **key field**.
23. Describe how you would prevent a computer virus from affecting your computer system.
24. What is a hacker?
25. Name
    a) two jobs which have been created by the increased use of ICT;
    b) two jobs which have been changed by the increased use of ICT;
    c) and two jobs which have been replaced because of the increased use of ICT.
26. Describe video conferencing.
27. Describe teleworking and explain why it is an advantage to telework.
28. Computer crimes are on the increase due to the expansion of the Internet. Name two crimes which could happen when using the Internet.
29. Name two health problems caused by continued use of ICT equipment and describe how they might be prevented.
30. Name two safety issues to be considered when installing a new ICT laboratory.

Section

B

ICT Applications, Systems, Networks and computer technology

This section is an extension of Section A and covers in more detail the technology and applications found in the home, at work and in everyday life. There is also more detailed coverage of legal issues relating to the use of computers and networks. Notes on hardware, software, input, storage and output are also extended. Finally, to support the major coursework and provide the foundation for further study of Section E, Chapter 9 is devoted to information systems theory.

In Chapter 7 some example applications are briefly described. However, Computer Aided Learning (CAL) and process control systems are included as examples with the relevant technology section. The text does not cover details of all applications you may study but the following list provides you with advisory notes about areas that you need to know about for the examination.

- Electronic communications: make sure you use e-mail and the Internet.
- Process control: look at robots and how they are used in factories to produce goods.
- Billing: look at mail order catalogues and how they advise customers about how much they owe or look at your electricity/gas bills at home.
- Crime: electronic fraud and security systems, tagging and the police computer system (see Chapter 8)
- Sales, stock control, purchasing and payroll. In particular look at supermarket stock control and point of sale terminals (Chapter 7).
- School administration: reports, records and registration are all systems found in schools. How do they work in your school?
- Booking systems: theatre and travel, banking systems (EFT), cash machines and home banking (Chapter 7).
- Medical applications and library systems – these systems we see in use in everyday life (Chapter 7).

Computer technology

Types of computer

Microcomputers

Desktop personal computers and notebook/portable personal computers have already been discussed in Chapter 1. Both of these types of computer are based on a single microprocessor. In addition to these types of computers, microprocessor technology (tiny circuits – sometimes called 'chips') appears in domestic appliances such as dishwashers and washing machines. Mobile telephones and other everyday equipment also contain these tiny little circuits which process input and produce some form of useful output. Palmtops and calculators fall into this same category of computerisation. There are many different manufacturers, with new products appearing all the time.

USES

- The home user, schools and small businesses all use microcomputers. Microprocessors are found in many home appliances.
- Schools, universities and other educational organisations also use microcomputers.

ADVANTAGES

- Microcomputers are an affordable way to improve efficiency by storing and processing data.
- Microcomputers are good at word-processing and using as a communication tool.
- Microcomputers provide access to the Internet for millions of users.

> **Microcomputers are small computers used by the home user and small businesses.**

Mainframe computers

In the early days of computer use there was no such thing as a small computer. The tiny circuits capable of processing many instructions in seconds had not been invented so the small microcomputers we know well today could not be built. Instead much larger machines occupied huge rooms or sometimes an entire floor of a building. This type of large computer is called a mainframe computer. Large mainframe computers were found in universities and larger businesses in the 1960s and 1970s. As microcomputer technology has advanced mainframe technology too has moved forward.

Today mainframe computers are also more compact than they were, but it is still common to see an entire site allocated to a mainframe computer with hundreds of disk drives, printers and other devices attached to it. A mainframe can support many thousand users. To do this terminals (sometimes these are microcomputers) are attached to it. Mainframes are very expensive and cost many hundreds of thousands of pounds. The top end of this category of computer is known as a *supercomputer* and they can cost millions of pounds to buy. Typical users of this type of computer are government establishments, the weather centres and very large commercial organisations.

USES

Large organisations such as banks, building societies and insurance companies often use mainframe computer technology.

Mainframe computers are used by large organisations such as banks and building societies for processing large volumes of data.

▬ADVANTAGES

- Using mainframe technology a large amount of data can be processed and hundreds of users may be able to carry out lots of different tasks at the same time. Often not only is it necessary to have a large processing unit, but also to be able store large volumes of data and produce many different reports.
- It is often more secure and convenient to have all this processing, storage and input-output capability located at one secure site.

Some applications at home and in everyday life where microprocessor technology is used

Today microprocessor technology is used in everyday life. As microchips get smaller and more powerful new uses are being found on a daily basis.

Portable telephones have microprocessors so that it is possible to save large address books, perform calculations and even automatically access the Internet.

Figure 7.1 A mobile phone

Many home users have their own computer and are able to send e-mail and access the Internet. They are able to word process their own letters and keep details of the way they spend their money.

Figure 7.2 Working with a PC at home

Some **central heating systems** use microprocessor technology. With these systems it is possible to *select the temperature* you want the room to be, so that the system knows when the boiler should be working. If the temperature of the room is less than the selected temperature of the room then it knows the boiler should be working. If the temperature of the room is greater than the selected temperature of the room then it knows the boiler should be switched off. For the system to make a comparison between the selected room temperature and actual temperature of a room we need to use sensors. Temperature sensors detect the temperature of the room so that it may be compared with temperatures programmed into the system. The processor then makes a decision about whether the boiler should be on or not.

It is also possible to tell the system the times when you want the heating and hot water to come on and off. A comparison is made between the *current time* on the system's clock with the times you have programmed into memory. The processor then makes a decision about whether the boiler should be on or off. If the *current time* = the time the heating should be **off** the temperature sensors are ignored.

> **Central heating** systems and home security systems use microprocessor technology to respond to data received from sensors. The sensor data is compared with the details programmed in by the user.

Figure 7.3 A central heating control panel with digital display

Security systems also use microprocessor technology. The home user may switch on the burglar arm when it is required. When the whole system is switched on, it will respond to data from a variety of sensors.

> **Security systems** have sensors to detect when doors or windows are opened. The microprocessor will make a decision to sound the alarm.

a) Sensors may be set up to detect a window or an open door. These sensors are usually *contact switches* which when they are no longer touching (because a window has been opened) send a signal to the microprocessor in the control panel of the burglar alarm;

b) A *passive infra-red* sensor (PIR) will detect if there is some movement inside a room. If movement is detected a signal is sent to the microprocessor. It then makes a decision to sound the alarm.

More details about sensors and control systems are to be found in Section C.

Most of us are familiar with the more common applications of microprocessor use in the home such as **dishwashers** and **washing machines**. A washing machine, for example, has many different programmes which we can choose using a control switch on the front of the machine. The control switch is the input. The machine wash, rinse and spin, together with the water temperature is then controlled by the processor. Switching on

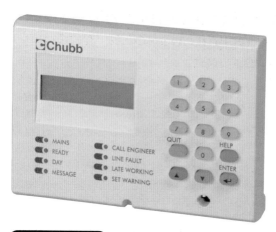

Figure 7.4 A security system control panel

the heater to heat up the washing water or turning on the motor to spin the washing are typical outputs from the processor.

Many of us have used a **digital watch.** Think about how you use the buttons. For example, we are able to set the alarm simply by pressing the buttons (the input). The processor knows when the watch time matches the alarm time (processing) and sounds the alarm (output).

Figure 7.5 A digital watch

However, today, new and exciting applications are being developed. Small microprocessors are being inserted into clothing or handbags as prototypes for use in a variety of ways as we go about our everyday business. A microprocessor personal assistant has also been developed which looks rather like a wristwatch. Additionally a prototype computer has been developed so that it is worn as part of a headset which helps you navigate around shopping malls or supermarkets. Manufacturers are looking at new and exciting ways to market **embedded microprocessors.**

Microprocessor technology can be used to repair damaged hearing. A tiny microprocessor is surgically implanted inside the ear of a person who has never been able to hear more than very muffled noise. The patient is now learning to process the messages that the microprocessor is sending to the brain and is virtually learning how to distinguish one sound from another and what it means. Such medical advances will no doubt continue and research into eyesight applications is becoming more promising.

Applications in the workplace where either microprocessor technology is used or where mainframe technology is used

Microprocessor technology is found in many small business and is used for example in:

- stock control;
- medical diagnosis (when you visit the doctor's surgery);
- dental records;
- video and library data;
- travel information.

Stock control

Many companies, such as gift shops, manufacturers and retail outlets, will use a micro-computer to record data about their stock. Often this means that as items come in from suppliers the details are recorded on the computer particularly how many of the item is currently held in stock. Each item will have a record of data such as: *a unique stock code, description, unit price, and the current amount in stock.* Records may be held in a simple file (see Section A). What is important is that when items are sold, the data in the record is changed straight away. For example, if two items are sold the *current amount in stock*, will be reduced by two. If the record also contains data about the *lowest amount in stock which is allowed* for a given stock item, it can print out details of all the stock which needs to be ordered at the end of each day.

If we also keep data about *the supplier who supplies the item of stock* and *the amount we usually order*, instead of printing just a list of items to order, the system can produce printed order requests for each supplier.

The method by which we read data into the system to allow us to process the data could vary according to the business concerned. Larger businesses may use bar codes (see below: data collection methods) whilst small shops with lower volume sales may just type in the stock code and amount sold. (Note the cylinder shapes ⬠ are disk files and printouts are shown as ⬡.)

> **Stock control** **is one of the most common computerised systems found in business today. Details of sales can be recorded.**

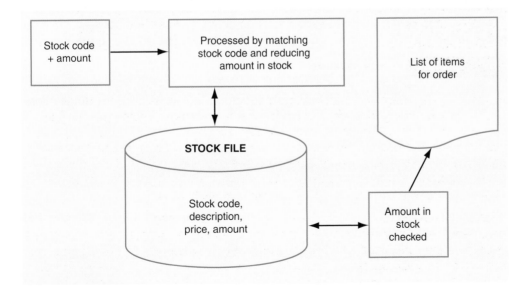

Figure 7.6 Typical stock control system at work

Medical diagnosis

A visit to your doctor's surgery today could result in a consultation with your doctor using a microcomputer to help. If diagnosis of your condition is not a simple matter because your problem is not so common details of your symptoms could be typed into the computer. The medical diagnosis system may offer a range of possible illnesses based upon these symptoms. Your doctor may use these suggestions to help him diagnose your problem. The system could help even more if the doctor selects the illness he thinks you have and asks for suitable medicines to help with the problem. The system could then display a suggested list of medicines and details of when certain medication may not be appropriately prescribed. For example, people with allergies or asthma may not be allowed to take certain types of medicine.

This is the simplest type of medical diagnosis system. The input is a list of symptoms and the output is a list of possible illnesses or medicines. The processing carried out by the computer is to take the symptoms and match it against the data it has stored about those symptoms.

More sophisticated medical diagnosis can be found in hospitals where the input is collected from sensors attached to the patient's body. It may be an electrocardiograph which measures heartbeat. Also tumours may be scanned using special scanning machines. Whatever the form of input the computer will process the input data and produce information that will assist with a diagnosis.

In intensive care units computers are also used to monitor vital signs of life, like respiration, heartbeat/pulse rate, brain signals and blood pressure. The processor matches this data against acceptable ranges stored in the computer's memory and raises the alarm if the readings are out of range.

> **Medical** diagnosis can be a simple process at the local doctor's surgery or it can be more sophisticated using complex sensors to detect changes in vital bodily functions.

Library systems

Computerised library systems have been installed in most libraries, for example, universities and public libraries. By keeping data about books and members it is possible to monitor the whereabouts of books and when they are overdue.

When a member joins the library their details are added to the members file. Similarly when new books arrive their details are added to the books file. When a member wishes to borrow a book the librarian scans the code (usually a bar code) on your membership card and the code in your chosen book. Because book details and member details are stored on the system the computer makes a link between the book and member record and stores details of the due date of return. The librarian stamps your book so that you know when to bring it back.

> **Library book** loans are recorded by reading the code on your membership card and the code stamped in the book.

When you return the book the librarian merely needs to scan the code in the book. If the return date is overdue the computer will display a message on the screen informing the librarian so that she can tell you if there is a fine to pay. If the book is returned on time, the loan details are updated with the date of return. Every so often loan details, which are old, are deleted. Some systems may immediately delete the loan record.

TRAVEL INFORMATION SYSTEMS

Travel information systems are usually *display systems*. For example at airports, major coach/bus stations and railway stations there are monitors which display information about due departures and arrivals. The information is taken straight from computer files and displayed for travellers to see.

Another example of a travel information system is where the user can use a special keyboard and make selections to see what sort of journeys are planned by tour operators at given times. Sometimes instead of special keyboards or keypads touch sensitive

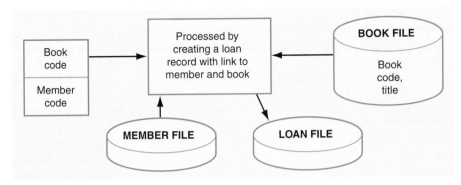

Figure 7.7 Library loan system

screens are in use. Most of these systems are connected to a mainframe computer with a large storage capacity so that many different users in different places can use the computer at the same time.

Figure 7.8 An airport information screen

Travel agencies also use travel information systems and the sales assistant can use the computer to find information for clients about the availability of flights and holidays. Sales assistants may also book a holiday for a client using the computer system. This type of travel information system operates nationally and requires a mainframe computer to support all the users making information and booking requests.

Another type of travel information system allows the client to select a destination from a list displayed on the screen. Then a presentation using video clips, text and sound can be started. This short computerised multimedia presentation will be displayed (see multimedia systems below) using the screen and speakers as output devices attached to the computer system.

Data collection methods

It is important that any data we input to a computer is accurate and relevant. Computers can only output accurate and relevant information if the data stored on them is accurate and relevant. It is often said that where computer systems are concerned if we put 'garbage in' we will get 'garbage out' often referred to as 'GIGO'.

We have seen in section A that common input devices are the mouse and keyboard. Often it is not convenient to use these input devices because we may need to do

Travel information systems vary in type, sometimes they are simple display systems with no user interaction, whilst others require an interactive dialogue with the user. Some travel information systems are used by travel agents.

more than type or point and click. Also using the keyboard to input data can result in errors being made. This is because sometimes there is a large volume of data to input. We are now going to look at alternative methods of inputting data into a computer – called *data collection*.

Optical Mark Readers (OMR)

Optical Mark Readers are able to detect marks on paper. A pre-printed document is prepared for users to select certain areas to insert a line or a mark. A document like this is scanned using reflected light to detect dark shadows.

USES

Universities and further education colleges often use pre-printed enrolment forms where students will enter a mark with a medium to soft pencil. Lottery tickets also work this way. You put a line through an area on the ticket to select a number. Also multiple choice questions on examination papers often require a candidate to make a mark to indicate their answer. The student will pencil a line through the option of their choice. Questionnaires and surveys may also use this technique.

ADVANTAGES

- Simply selecting and marking a choice in the right location on an OMR form is easier than typing in data.
- Documents can be scanned very quickly with only a few errors (only 2 or 3% of documents with modern OMR machines).

DISADVANTAGES

- Badly damaged, creased or folded forms may be rejected.
- Because every option must be catered for the forms are sometimes not very easy for the user to understand. This may introduce errors.
- They can only be used when the data to be input can be selected by marking with lines your choices.

Optical Character Readers (OCR)

Optical Character Readers (OCR) also detect patterns of marks which are in character format (numbers, letters, punctuation and some special characters like '-,@' etc.). The characters are more easily recognised if they are printed, not hand-written, because it is not easy to cater for every different style of handwriting. The characters are converted by a scanner from picture format into coded characters that the computer can work with. This is normally ASCII format (American Standard Code for Information Interchange). OCR software can be purchased separately for use with a standard A4 scanner.

USES

OCR is often used to scan text for use in a word processor.

ADVANTAGES

- When a computerised document has not been saved and only printed text is available, it is possible to use OCR to scan in the text for later editing and re-arrangement.

DISADVANTAGES

- Some characters cannot easily be interpreted and errors sometimes occur during conversion. This is especially true if there are a lot of diagrams and characters laid out in a way the software cannot interpret.

OMRs are devices which read marks on documents. They are used for speedy input of data from questionnaires, examinations and student enrolment.

OCRs are devices which read typed or printed characters. They are used to scan documents that may need later editing on a word processor.

Magnetic Ink Character Recognition (MICR)

Characters which have been printed using ink which contains iron and can be magnetised may be read using a Magnetic Ink Character Reader device. This type of data collection has limited use and is mainly restricted to banking systems because of the expensive equipment involved. Cheques are pre-printed with the sort code and account number and when a cheque has been written the data input clerk has to also mark the cheque amount in magnetic ink.

USES

Bank cheque processing.

ADVANTAGES

- Fast processing of large volumes of data.
- Cannot change the shape of the characters without expensive equipment, so is a fairly secure method of data collection.
- Low number of errors during the reading of documents so this method of input is very reliable.

DISADVANTAGES

- MICR is expensive to use because special equipment is needed to create the characters as well as to read them.

MICR is used in banking systems for reading data recorded at the bottom of cheques.

Bar-code readers

Bar codes are a series of thick and thin vertical lines grouped together. Bar code readers are often used as a fast and effective way to input data. The reader itself uses a laser beam to read the series of thick and thin lines which represent the bar code number. Almost every product we see on supermarket shelves has a bar code. The bar code is 13 digits long and there are four main divisions. The first part of the bar code (two digits) represents the country, the second part represents the manufacturer's code (five digits), the third part represents the product code (five digits) and there is a final digit, which represents the **check digit**. This last digit is a calculated digit to ensure that the bar code is read properly. If there is an error, the reader usually beeps and the operator must key in all the digits manually. When the bar code is read it locates the correct product on the stock file, stored on

Bar code readers are often used as a fast and effective way to input data. A laser beam scans the series of thick and thin lines in order to detect numeric coded data.

Figure 7.9 A bar code

the computer's disc. The price is read from the file and a sale is registered, producing a record on the customer's receipt. The number in stock field is reduced by one.

USES

Bar codes are used on library tickets, airport baggage labels, supermarket products, clothes and on many other retail items. Bar code readers are used in most situations where there is an Electronic Point Of Sale till (EPOS till), for example: department stores, supermarkets.

ADVANTAGES

- Fast, accurate data entry.
- It is possible to store all the details about the country of origin and manufacturer as well as the product code itself. These are recorded in a standard format within the bar code.

DISADVANTAGES

- If the bar code is damaged the bar code reader cannot read it. It is then time consuming to enter all the separate digits using a keypad.

Touch screens

Touch screens are monitors which detect where it is being touched. The user makes selections by touching the screen, rather than moving a cursor to the point on the screen with a mouse, joystick, touchpad or tracker ball.

> Touch screens are useful for selecting options from menus especially when computer users are likely to have little experience of using mice and keyboards.

USES

Touch screens are often used in situations where users are likely to have a low level of competence in using computer keyboards. Touch screens are sometimes used in restaurants, building societies and travel information systems.

ADVANTAGES

- No computer literacy is required. It is simple to select your requirements by just touching a picture on the screen.

DISADVANTAGES

- Touch screens are not robust and can soon become faulty.

Graphics tablet

These are flat and rectangular in shape. A stylus or 'puck' is used to draw on the tablet often tracing over a diagram on paper. The drawing is transferred onto the computer by

Figure 7.10 A graphics tablet

taking x-y co-ordinates (the address of each point) for every contact that the stylus makes with the tablet.

USES

Graphics tablets are used in drawing environments and are often used with Computer Aided Design software perhaps for designing buildings in an architect's office.

ADVANTAGES

- In a design environment where it is more natural to draw diagrams with pencil and paper it is an effective method of inputting the data about diagrams onto the computer.

DISADVANTAGES

- This method is really only useful for inputting data about line diagrams.

Voice input

We can now input data by simply talking into a microphone and using special software to recognise the voice. Software must be taught how each user pronounces the words before the speech can be interpreted and transferred to the computer. Some computer systems can respond to voice commands and can carry out tasks because the spoken word is interpreted by software and converted to instructions.

USES

- Inputting text to word processing software.
- Controlling devices such as electronically controlled doors and machines.

ADVANTAGES

- Voice input is extremely useful for those users unable to use keyboards or mice.
- Software is now affordable by the home user

DISADVANTAGES

- The system must be able to recognise the voice of each user. Teaching the software can be tedious and time consuming.
- Speech recognition software is still not very accurate.

> Voice input is an extremely convenient form of data input but it is not yet fully reliable and time has to be spent teaching the computer to recognise the way each individual user speaks.

Backing storage devices and media for large data file and applications

CD-R and CD-RW

These are optical storage devices (see Section A) belonging to the same family as CD-ROMs. CD-R (Compact Disk Recordable) can be written to only once whilst CD-RW are CDs which can record data more than once. It is possible to write 650Mb of data to this type of disk and it makes them very good for high volume data.

A CD-R disk has a layer of special dye covered by a layer of gold. It also has a protective plastic coating. To write to the disk a powerful laser beam directed on the disk affects the dye and changes its structure so that the gold layer no longer reflects light when the disk is read. The change in structure is permanent. CD-RWs differ because the laser beam changes the chemicals on the surface to be reflective or non-reflective when heated by the energy from the laser beam.

> CD-R and CD-RW are optical storage devices, which are capable of storing large volumes of data when compared to floppy disks. They are portable but have slow access times when compared to hard disks.

USES

Large volume applications may be recorded to CD-R when they are finalised, for example a tailor made database system or a catalogue of student work for display. CD-RWs may be used in situations where you need to record the final result and keep it for quite a long time before replacing it with another result. A typical example might be a monthly school magazine which may be required for a number of sessions before being replaced with more recent work.

ADVANTAGES

- A portable record of a final result that is fairly secure is created with CD-R because once it has been created the disk becomes a CD-ROM.
- Large volume data is stored safely and securely.

DISADVANTAGES

- Writing to CDs is time consuming. It may take more than 15 minutes to fill a CD. Consequently they are unlikely to replace hard disks which have a much faster access time.

Zip drives and jaz drives

Zip disks are a high capacity disk, that are slightly larger and thicker than normal floppy disks. They have their own special drive which can be attached to a parallel port (socket at the back of the computer that the printer usually connects to), so it can be plugged in when you need to use it. It can also be a permanent fixture in a computer like a floppy disk drive. A zip or jaz drive has to have its own software installed so that the computer can see and use it.

A jaz drive is a removable disk drive capable of taking large capacity disks. They have a fast data transfer rate.

USES

Zip and jaz drives can be used for backing up hard disks and transferring large volumes of data from one machine to another.

ADVANTAGES

- Using these devices it is fairly fast to back-up data. Data is also portable.
- These devices have a large capacity.

DISADVANTAGES

- Disks must be kept safe and are subject to the same hazards as floppy disks such as heat, magnetic and fluid damage.
- Compared to hard disk access to stored data is slow.

RAM and ROM and their uses

IAS has both ROM and RAM memory. ROM is non-volatile and stores the bootstrap program whilst RAM is volatile.

Random Access Memory (RAM) is the type of memory used for Immediate Access Storage (IAS). Any data stored in RAM is only stored there temporarily therefore this type of memory is known as volatile memory. When the computer is switched off all data in RAM is lost.

Another type of memory which is also used for IAS is Read Only Memory (ROM). The data stored in ROM will not be lost when the machine is switched off and it is known as non-volatile memory.

Data held in IAS is immediately available to the computer. It is essential that the basic instructions that contain or load the **operating system** are always present in the computer system. These instructions to load the operating system are known as the *bootstrap program* and this is stored in ROM. The user cannot change these instructions.

USES

ROM is used for the bootstrap program whilst RAM is used to store data and instructions which are required immediately by the computer.

Multimedia systems

Multimedia systems combine text, graphics, sound and video using a computer.

Multimedia systems are systems that combine text, graphics, sound, animation and video using a computer. Usually a fairly powerful computer is used and this will have a built in CD-ROM or DVD drive, speakers, sound card, large memory, powerful graphics and video cards and a fast processor.

USES

Multimedia systems are used for presentations, reference material and educational software sometimes known as Computer Aided Learning software (CAL).

ADVANTAGES

- Using a variety of media like sound and video means that multimedia material is interesting and more illustrative than normal text presentations.

Computer Aided Learning (CAL)

Computer Aided Learning is sometimes confused with Computer Based Training (CBT). CAL is software which helps you learn a subject, whilst CBT is more concerned with training people how to do a task. Both types of system may present material or tasks to be learned using a multimedia computer system. The important part of such a system is that it will give students a chance to test their own knowledge and give them immediate feedback about how well they have performed. Feedback can be visual (a graphical pop up display could be used), involve sound (voice or other types of sound) and it could be text based (in the form of a score displayed on the screen or a message area at the bottom of the screen).

USES

CAL is beginning to be used much more frequently in schools. There are many types of packages for different subjects and catering for different age groups.

ADVANTAGES

- There is individual tuition using a wide range methods, media and feedback.
- Students can go over the material again and again in their own time including repeating test material to improve their score.
- Due to the different media used it helps to motivate students and keep their interest.
- It generally improves student performance.

DISADVANTAGES

- Sometimes the teacher may have difficulty getting students to pay attention in class because they will not stop using the software when asked.
- The teacher and student may not communicate problems to one another quite so often.
- Students may not diskuss topics in class so often and this may reduce social interaction and valuable group diskussions.
- CAL can be expensive although due to competition from software writers, titles are becoming cheaper.

Voice output

Voice output is when a computer system generates the spoken word by putting together a sequence of sounds to match, for example, words which have been typed into the computer. Special software is required to make the conversion.

USES

Voice output is useful for people who are partially sighted. The computer can read word-processed documents and communicate by sound output from the computer. Voice output is also useful for those who are physically handicapped and cannot speak. By typing on a keyboard they are able to communicate using the spoken word. Directory enquiries at British Telecom use voice output to tell the caller the number that the computer system has found. Voice output is also used in multimedia presentations and provides a valuable means of communication.

> **Voice output** is particularly useful when the user cannot see the result the computer wishes to display, such as when a telephone user is making a directory enquiry.

ADVANTAGES

- When the user cannot see the result on the computer screen, either when the user is not able to see the result because they are located far away from it, or when they are visually handicapped.

DISADVANTAGES

- The quality of voice output is getting better but it still sounds like a set of small sounds strung together and is therefore obviously electronic and rather unnatural.
- Sound files used for voice output occupy a large amount of memory.

Sound

Sound input and output has already been mentioned in Section A.

A review of what we have said so far.

- A sound card is the hardware required inside the computer. It must be installed correctly for your computer to be able to reproduce sound.
- Sound starts in analogue format as sound waves.
- In order for sound to be stored on computer it must be changed into digital format. This is done by sound sampling.
- To reproduce the sound we also need a speaker.
- To record sound we use a microphone or on some occasions rather than using sound sampling and a microphone, we may use a Musical Instrument Digital Interface (MIDI) with an electronic musical instrument such as a music keyboard.

Sound is an important part of a multimedia system. It brings multimedia presentations to life with voice commentary or music.

USES

Sound is used in multimedia presentations and is particularly useful in CAL presentations.

ADVANTAGES

- Valuable audio feedback is given to the user.
- Sometimes audible alarms can be given when necessary.

DISADVANTAGES

- Other users can be distracted by the noise.
- If sound is overused it can be annoying for the computer user.

Video and animation

Multimedia systems often use video clips and animation. For both these, individual picture frames are played in sequence. Video images are simply a set of still images (or frames) taken over a set period of time. When played back at the same speed as the images were recorded the whole thing can be viewed in much the same way as they would if they had been seen live.

Animation is usually when drawn images (possibly a cartoon) are put together in sequence to simulate (mimic) movement. In the past it was necessary to draw every single image to create smooth action replays for cartoon films. Nowadays it is possible for animation software to have a start and end frame. The software then produces the image frames necessary to produce high quality animation sequences. For both video and cartoon ani-

Sound is an important part of a multimedia system. It requires a sound card, speakers, microphone and software to operate.

Although video and animation sequences require expensive equipment to run them they greatly enhance multimedia presentations.

mation a large number of images are required even for the shortest sequences so a computer with a large disk capacity and powerful processor are required.

USES

Video and animation can be used in CAL and other multimedia presentations. Sometimes entire films are produced so that users can watch them on their computer. Video images are also used in video conferencing systems.

ADVANTAGES

- Realistic moving images can be created to add interest to computerised presentations.

DISADVANTAGES

- Can be expensive due to the equipment and software required.
- Some lower specification machines may not be able to run the sequences since the image quality can be low and the sequence too erratically displayed.

Different types of software

There are many different types of software but mainly there are two categories: systems software and applications software.

The first category, *systems software*, is concerned with keeping the computer system working. The main items of software that you will find in this category are operating systems, user interfaces, programming languages, translators and utilities.

The second category is *applications software*. This type of software may be general purpose (sometimes known as generic applications software) or it may have been written for a specific task like stock control.

Operating systems

Operating systems software is the instructions which control the general day to day running of the computer. It looks after the way memory is organised, schedules all the tasks running on your computer and allows the user to communicate with the computer. Sometimes the operating system comes together on one CD-ROM with the user interface software (the user interface software is software which allows the user to communicate with the operating system – see below). Both are installed at the same time.

User interfaces

The user interface allows us to give commands to the computer. Today most personal computers have a graphical user interface (GUI).

The interface allows the user to communicate with the computer's operating system, so providing the user with overall control of the tasks. A GUI is also known as a WIMP interface (Windows, Icons, Menus, Pointer) and this is because each task is displayed in an individual window (which is basically a rectangular box on the screen with a process's output or folder's contents displayed in it).

Windows can also display the contents of folders (directories), which may contain software like a word processor or documents like a letter you wrote using the word processor. A picture (icon) represents each item such as a document or piece of software. An icon is just a small graphical picture. (Note that a folder usually contains a selection of documents, programs/software and perhaps, other folders).

In addition at the top of some windows you may see words which, when you click on them, give you a series of options to click on. These are called '*Pull Down Menus*'.

> **Systems** software is concerned with keeping the computer working whilst applications software is concerned with particular tasks like word processing or stock control.

> **An operating** system controls the general day to day running of the computer. A computer system cannot work without it.

> **A software** interface allows the user to communicate with the computer.

> **A GUI is** sometimes known as a WIMP environment because it has Windows, Menus, Icons, Pointers.

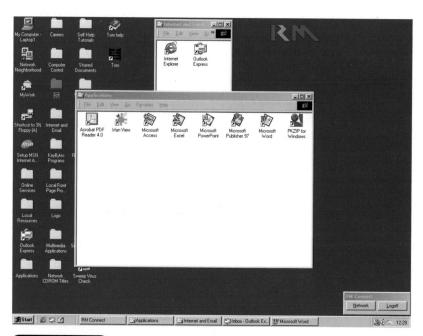

Figure 7.11   A window on a screen

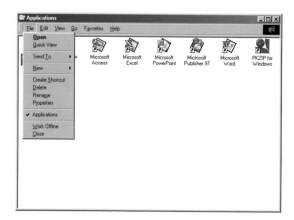

Figure 7.12   Icons and pull down menus

Finally the 'Pointer' referred to in a WIMP environment is the pointer displayed on the screen as a result of moving the mouse. As the pointer moves over an object it is possible to click and select that particular object.

These basic features of a GUI allow you to easily communicate with the computer. An alternative user interface might be a command line interface. There are no windows or graphics just a basic command line prompt such as: 'C>'. This indicates that the computer is waiting for an instruction. The user must learn the command necessary to carry out a particular task. For example to display the contents of a folder, which is equivalent to a directory, you may have to type 'DIR' and press ENTER or CAT and press ENTER.

Comparing command line interfaces and GUIs

The main advantage that GUIs have over command line interfaces is that they are easy to use for inexperienced users because *they are very 'user friendly'*.

They are however *slow in some ways because sometimes a sequence of actions is necessary in order to find one item or do one task*. For example if you wish to find a document which is stored in a folder it may be necessary to operate several mouse clicks and open several windows in order to find it. One of the biggest problems that users have is finding documents. Also if you use a pull down menu there may be several other sub menus to negotiate before you can select the option of your choice.

The main advantage of command line interfaces is that experienced users find them very quick to work with compared with GUIs. There is no extra software to worry about and *providing you are an experienced user who knows all the commands, it is a very efficient way to give commands to the operating system*.

Utilities

Utility programs are quite varied and mainly help the user with general maintenance and housekeeping tasks, such as formatting disks, repairing damaged files, compacting disk storage which has got messy due to lots of different additions and deletions of files.

Virus checkers may also be regarded as a utility program since they too help to keep your system in good working order by detecting and disinfecting your affected files.

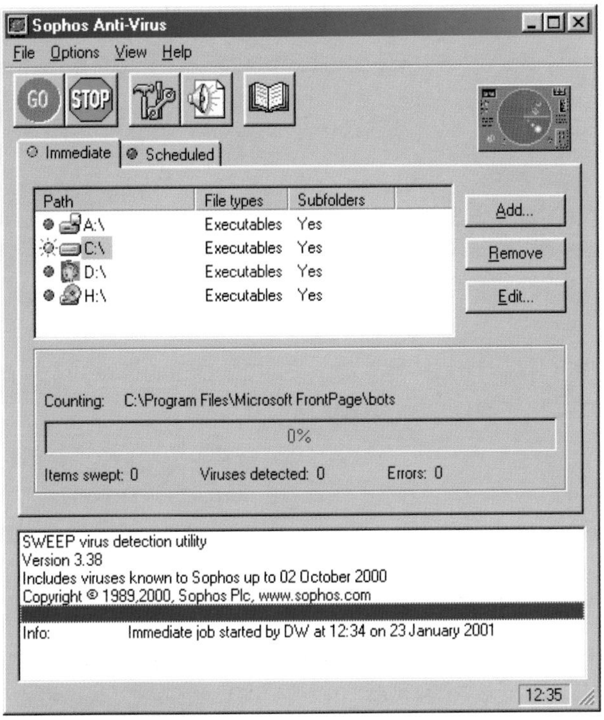

> Utility programs carry out many general tasks on your computer such as formatting disks, virus checking disks and re-arranging the way files are stored on disks.

Figure 7.13 A virus checker

Programming language translators

Programming languages such as Pascal, C, Fortran and COBOL are used to write software applications. In the 1960s and 1970s many computer programs were written in COBOL to handle large files, like payroll files. Today more popular programs are those which are designed for writing software which is user friendly, such as Visual Basic and Visual C++. Program instructions written in these languages cannot be understood by the computer and must be converted to machine code. Machine code is the binary 0s and 1s that the computer is able to read.

> A programming language translator is required to convert programs written in high-level languages (such as C++) into a machine readable format.

Programming languages like these are known as high-level languages. There are other languages, which are more like machine code, and these are known as low-level languages or assembly languages.

Programming language translators are sometimes known as compilers although there are also those translators which are known as interpreters because they interpret the code a line at a time rather than creating a complete version of the program in machine code (binary code) for later execution.

Applications software

Applications software usually carries out specific tasks such as stock control or payroll. An application may be written using either a *programming language* or a more *general purpose piece of software* such as database software. Applications may also be purchased 'off-the-shelf' as a pre-written package. For example there are many accounting packages which can be bought 'off-the-shelf'. With this type of package you only need to enter the data before starting to use it regularly. Sometimes companies want a system specially written just for them. These are called 'bespoke' or 'tailor-made' systems.

General purpose/generic applications software

Commonly available packages such as word processors, spreadsheets, databases, desk top publishers, graphics and design packages (such as Computer Aided Design (CAD) software) are used to generate documents or applications. Examples are on the next page.

Programming languages

Programming languages may also be general purpose or they may be designed for a specific type of applications. For example Fortran was designed for scientific applications whilst COBOL was designed for large-scale file handling such as payroll. Visual Basic is another language designed to develop applications which respond to interactive events such as a mouse click or key pressed on the keyboard.

Relative advantages and disadvantages of purchasing a bespoke systems vs an off-shelf system

- Bespoke systems are more expensive than an off-the-shelf system.
- Off-the-shelf systems cannot be edited. They are a 'one off' purchase and any upgrades to the software must be purchased separately.
- Bespoke systems are tailored exactly to your needs and may be edited as your needs change.
- Off-the-shelf systems have been bought by others and have been tried and tested. They are readily available. Bespoke systems break new ground and will take time to create.

> Programming languages may be used to create applications but some expertise in programming is required. A more general purpose piece of software is slightly easier for the developer to use.

> Bespoke systems are more expensive to buy but are tailored to your exact needs, whilst off-the-shelf systems are readily available, tried and tested and much cheaper to buy.

Software	Purpose	Examples
Word processor	To create and edit written documents.	Letters, reports, memos, theses
Desktop publisher	To create well laid out informative documents of various types using visually appealing graphics and text.	Flyers, brochures, newsletters, business cards, invitations
Slide show software	To create interactive presentations.	Local tourist guide, CAL package for teaching the alphabet
Spreadsheet	To create computer models using primarily data, formulae and rules.	Break even analysis, personal finance, cash flow model.
Database	To create a structured set of data for searching, sorting and producing informative reports.	Pupil record keeping, stock control, customer records
Graphics packages	To produce and edit drawings, photos and other images.	To draw pictures for a brochure, to edit a scanned image.
Design packages (CAD)	To create technical drawings/ /design specifications.	To design a building or bridge

Summary

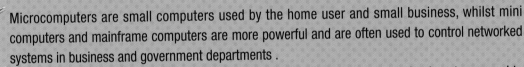

Computor systems: components and types

- Microcomputers are small computers used by the home user and small business, whilst mini computers and mainframe computers are more powerful and are often used to control networked systems in business and government departments .

- Central heating systems and home security systems use microprocessor technology to respond to data received from sensors, according to details programmed in by the user.

- The simplest type of medical diagnosis system is where the input is basically a list of symptoms and the output is a list of possible illnesses.

- Stock control is one of the most common computerised systems found in business today. Details of sales are recorded by decreasing the quantity in stock.

- Library book loans are recorded by reading the bar code on your membership card and the bar code stamped in the book.

- Travel information systems vary in type. Sometimes they are simple display systems with no user interaction, whilst others require an interactive dialogue with the user.

- OMRs are devices, which read marks on documents. They are used for speedy input of data from questionnaires, examinations and student enrolment.

- OCRs are devices which read typed or printed characters. They are used to scan documents which may need later editing on a word processor.

✓ MICR is used in bank clearing systems for reading magnetised characters at the bottom of cheques.

✓ Bar code readers are often used as a fast and effective way to input data. A laser beam scans the series of thick and thin lines in order to detect numeric coded data.

✓ Touch screens are useful for selecting options especially when computer users are likely to have little experience of using mice and keyboards.

✓ Graphics tablets are used in drawing environments and are often used with Computer Aided Design software, perhaps for designing buildings in an architect's office.

✓ Voice input is an extremely convenient form of data input for those users unable to use keyboards or mice.

✓ Optical discs such as CD-R (Compact Disc Recordable) can be written to only once whilst CD-RW are CDs which can record data more than once.

✓ Any data stored in RAM is only stored there temporarily and is volatile whilst the data stored in ROM will not be lost when the machine is switched off and it is known as non-volatile memory.

✓ Multimedia systems combine text, graphics, sound and video using a computer system.

✓ CAL uses multimedia to present material or tasks to be carried out.

✓ Sound is an important part of a multimedia system. It requires a sound card, speakers, microphone and software to operate.

✓ Video and animation is when individual picture frames are played in sequence.

✓ Video and animation sequences require equipment to run them but they greatly enhance multimedia presentations.

✓ Systems software is concerned with keeping the computer system working such as operating systems, user interfaces, programming language translators and utilities.

✓ Operating systems software are the instructions which control the general day to day running of the computer.

✓ The user interface allows us to give commands to the computer. Today most personal computers have a graphical user interface (GUI).

✓ A GUI is sometimes known as a WIMP environment because it has Windows, Menus, Icons, Pointers.

✓ Command line interfaces are where the user types a command directly communicating with the operating system software.

✓ The main advantage of command line interfaces is that experienced users find them very quick to work with compared with GUIs.

✓ Commonly available packages known as generic applications software, such as word processors, spreadsheets, databases, desk top publishers, graphics and design packages (such as Computer Aided Design (CAD) software) are used to generate documents or usable applications.

✓ Utility programs mainly help the user with general maintenance and housekeeping tasks, such as formatting discs or controlling virus attacks.

✓ Programming languages are designed for creating all types of different applications. They need a translator to change the instructions to machine code that the computer can understand and execute.

✓ Programming languages may be used to create applications but some expertise in programming is required whilst a more general purpose piece of software is slightly easier for the developer to use.

✓ Programming languages are also used to create both bespoke software and off-the-shelf software.

✓ Bespoke systems are more expensive to buy but are tailored to your exact needs whilst off-the-shelf systems are readily available, tried and tested and much cheaper to buy.

Test and review

1. List some typical uses of microprocessors. _____

2. List the main uses of mainframes. _____

3. Describe how a central heating system works. _____
   _____
   _____

4. State the typical input and output of a medical diagnosis system found in a doctor's surgery _____
   _____

5. Describe how a computerised stock control system works. _____
   _____
   _____
   _____

6. State two typical uses of OMR. _____

7. Describe the main difference between OMR and OCR. _____
   _____

8. MICR is used in b_____ for reading magnetised characters at the bottom of c_____.

9. Tick the correct items which accurately describe bar codes and bar code readers.
   a) They are often used as a fast and effective way to input data.
   b) You type in the numbers with a keypad.
   c) A laser beam scans the series of thick and thin lines in order to detect numeric coded data.
   d) If they are damaged you cannot input data.

10. When are touch screens likely to be used? _____

11. When are graphics tablets likely to be used? _____

12. Examples of optical disks are: (tick the relevant examples)
    a) CD-R (Compact Disk Recordable)
    b) Zip disks

c) CD-RW

d) Floppy disks

e) CD-ROM

13. Select TRUE or FALSE (T/F) for the following statements.

a) Data stored in RAM is volatile.   T/F

b) Data stored in ROM data is non-volatile.   T/F

c) CAL means Computer Aided Lessons.   T/F

d) Multimedia is when a document combines text and CAL.   T/F

e) Sound is an important part of a multimedia system.   T/F

f) Sound requires only a sound card and speakers to operate.   T/F

14. Video and animation works by capturing still images and _____

_____.

15. Tick the correct members of the systems software category:

a) operating systems

b) user interfaces

c) programming languages

d) applications programs

e) translators

f) utilities.

16. List the main tasks of an operating system. _____

17. The user interface allows us to give commands to the computer. Today most personal computers have a graphical user interface (GUI). Give one other name for a GUI._____

18. When the user types a command directly to the computer after the system prompt, this is known as a C_____ L_____ Interface

19. The main advantage of command line interfaces is _____

_____.

20. List three commonly known generic applications packages. _____

_____

21. Utility programs carry out the following task (tick correct options):

a) formatting disks

b) virus checking

c) saving space on disks

d) clearing the screen

22. Why do programming languages need a translator? _____

_____

23. What are bespoke systems? _____

_____

24. What are the main advantages of buying an off-the-shelf system rather than a bespoke system? _____

Review and thinking tasks

Which utilities have you used on a computer? Think about what they are and how you used them.

It is more than likely that you use a computer system with a GUI (pronounced goo-ee)? Have you tried to use a command line interface? Ask your teacher if it is possible to see what it is like to type commands directly to the operating system.

Next time you go to the supermarket take note of what happens at the checkout. Does the bar code scanner work every time? What happens when it doesn't? What do you think happens each time that an item is put through the checkout?

Legal, economic and political issues relating to the use of ICT

There are many laws that have been passed to encourage people to use ICT responsibly. We have already looked at copyright law and how it is illegal to copy, use and distribute software without a licence. We are now going to look more specifically at the law which controls the storage and use of data. This is known as the Data Protection Act.

Additionally this chapter covers in more detail the changing work patterns in commerce and industry.

The Data Protection Act

The Data Protection Act was first introduced on the 12 July 1984. It contained eight principles, which were introduced to help control the way people collected, stored and used data about others (data subjects). The Act was considered necessary because more and more data was being stored in computer files. In 1998 a new Act was passed which now also deals with manually held data and other data transferred over the Internet, or held on large customer databases for marketing purposes.

The principles of the new Act

1. Personal data must be obtained and processed fairly and lawfully, and must not be processed until at least one of the following conditions are met:
   a) the data subject has given their permission for the processing;
   b) the processing is necessary to fulfil terms of a contract with the data subject;
   c) the processing is necessary for legal reasons;
   d) the processing is necessary to protect the data subject, for example to extract data necessary for emergency medical treatment to be given;
   e) the processing is necessary to carry out the work of a government department or for the administration of justice;
   f) the processing is necessary in the normal work of the data controller and it does not conflict with the rights of the data subject.

2. Personal data shall be held only for one or more specified and lawful purposes and must not be processed for any purpose incompatible with the specified purposes.

3. Personal data held should be relevant, adequate and not excessive in relation to the stated purpose(s).

4. Personal data must be kept accurate and, where necessary, kept up-to-date.

5. Personal data must not be kept longer than it is necessary to fulfil the stated purpose(s).

6. Personal data must be processed in accordance with the rights of the data subject.

7. Personal data must be kept secure against unauthorised access, alteration, destruction or disclosure whether accidental or deliberate and appropriate technical and organisational measures must be taken to ensure that there is no accidental loss, damage or destruction of data.

> **The Data Protection 1998 has eight principles which state in general that data must be obtained and processed lawfully, be secure, relevant, accurate and up-to-date, used for only the specified purpose and kept no longer than necessary to fulfil that purpose. The rights of data subject must also be observed.**

8. Personal data cannot be transferred out of the European Economic Area unless the country it goes to has adequate protection for the rights of data subjects.

Sensitive personal data

The Act classifies sensitive personal data.

- Racial or ethnic origin about the data subject.
- Political opinions of the data subject.
- Religious beliefs of the data subject.
- Details about trade union membership.
- Physical condition or mental health of the data subject.
- Details of any alleged offences or offences the data subject may have committed.
- Details of any convictions, proceedings or sentences resulting from alleged offences or offences the data subject has committed.

If the data is sensitive then it can only be processed if one extra condition is met.

- The data subject knows what data is being processed and how it is being used and has given explicit consent.
- The processing of data about the data subject is necessary as a result of employment law where it is required for the data controller to provide certain information.
- The processing is necessary to protect the data subject and he cannot give consent, or to protect someone else if consent is refused without good reason.
- The processing is carried out by a political, religious or trade union organisation and related only to its members.
- The information has been made public deliberately by the data subject.
- The processing is necessary for legal reasons.
- The processing is necessary to carry out the work of the government or the justice system.
- The processing is necessary to check that equal opportunities are available and the processing respects the rights of the data subject.

The Data Protection Commissioner (DPC) is responsible for maintaining the details of the particulars of data held by data controllers (those organisations using the personal data on 'data subjects'). The DPC is also responsible for investigating complaints and initiating prosecutions if the regulations are broken.

To notify the DPC organisations must fill in the relevant forms and provide:

- details of their name and address;
- a description of the data being processed;
- a description of the purpose for processing the data;
- a description of the recipients to whom the data controller intends to disclose the data to.

If an organisation does not notify the DPC of its use of personal data they may be taken to court and fined. In some instances this fine is unlimited. Additionally the courts may rule that organisations must pay compensation to the data subject if the damage is considered to be serious enough.

Some data is regarded as sensitive such as racial or ethnic origin, political and religious beliefs, any crimes or alleged crimes committed, trade union details and the mental and physical health of the data subject.

The Data Protection Commissioner (DPC) is responsible for ensuring that organisations who notify him about the data they process do so under the conditions specified in the Act.

New rights for data subjects

1. The right of access to data being kept about the data subject and the purposes it is being used for.
2. The right to prevent processing if it is likely to cause distress (this right does not apply if the data subject has given permission, processing is necessary to enter a contract, for legal reasons or it necessary to protect the rights of the data subject).
3. The right to prevent processing for direct marketing.
4. The right to prevent any automated decision making based on personal data kept. Data subjects must also be told when decisions are made using this method.
5. The right to compensation if a data subject suffers damage, or in the case of sensitive data suffers distress.
6. The right to request correction or destruction of inaccurate personal data.
7. The right to ask the DPC to check that processing of personal data by a data controller is being carried out in accordance with the Act.

There are exemptions from the new Act, which means that you do not have to notify the (although many of these exemptions have conditions attached or parts of the Act which do not apply). In general these are:

Exemptions

1. For reasons of National Security.
2. To prevent and detect crime, catch and prosecute offenders.
3. To work out and collect taxes.
4. To carry out regulatory activity, for example any organisation which makes sure other organisations carry out their business according to their membership rules and regulations.
5. For artistic, literary, research, historical or statistical purposes and generally where information is public.
6. Where data is used for domestic purposes such as home accounts.

Extra rules and rights of the new Act are applicable from 1 January 1999 particularly to new uses of data, although for data which is already registered there is a transition period of several years.

Unauthorised access and data encryption

Hacking has already be described in Section A, as unauthorised access to a computer system and data which belongs to someone else. There are many reasons people have for hacking but sometimes people break into computer systems just for the challenge, that is, to prove that they can do it. Some people are actually employed by companies to try and break into their own computer systems, in order to prove that company security measures are sufficient. Some hackers intend to commit a crime, and hack into computer systems so that they can use the data to commit fraudulent crimes (cheating others so that they can steal money) or commit other serious crimes. Crimes committed as a result of hacking are punishable by law (see Computer Misuse Act).

To prevent unauthorised access a user identification/network identification and a password is issued to each user of the computer system as discussed in section A. However there are other methods to assist in preventing unauthorised access.

> There are new rights for data subjects, which in particular included the right of access to data kept and processed. Also any decisions which are made automatically, based on data kept can be prevented.

Physical methods for prevention of unauthorised access

Sometimes people within the same organisation want to hack into other users' work areas. To prevent this users must be watchful and make sure no one obtains their password. It is also wise for some organisations to put special locks on doors into certain areas of the building so that only authorised users (with the keys) are allowed access to particular computers. These computers could also be the only machines which have the capability to give access to certain parts of the computer system.

Additionally each terminal could have its own lock and key which activates the computer only if the user inserts the key into the lock and turns it. Often some government departments will employ this type of security because only certain administrative staff need access to particular parts of the computer system.

Encryption

Another means of preventing unauthorised access is to use *encryption*. This means that data has been mixed up or converted according to certain rules. Once the data has been encrypted this way it no longer makes sense to the reader. This particular method is very useful if data is likely to be intercepted (captured as it is being transferred from one place to another, perhaps along telephone lines) either by someone within the organisation using another computer on the network or from outside the organisation over the Internet.

Electronic Fraud

As ICT spreads in use and more applications are implemented there is more opportunity for the criminal to commit electronic fraud. Electronic fraud is a term which means that people us ICT to obtain money or goods that they are not entitled to.

For a long time a well-known crime is for people to obtain other people's credit cards or bank cards to obtain money. Once a thief has managed to obtain a cheque book and cheque guarantee card it requires very little expertise to copy the signature on the cheque guarantee card.

Credit cards can be stolen long before they reach the new owner, during postal transit, or later from the owner. Once this has been done the thief can use the card for transactions. Similarly credit card details can be copied from a receipt or intercepted in some way as a transaction is being made. Goods can then be ordered over the telephone or the Internet. It is less likely for someone to obtain cash on a stolen bank or credit card because a personal identification number (PIN) is required. This is why keeping you PIN private is so important.

There has been a great deal of concern about fraud on the Internet. Traders have been known to pose as large, well-known retail outlets and obtain money for goods, later disappearing and never supplying the goods. It is important to ensure that when purchasing goods on the Internet that the site is secure (indicated by a message or padlock displayed on screen). This means that any data transmitted to or from the site is encrypted and secure.

There have also been cases where people have put fictitious employees onto the company payroll and paid money into false bank accounts. Others have slowly taken small amounts of money from everyone's pay (such as a few pence) and paid it into a separate bank account. Due to the large volume of people paid on a regular basis over a long period of time this has soon mounted into many hundreds of thousands pounds.

Computer Misuse Act (1990)

The Computer Misuse Act (1990) was first passed in order to make it official that it was a crime if people hacked into other people's computer systems in order to steal data.

There had been a number of data thefts as a result of hacking, including students who had logged into hospital computers and stockbrokers' computers.

A famous example of hacking hit newspaper headlines where the motive was reported to be obsession with the search for alien spacecraft. A programmer hacked into US Air Force computers believing that they were hiding a captured alien spacecraft. He hoped to find information about the capture by gaining unauthorised access to data held on the computer. The case was eventually dropped although he and his helper were charged with three offences under the Computer Misuse Act of 1990.

The Computer Misuse Act covers a number of misuses of computers.

- Hacking into someone's computers system with a view to seeing data, changing or deleting it.
- Using computerised equipment to commit fraud.
- Software piracy–copying programs for own use or re-sale.
- Using time on someone's computer to carry out any type of work, which the computer owner has not authorised.
- Deliberately spreading a virus onto someone else's computer system.

Changing pattern of commerce and industry due to increased use of ICT

There have been many changes as the use of Information and Communication Technology has increased. From the simple introduction of data processing which was introduced in the 1960s to the more sophisticated interactive on-line banking systems we see today each new use of ICT has meant a change in the way data is collected and stored. It has also affected the way people work.

Advances in Communication Technology have expanded the possibilities for increased use of ICT. Better communications technology couple with better and increased use if ICT has resulted in a change in the way businesses work. Now we see automated decision making, computerised production lines, automated document production and automated monitoring systems. Automated Teller Machines (ATMs) dispense cash at the touch of a button and now we can carry out most banking transaction on-line.

All these new products and services together with automated clerical and manufacturing processes mean that organisations have changed. Some effects that we may see are:

- Businesses have fewer staff making decisions meaning fewer managers may be required.
- Staff are required with technological expertise rather than basic clerical skills.
- Some businesses are expanding far faster than they would without the use of ICT.

Just browsing on the Internet one can see an example of the changing face of business. Many large organisations are now selling direct to the customer over the Internet. Even supermarkets are selling goods and arranging home delivery. Superstores, for example have set up a trial *virtual supermarket*, where shoppers browse around a virtual (imaginary) store and arrange for the delivery of goods which have been bought. Many small businesses are able to sell their goods internationally, when normally they would be limited to a few local shoppers.

Banks, in particular have been very keen to get customers to check their bank balance, check which direct debits are set up, transfer money and carry out many other everyday transaction over the Internet.

The Computer Misuse Act was set up to legislate against deliberately spreading viruses, hacking, computer crimes such as electronic fraud and software piracy.

ICT has changed the face of business with automated decision making, computerised production lines and automated monitoring and document production.

Businesses have changed with fewer staff making decisions and working in clerical jobs and factories. Instead the smaller number of staff required are expected to have ICT skills.

Computer Aided Design (CAD) systems allow models of a system (which could be a large engineering construction like a bridge or a smaller construction such as a house) to be created. The software allows designers to build very detailed models with accurate measurements or dimensions. The model can be rotated, flipped and looked at from every angle in three dimensions. With CAD drawings can be:

- scaled or resized;
- rotated to give different views;
- developed with a high degree of accuracy.

Additionally, the designs may be tested in a variety of situations.

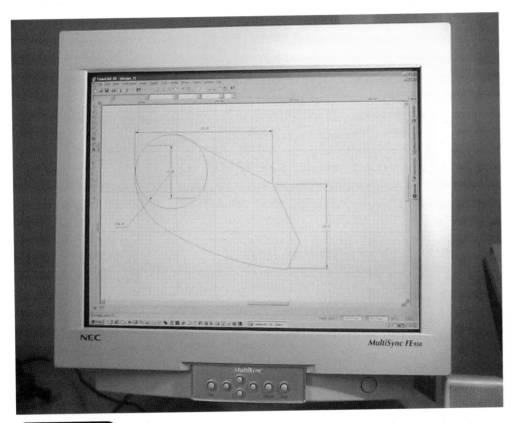

Figure 8.1 CAD

Computer Aided Manufacture (CAM) is when the manufacturing process is controlled by ICT. There may even be an integrated (joined) CAD and CAM system. A major feature of CAM systems is the control of mechanical equipment. Robots are mechanical devices, which operate under the control of a computer system. Generally robots operate in the following way.

- They have sensors, which capture data from the environment.
- A microprocessor processes the data from the sensors.
- Actuators produce movement, for example turning a switch on or off.

The first robots were famous for their increased throughput in the car manufacturing industry.

Use of I.T. has had a major effect on businesses involved in design and manufacturer. In some cases, integrated CAD/CAM systems mean that both the design and production process are automated.

Some of the main changes to commerce and industry.

- Increased efficiency: information is produced on time and up-to-date as and when it is required.
- Increased accuracy and reliability: information produced is usually consistently accurate and up-to-date, improving the chances that correct decisions are going to be made.
- Less necessity to employ large numbers of staff, who will need more support, breaks, health checks, holidays etc.
- Sometimes ICT systems can work in hazardous situations that it is unlikely a human worker would be able to work.
- The need for premises is reduced: for example businesses operating a direct service to the consumer on their home computer will not need to display goods at a shop.
- There are less heating, lighting and rental costs if there are fewer offices and retail outlets required.
- Staff requirement is reduced: so there is a reduced payroll where robots do the work or for example in banking where automated systems are replacing bank clerical staff.

Changing pattern of employment due to increased use of ICT

In addition to the changes in commerce and industry there have been changes in the way people work. In almost every business, computers are used in some way. This means that more people use computers and less people are required to do manual work – a change in the pattern of employment.

The changing patterns of employment include *reduced clerical staff and manual workers* meaning that there has been some *unemployment*. Due to the introduction of computers thousands of office jobs have been lost. Instead of an army of payroll staff or filing clerks we have automated computerised payroll systems. Many of these jobs were lost in the 1960–70s when computers were first used in larger businesses to cope with the ever increasing burden of calculating pay for a large number of employees. For some of these businesses it was becoming impossible, even with a large number of people, to make sure all the pay had been calculated and prepared accurately and on time.

More recently banking systems have become more automated with more and more Automatic Teller Machines (ATMs) reducing the number of banking staff required to deal with customers.

It also means that those workers left in jobs working with computers now have *different jobs and have to be trained to use computers*. For example, a secretary may need to be trained to use a word processor rather than use a typewriter. In some instances because the computers need to be maintained and users need support there has been an *increase in computer industry related jobs*. For example, much more software is now available and computer programmers are now in demand. Computer repair centres and advice lines have provided new jobs. In fact there is a whole new industry related to computer manufacture, maintenance and development.

We have already mentioned teleworking/telecommuting in Section A, where people work from home using a computer and telephone line rather than commuting to an office. Businesses still are a little slow to benefit from this type of work situation because

In general the changes to business today are also as a result of advances in communications technology with increased marketing and reliance on the Internet for customers.

The changing patterns of employment include reduced clerical staff and manual workers meaning that there has been some unemployment.

The requirement to train and re-train staff has been a major effect of the increased use of ICT.

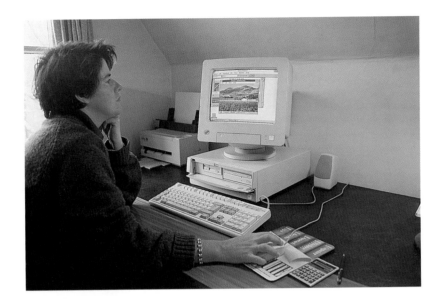

Figure 8.2 Working from home

they fear that it may be difficult to control the workforce. Some workers also prefer to have daily social contact with colleagues especially if they are working in a team. They are also unable to separate home and work commitments and are not able keep to their work schedule. However, workers save commuting time and costs and work more flexible hours.

> Flexible working hours, videoconferencing and teleworking are now becoming more commonplace as a result of the increased use of ICT.

Summary

Computor systems: components and types

✓ The Data Protection Act 1998 has eight principles which state in general that data must be obtained and processed lawfully, be secure, relevant, accurate and up-to-date, used for only the specified purpose and kept no longer than necessary to fulfil that purpose. The rights of data subject must also be observed.

✓ There are new rights for data subjects under the Data Protection Act of 1998, which in particular included the right of access to data kept and processed. Also any decisions which are made automatically based on data kept can be prevented.

✓ Encryption and physical locks as well as passwords and user identification are methods used to protect computer systems from unauthorised access.

✓ The Computer Misuse Act was set up to legislate against deliberately spreading viruses, hacking, computer crimes such as electronic fraud and software piracy.

✓ Businesses have changed with fewer staff making decisions and working and ground level, instead the smaller number of staff required are expected to have ICT skills.

✓ ICT has changed the face of business with automated decision making, computerised production lines and automated monitoring and document production.

✓ Information is more likely to be produced on time, accurately and be up-to-date.

✓ As a result of advances in ICT and marketing over the Internet there is less need for retail premises and storage of goods.

✓ Reduced requirements for clerical staff and manual workers meaning that there has been some unemployment.

✓ There has been an increase in computer industry related jobs.

✓ The requirement to train and re-train staff has been a major effect of the increased use of ICT.

✓ Flexible working hours, videoconferencing and teleworking are now becoming more commonplace as a result of the increased use of ICT.

? Test and review

1. The Data Protection 1998 has eight principles. Briefly state what they are:

   _____

   _____

   _____

   _____

2. There are new rights for data subjects under the Data Protection Act of 1998. Describe what they are._____

   _____

   _____

   _____

3. A password and user identification is one method used to protect computer systems from unauthorised access. State two other ways in which it is possible to prevent unauthorised access. _____

   _____

   _____

4. Electronic fraud and software piracy are two computer crimes which are covered by which Act?_____

   _____

5. Describe how businesses have changed with the increased use of ICT.

   _____

   _____

   _____

6. Because ICT is used to provide information it is more likely to be produced on time. It is also more likely to be a_____ and u_____.

7. Name two jobs which have been lost due to the introduction of ICT in business._____

8. Name two jobs that have been created as a result of the introduction of ICT in business. _____

9. **Name two jobs that have been changed as a result of the introduction of ICT in business and where training is inevitably required.** _____

   _____

10. **ICT in business has affected the way we work. State three ways employment has changed.** _____

    _____

Review and thinking tasks

Think about what the new rights you will have as a data subject under the new DPA 1998. What difference do you think it will make to you when examination results are published?

Do you have a network/user identification number for your network at school? If so, when was the last time you changed your password? Is it too long since you changed your password? Ask your friend to try and guess your password. Is it easy to work it out because it is the name of your pet, or something else dear to your heart!

Look at the jobs that supermarket cashiers now do. Have they changed with the introduction of computers? Are their jobs easier or more complicated? Can they work faster or does it take more time to manage the point of sale terminal? What other forms of ICT are used in supermarkets?

What do you think happens when you pay your supermarket bill using your bank/switch card (not credit card)?

Information systems and applications

This chapter discusses different types of information system and many issues regarding the processing, security and accuracy of data. The system cycle is also discussed in some detail so much of the chapter content is very valuable background and support material for the major coursework component of GCSE work.

Back-ups vs archiving of data

Data is very valuable. We have already seen that to have our data infected by a virus or deliberately destroyed by someone can be very harmful for an organisation. For example think about the consequences of the following situations. What do you think will happen?

a) A business loses payroll details for each employee.

b) A customer rings to find out how much they owe and all customer data has been lost.

In medical situations accurate and secure data can mean the difference between life and death, so it is not only financial problems that are caused by lost data.

In Section A, we discussed the possible causes of lost data and the use of a back-up copy to help us recover lost data. It is important to have detailed instructions about how often back-ups should be taken, where they are to be stored and how to recover from a situation where the original data has been lost. All this information is written down (documented) and called a *back-up strategy*.

A good back-up strategy is clearly necessary for protection against the loss of data. We must remember that our systems would not operate without software. It is also important to keep a back-up copy of any software we use.

A typical back-up strategy for a business with two network servers (one with software and user details (server 1) and one with all the customer and product data on it (server 2)) and 50 terminals, may be as follows.

> A good back-up strategy should be written down (documented) for others to use. It will contain details of the sort of back-ups to be taken, their frequency and where they are stored.

1. Every evening at 6pm when no more business transactions are carried out, a back-up tape is taken off the whole disk on server 2 containing customer and product data. Server 1, which has applications and user data is backed-up once a week, since there are only one or two changes to users data and applications each week.

2. Every morning the network manager checks the network server 2's display screen to ensure that there have been no errors during back-up. On Monday both servers' screens are checked.

3. If there have been any problems, because the company has a service and support agreement with a local computer specialist, they are contacted to investigate and fix the problem.

4. The storage of back-up tapes is in a fireproof safe located in a separate building on the same site. However, just in case of total disaster, the network manager takes a duplicate copy of all back-ups home at the weekend, only returning them when

they are replaced by the next two-week cycle. Back-up tapes are kept for two weeks before they are recycled to be used again, so the company always has two weeks of back-ups to go back to.

Specification of this simple back-up strategy:

1. The media for the back-up: *tapes*, and how the media can be re-used: *every two weeks*.
2. The frequency of taking the back-ups: *every night and once per week for two different servers*.
3. Who is responsible for the back-ups: *network manager*.
4. What must be done in the event of back-up failure: *contact support centre*.
5. Where backups are stored: *both a fireproof safe and off site with the network manager*.

It is important to remember that unless a record of transactions is taken during the day it will be impossible to recover the situation completely from a backup of the servers' disks. The back-up will restore the situation to what it was the previous day. If a customer has bought thousands of pounds' worth of products it is extremely important that data is not lost. We must also therefore take copies of transactions during the day to ensure that we can completely recover from any failure. Copies of transactions must be taken onto disk or magnetic tape which does not belong to the server.

In school it is important that you have your own duplicate copies of your work. The back-up copies you take must be frequent to ensure you do not have to repeat the work over and over again. It is particularly important for you to take frequent back-up copies of your coursework, making sure you label your disks to indicate which copy of the work is most recent!

Archiving of data is also carried out by many organisations. We still may use the same type of storage media, such as tapes or zip drives, but archive data is more concerned with taking a final copy of the data we are using currently because we no longer need to use it regularly. If we use our example company with two servers, notice they have a set of customer data with accounts. When customers have indicated that they no longer wish to deal with the company any longer and would like to close their account, their data will be archived. This means the data is removed from the customer data file and put onto a separate file of past customers.

In school it is common to archive data about past pupils. Each year, in September when year 13 pupils go off to university or to start work, a new set of year 7 pupils joins the school and everyone moves up a year. The year 13 pupil data will be archived and kept for a specified period of time.

It is important not to confuse back-up data with archive data. Back-up data is a copy of currently used data whilst archived data is a copy of data which we are not currently using on a daily basis but which we may need to look at occasionally.

Archive data is a copy of data which is no longer in regular use but which we may need to look at occasionally.

Integrity and security of data

It is important to distinguish between data integrity and data security. Data security is all about trying to ensure that data is safe and this is why we need to have copies of data kept safe and why we must try and prevent unauthorised access. We must keep our data safe from various hazards, which could destroy it for example viruses, user error, deliberate destruction from a hacker or hardware failure.

Data security is about the safety of data whilst data integrity is about the accuracy of data.

Data integrity is about the reliability of data. We need the data to be reliable and we can only rely on accurate data. To try and make sure that data is as accurate as can be reasonably expected, we must carry out many checks as the data is input to the system and sometimes as the data is processed. The methods we use to check the data are known as *verification and validation*.

Verification and validation methods

Verification and validation are two ways in which we can take every reasonable precaution against storing inaccurate and unreliable data. However even when we take all these precautions, it is important to note that we cannot *ensure* that our data is absolutely accurate and reliable. We can only ensure that data entered is *reasonably* accurate and reliable.

Verification and validation checks are used to help prevent against erroneous data getting put onto our computer system.

Types of error

There are many types of error that could occur when inputting data.

a) The person who is responsible for reading a document, from which data is copied, may not read it properly.

b) The person responsible for copying the document into computer readable format may make a mistake, for example, mis-spelling a word.

c) The person responsible for entering the data onto a document, which is later used to input data to a computer system may not write down the details accurately.

d) There could also be a faulty connection between hardware components causing an error in the way data is transferred between the components.

The types of error that could occur when transforming data to computer readable format (onto disk for example).

a) Omitting an item which must be entered.

b) Entering the data twice by mistake.

c) Switching characters in a word around: this is called a transposition error, for example instead of typing '121087' for a date of birth, typing '101287'. This would give an entirely different date of birth, simply by switching the positions of 0 and 2.

Transcription errors are errors which occur as a result of transcribing the data from its original format to computer readable format.

d) Typing extra characters such as an extra 0 at the end of a value.

e) Typing a different character because it has been mis-read, for example, typing 'Hattods' rather than 'Harrods'.

f) Typing the wrong letter or missing a letter because of the speed at which the keyboard is being used, for example typing 'Jnes' or 'Jines' instead of 'Jones'.

All these types of errors are called *transcription* errors – errors which happen when we copy details from a document to convert into digitally stored data.

Verification checks are the checks made when the data is first input to the system. Verification ensures as far as possible that the original data (known as source data) is put into the correct format for the computer (transcribed) as accurately as possible.

Verification is when the original data on a document is checked against the final computer readable format to try and ensure that it has been accurately transcribed.

For example if a we wanted to enter a new pupil onto a pupil record system, a form (see below) may be use with space for name and address, date of birth and any other data we need to store on our system. The school secretary will *transcribe* this data from the form (*source document*) by copy typing the details using the keyboard of the computer.

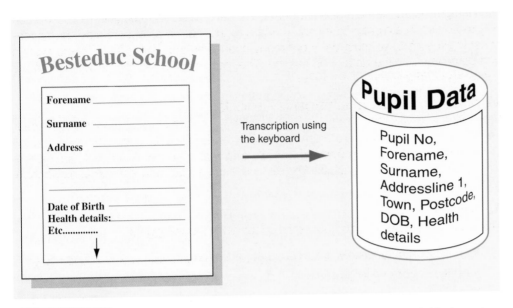

Figure 9.1 Transcribing data from a pupil's form to computer readable format

Visual checks will be made by looking at the monitor to ensure that what she has typed is what is on the source document. However, if the source document contains inaccurate data, this type of check will not detect that any error has been made. This type of check is very good when a small amount of data has to be entered.

When large volumes of data are going to be entered many data entry clerks will be entering data from a lot of source documents (many thousands of documents per day). These data entry clerks do not perform visual checks by looking at the monitor. They type very quickly and will only look at the source documents. In this situation, in order to verify data, it is much faster for two clerks to enter the data with an alert (beep sound) sounding when the second data entry clerk types in something different to the first data entry clerk. The second clerk will ensure that the error is corrected.

The next step is to *validate* the data. This can be done as the data is being keyed in and it can also be done later on when the data is processed. When there are large volumes of data and two operators, it is more common for the validation checks to be carried out at a later stage when all items have been stored away to disc. With small volumes of data where a single operator keys in small amounts of data the validation checks can be carried out as the data is typed.

The software performs validation checks and when there are small volumes of data a single operator error message is displayed on the screen. This means that verification and validation are carried out simultaneously. When large volumes of data and two operators are involved the software performs validation checks at a later stage usually producing a printed list of all errors found (see batch processing notes on page 96).

Typical validation checks

1. *Picture check* (or format check): for example the postcode may have 2 letters and a number, followed a space, then a number and 2 letters.

2. *Presence check*: some data may be essential and if the item has no characters entered this may be unacceptable, so an error message is printed and the input rejected.

> **Validation checks are performed by the software in order to check as much as possible, that data is reasonably accurate. There is no guarantee that all errors will be detected.**

3. *Range check*: there may be a lower and upper limit set on a data item, for example for a test result, the maximum mark may be 60 so a range check may be set at greater than −1 and less than 61.

4. *Comparison check*: there may be a specified set of values, which the software will reject if the data entered is outside this set of values, for example: a list of possible subjects the pupil may wish to take is limited by the range of subjects on offer at the school.

5. *File look up check*: this is when we look for a match on they key field (e.g. customer number). For example, a customer buys some goods and we wish to add the transaction details to the customer record we have on file. The software will look for the customer identification number keyed into the system by the operator to see if it exists. If a match is not found when the file look up takes place the customer identification number may have been entered incorrectly. This is the sort of validation check which is carried out during processing of the data transaction and in a batch system which is done later on (see page 98).

6. *Batch header checks*: when we have large volumes of data, details from the source documents are keyed in batches. A group of documents are put together with a starting document called a **batch header**. The batch header will contain numerical data for example, about the number of documents in the batch. The computer performs calculations as the documents in the batch are processed. The batch header numerical data is checked for a match. The whole batch will be rejected if the computer calculated values and the batch header values do not match (see batch processing on page 97). Other numerical values commonly found on a batch header are **hash totals** and **control totals**. A *hash* total is a total of numerical values in the batch which produces a meaningless value for example a total of all customer numbers would be meaningless. A *control total* is a *total* of numerical values in the batch which produces a meaningful value, for example a total value of all the transactions made.

7. *Check digit check*: this type of check uses a calculation to create an extra digit at the end of a number. Its purpose is to determine whether the data entered is reasonably accurate and any transposition of digits and incorrect typing of digits within the number will normally be detected using this method. Key fields such as customer number, pupil number and product code usually have a check digit built into them. The best known method of calculating a check digit is the modulus-11 system. It detects 99% of all errors and works in the following way.

a) Each digit of the number is weighted as follows, the rightmost (least significant digit) is weighted 2, which means it is multiplied by 2, the one to its left is weighted 3, multiplied by 3, the one to its left is weighted 4 and so on, for example 3421 would be weighted as follows: 3×5, 4×4, 2×3, 1×2.

b) All the results of these calculations are added together, in our example, $(3 \times 5 = 15) + (4 \times 4 = 16) + (2 \times 3 = 6) + (1 \times 2 = 2) = 39$

c) The result is divided by 11, in our example $39/11 = 3$ remainder 6.

Typical validation checks carried out by the software are: picture check, presence check, range check, comparison check, file look up, check digit check, batch header check.

d) We then subtract the remainder from 11 to give the check digit: $11 - 6 = 5$.

e) The check digit is then the fifth and last digit of the number: 34215.

To check that the number is valid the software simply needs to weight all the digits, but this time the least significant digit (now the check digit) is weighted by 1. The results are again added together and if the final sum is divisible by 11 with a remainder of 0, the number is valid. Hence the computer check in our example will be:

$(3 \times 5 = 15) + (4 \times 4 = 16) + (2 \times 3 = 6) + (1 \times 2 = 2) + (5 \times 1) = 44/11 = 4$ remainder 0.

Parity checks

As well as validation and verification we may also check the transfer of data between hardware components using *parity checks*. Parity checks work by ensuring that the character transmitted has not been changed by interference on the line. If the character format is invalid then it is re-transmitted.

Remember that each character must be turned into a format the computer can deal with. We have already seen that this means using something called ASCII format (see page 00). Each coded character (known as a byte) will be made up of several 0s and 1s called *bits*. For example the character '$' which is represented by 0100100 will have an extra 1 added to the end of it to make it a valid ASCII code because ASCII uses odd parity. Odd parity is when an odd number of binary 1s form the entire coded character. Even parity is when an even number of binary digits is used. If the code had represented the character '£' it would have already had an odd number of binary digits: 0100011 so an extra digit of 0 would have been appended to it.

> **Parity checks** also check that there are no errors introduced when data is transferred from one hardware component to another.

Batch processing, on-line and real-time processing

Data may be processed in different ways. We have already mentioned that large volumes of data may be put into batches for later processing. This is known as *batch processing*. When small volumes of data are involved it is more common to enter data straight onto the computer. In some circumstances the data will be processed immediately and this is known as *real-time processing*.

On-line and off-line processing of data

First let us look at what we mean by the terms *on-line and off-line*. *On-line* means we are connected to the computer that is going to process the data we wish to put onto the system (or extract from the system). *Off-line* means that we are working with data that will not be processed by the computer we are working on at present.

> **On-Line** means that our computer is not connected to the computer processor responsible for the main processing of our data and off-line means we are working on a computer without being directly connected to the main computer processor.

You may have noticed this if you have used e-mail software. Sometimes you can connect to the e-mail server that looks after all your mail which means that you are on-line. Later you can view the messages that your own computer has downloaded (transferred from the mail server to your own computer via a communication line) without being connected to the mail server any longer. You are now working off-line from the computer that deals with your mail despite the fact that you are still working on a computer. A computer used in his way is sometimes called a terminal when it is talking to the main computer or network server.

Sometimes we may look at data stored on computer files. We are on-line to the data. If you go to the bank there are sometimes machines you can use which when you insert your bank card and enter a PIN number (Personal Identification Number), it will give you access to your bank details. This means you can check your balance and look at other data, perhaps look at the last few transactions on your bank account or print off a small bank statement. The cashiers at the bank can also provide you with this information just by looking at your bank details on-line.

It is also possible to look at your bank details on-line over the Internet. If however, you withdraw cash, although you do this on-line, the transaction is recorded in a file and the processing of that transaction is carried out later, perhaps overnight. On-line systems are sometimes referred to as *interactive* systems.

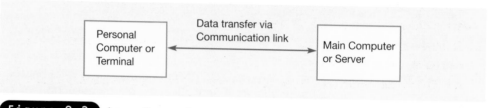

Figure 9.2 An on-line system

Real-time processing

Where it is absolutely crucial for data to be up-to-date all the time or where the data volume is so low it is possible to process transactions a few at a time, the systems are usually working in real time and are called real-time processing systems.

The main characteristics of real-time systems.

- Low volumes of data are processed.
- Immediate response to events or transactions entered.
- Data on the system is always up-to-date.

Real time systems must also be interactive. Examples of real-time systems are: patient monitoring systems, greenhouse control systems, aircraft onboard flight control systems, defence systems and nuclear power stations. Any computer system which has an application regarded as 'mission critical' where an immediate response to events or data input is required must be a real-time processing system.

Batch processing systems

Batch processing is where a group of transactions are gathered together over a period of time for later processing. The data from the transactions may be gathered via an on-line system so that a single operator verifies data. As data is collected software validates the data. It may then be stored on a transaction file for processing.

Alternatively data can be gathered off-line using the common method of key-to-disk systems. Validation programs may be present on this type of system too so that both verification and validation can be carried out on the same system. This method of data input usually involves two operators (see verification on page 93). Whatever the situation, data is put into batches to assist with checking for validity. Batch headers are really a separate document used for controlling the data in the batch. A batch header contains batch totals (see verification on page 93) which are checked during processing of the data.

The stages in batch processing where documents are prepared off-line

1. Documents are gathered together and a batch header document is created by manually working out what totals are needed for each batch.
2. The data is keyed off-line where most of the checking of data is carried out (note file look-up cannot be done at this stage because the main files are not present).

3. The transaction file is transferred to the main computer. Often transaction files are downloaded from one system to another.
4. Processing starts at a specific time. Often batch processing runs are carried out overnight.
5. During processing the first step after validation is sorting the transactions into the same order as the main file (master file).
6. The transactions are matched in order. As records are matched updates to the master file can take place.
7. Any file look-up errors are printed out and rejected transactions are written to a separate file. Other specified reports are also produced.

In batch processing systems it is usual for a large proportion of master file records to be updated. This will give you some idea of the amount of processing involved. Because usually nearly every record is updated we say the *hit rate* is high. Hit rate is the number of file accesses there are. In a payroll system when everyone is paid each week the hit rate will be 100%. The higher the hit rate on a file, the more likely it is that batch processing will take place. High percentage hit rates mean that it is sensible to keep the master data sorted and therefore it is necessary to sort transaction data so that matching of records easier.

A payroll batch processing system

If we imagine a business with many employees working in several factories around the UK all the shifts and hours they work will arrive for processing by the main payroll processing system based in London each week. The details of the hours worked and any overtime are prepared locally at each factory site. The hundreds of daily worksheets and clock card data have to be transcribed onto computerised transaction files. In this case batch headers are prepared and two operators will key in data to verify it.

Simple validation checks are made. The employee's identification number has a check digit which must be checked and the hours and overtime hours must be within a sensible range.

Once the data has been prepared the valid transaction files are submitted by logging on to the main computer at the London Head Office and transmitting the data over the normal communication channels. In this case ISDN lines are used. The transaction files from each location are put together and sorted into employee identification number order.

The data is then processed by matching the sorted transaction file with the sorted master file so that payslips can be printed, together with a full a report detailing all pay for that week's payroll. The annual amount earned, National Insurance and tax paid for the year is also updated on each employee's master record. Any errors in processing are reported and these must be corrected straight away so that a second batch run can be carried out if necessary. This will ensure that people are paid when wages are due.

The processing involved in this system is illustrated in Figure 9.3.

> **Batch processing** is where large volumes of data are verified and validated before they are sorted for processing against a master file. The hit rate is high, which means that most records on the master file will be updated during the course of a batch-processing run.

> **In a payroll** system where a large number of employees are paid every week batch processing is essential, since the hit rate will be 100%.

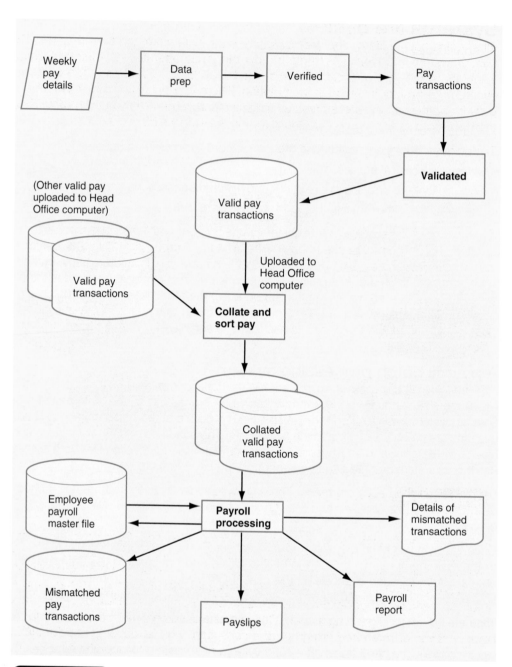

Figure 9.3   Batch processing example of a payroll system

Systems life cycle

All systems have a life cycle. They are born, have a life span and then they die. The human system is a typical example of how this cycle operates. Computer systems follow the same type of cycle. The 'systems life cycle' in ICT, refers to the course of events from project initiation to completion. There is a period of development and growth and then a period of stability as maturity approaches, followed by decline. Keep this concept in mind as we look at the stages in the systems life cycle.

The stages of the systems life cycle are:

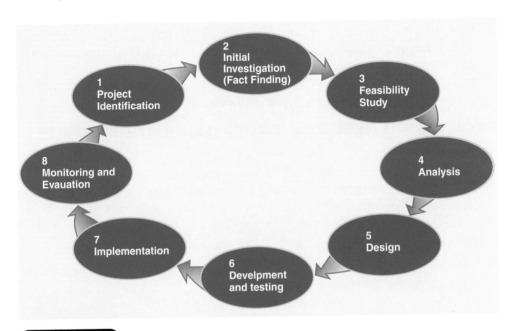

Figure 9.4 Systems life cycle diagram

1. *Project Identification* is when there is a problem identified. Perhaps there is some inefficiency in the way data is managed, customers may have complained or it may simply be that the managers want a more up-to-date and modern approach to dealing with a certain aspect of their business. Sometimes the identification of a project may be informal, perhaps a business discussion suddenly identifies an area for development and the go ahead is given right away. Other times a document may be prepared so that proper *terms of reference* are given to a consultant who has been given the task of investigating whether it is sensible to develop a new system for a particular aspect of the organisation. Terms of reference simply mean that the consultant is given the main points of what is expected, for example customer information should be available at a moments notice and orders must be processed the same day. The terms of reference will be part of the project identification which will also give a little more detail about what the initial problems appear to be and also it will detail the main activities and people involved in the area targeted for initial investigation.

> **Project identification is the initial step in identifying an area within an organisation that may have problems.**

2. *Fact finding.* Armed with the initial briefing it is then necessary for the consultant to decide how to investigate the problems identified a little more. Some of the questions that need to be answered.

a) Why do these problems exist and are the current methods (if any) used for processing data and carrying out tasks appropriate?

b) What are the current tasks?

c) Where is the data currently stored?

d) How is the data currently stored (what is its structure? Records? Files? database?)

e) How is the data collected?

f) Are there any computers used at present and if so what are they and which software is used?

g) What documents are used at present? How are they used? Where are they filed? Who uses them?

h) What reports are used? Who uses them? Are they useful?

From this basic set of questions more questions may arise. It may be necessary to talk to many different people many times. It may also be necessary to watch people working or ask customers and staff to fill in questionnaires. These are the main methods used during an investigation or initial fact finding exercise.

Information systems investigation methods

Questionnaires

These are a set of questions which may be prepared on paper. The person investigating the problem area of the business may issue a written set of questions for people to fill in or may use them as the basis of an interview. The written questionnaire is very popular for initial data gathering where there are a large number of people involved.

ADVANTAGES

- The questionnaire is an efficient method for gathering basic information about data and tasks within a problem area.

- It saves time because every individual is not being taken away from their job to discuss individual issues.

- It also assists the people working within a problem area to focus on the issues in the questionnaire.

DISADVANTAGES

- Sometimes people do not submit completed questionnaires within a given time scale. They also may have difficulty understanding the questions. The consultant has to sit down and develop a well designed questionnaire that is not too time consuming for people to fill in and also is easy to understand.

- Some issues may not be explored because the questionnaire is so focused.

Observations

These are sometimes the best way to obtain information about tasks and procedures. Observations may be carried out for short specific periods or it may be necessary for a longer, more intensive observation session. The sessions must be agreed with the person carrying out the tasks and the observer must be aware that behaviour could be modified just because the person is being watched. Observations are sometimes carried out by the consultant watching the person concerned or by arranging a video recording.

ADVANTAGES

- A clearer picture of the tasks and processes are obtained.

DISADVANTAGES

- The person being observed may resent being watched or they may modify their behaviour because they are being watched.

Interviews

These are often a necessary part of fact findings because initial findings may require further discussions. Interview times will need to be arranged and agreed with the people concerned. It is important to keep to the specified times agreed for starting and finishing. During the interview it is essential to take a record of what has been said for future analysis. It is also essential to ascertain whether it will be possible to come back to ask further questions.

ADVANTAGES

- It is possible to explore some facts in more detail.

- Certain issues may also be raised which the consultant was unaware of.

DISADVANTAGES

- They are time consuming for both the consultant and the person being interviewed.

- It may also be impossible for staff to find a time slot during their working day if they are very busy.

- Sometimes it can be difficult to keep the focus of the interview when the person being interviewed raises other issues.

3. *The feasibility study*. This is the result of initial investigation. The question that must be answered is: 'Is it sensible to proceed with the further analysis, design and development of a new system?' To do this feasibility report is written.

1. A cost/benefit analysis: an outline of the costs to develop and implement the system together with details of all the benefits to be gained.
2. The initial fact finding with a preliminary analysis and possible designs.

4. *Analysis*. A full analysis which will involve further detailed investigation using the same type of techniques: observation, interviews and questionnaires, together with an analysis of the facts discovered. The analysis will give a clear picture of the current situation: inputs, data stored, processed and used to create information. The analysis will also identify any constraints the restrictions that will not change, and any aims. All these details will be documented and a clearer picture of the problems and user requirements will be documented. The final summary of the analysis is a *requirements specification*. In simple terms this could be a numbered list of requirements that the new system will need to fulfil.

5. *Design*. The next step in the cycle is to fulfil the requirements specification. Suggested designs will be finalised and a preferred design will be agreed upon with the user. The final design will be specified in terms of inputs, outputs, data structures (such as files or a database), processes and security and recovery procedures. Additionally the hardware and software to support and run the system will be specified. All these details will be included in the design documentation, known as the *design specification*. It is also usual to design a test strategy when the details of the design are specified.

6. *Development and testing*. At this stage in the system life cycle the data structures will be set up and the software used to develop the processes specified in the design specification. At the same time as the design specification is finalised a test strategy must be decided upon. The test strategy is a plan for testing that the system will work. Test data will need to be selected to test a specific purpose and the expected outcome

Fact finding involves finding out about data and processes within the area of the organisation under investigation. Questionnaires, observation and interviews may be used to fact find.

A **feasibility** study report contains details of costs, benefits, a preliminary analysis and possible initial solutions or designs.

Analysis of the system or area, under investigation will be summarised in the requirements specification and should include details of the current system, problems and user requirements.

A **design** specification should meet the user requirements and contain details of inputs, outputs, data structures, processes, hardware, software, and security and recovery procedures.

is identified. Later when the system is tested, the results of each test will documented with any action to be taken, if the test did not work. User instructions will also be developed and part of the testing will involve potential users of the new system, obtaining feedback and amending any user documentation as necessary.

7. *Implementation*. At this stage the system has been tested and is considered to be working. Introduction of the new system must be planned carefully and any training which users may need must be given before any final implementation is carried out. Additionally it is necessary to convert any data from the old system to the format required for the new system. There are a number of system implementation strategies we may adopt.

a) *Direct changeover*. This is an all or nothing situation. Any old documentation, data and procedures will cease to exist and overnight the new system is put into use. It has the advantage that the system must be used because there is no alternative. However if the system fails then there is no alternative option to turn to.

b) *Phased changeover*. This is when parts of the system are implemented a little at a time. It gives users the opportunity to gradually get used to the new system and any errors still apparent when real data is put into the system can fixed. Because the system is introduced a little at a time the changeover is much more manageable.

c) *Parallel running*. This is when the old and new system will run together in parallel. It means that data must be processed twice which is a real disadvantage, but any errors or user problems can be pinpointed and dealt with without affecting the normal output from the system.

d) *Pilot running*. This is when the new system is run on a trial basis by a small number of users before the whole system is implemented. It gives new users a chance to report upon the success or failure of the new system so that any minor modifications can be done before the whole system is implemented.

8. *Evaluation/maintenance/monitoring*. When the system has been implemented it is important to evaluate how it is working. Are users happy with the system, how efficiently does the system work? Have there been any unexpected errors?

Over time it is necessary to constantly monitor the performance of the system. Information requirements may grow. Data input to the system may change and data structures may also have to change because of the evolving needs of users.

Inevitably as the life of the system progresses, performance will become weaker as the demands upon it change and grow. For this reason data structures and procedures may need to be changed or added to. This is when maintenance work will be required, until eventually the system maintenance will cause further weaknesses to occur. As time progresses the system will become so weak that it will not be sensible or economically viable to maintain it any longer. A new system will be required to replace it.

Prototyping

The system life cycle looks a little different if a prototyping is used to determine requirements or if it is used to check whether a possible design could work. A prototype is a mock system which looks like the real thing. For example it is possible to build several screen designs with links to imitate the way a user would navigate the interface. Prototyping is often used to establish the users' requirements or in determine which design approach the user prefers.

Development and testing is concerned with using software to set up the interface, data structures and processes, making sure that they work as far as is possible before the system is introduced to the users.

Implementation is concerned with training, data conversion and system changeover.

Evaluation, Monitoring and Maintenance are concerned with ensuring the system operates effectively and users are satisfied in the long term period after implementation.

A prototype computer system is usually built using several screen designs and reports in order to give users an idea of the way the system will look and feel to use. Its capability to process any data is limited.

The control-feedback loop

The control-feedback loop is usually present when systems are closed. A closed system is one which operates without interference from the user. Often this type of system is found where sensors monitor a situation to provide *feedback*. The system responds to the input from the sensors by producing output which will in turn affect the situation. An example might be greenhouse environmental control. Sensors measure the temperature and humidity and the system controls the heaters, windows and sprinkler system to maintain pre-set values for the temperature and humidity. The processor makes the comparison between the pre-set values and the readings from the sensors.

Figure 9.5 Input-process-output-feedback loop often found in control systems

We have also discussed the central heating systems found in the home. Again the only input from the user is to set the values for comparison by the processor – times and room temperature. The system then switches itself on and off depending on the whether the processor identifies any matches between the temperature sensors, the system time and the respective pre-set values.

Another way in which feedback is used is when the system generates what is known as a *turnaround document*. This is when part of the document, which is printed by the system, is used to capture the next input. A commonly quoted example of a system with a turnaround document is a utility bill, like an electricity bill. This document is sent to the customer detailing the units of electricity used and the total amount the customer is required to pay. There is a tear-off portion at the bottom of the printed bill which the customer sends back with any accompanying payment. This is the turnaround document and the second input is the payment data (see figure 9.6).

Form design and the user interface

When we design our system it is necessary to specify the way that data is going to be entered into the system. This may be using any one of the data collection methods we have already discussed. The user interface design is extremely important. A badly designed interface can mean that the user will avoid using the new system once it has been implemented. We often refer to 'user friendly' or 'intuitive' user interfaces. This simply means that the interface works logically and consistently so that there are no unexpected surprises for the user and it is always clear what the user should do next.

Good user interfaces often have on-line help systems (this usually displays help on the screen when the user needs it) built into them which are often rarely needed if the design is very good. Menu structures are also sometimes a feature of user interfaces. An introductory screen may present the user with a set of options. These are known as menu options. Further menus may appear on screens as the user makes selections. Often these menu screens are arranged hierarchically as shown in figure 9.7.

Features of good interface design

a) *Consistency of layout*. The user will always find similar features in the same place from screen to screen, for example the exit button may always be in the right hand bottom corner of the screen.

> **Feedback**
> is when some aspect of the output is used later as input. It could be used in a control system or using **turnaround** documents in a data processing system.

> User interface design is an extremely important part of system design. A good, 'user friendly' interface, which is intuitive, can make the difference between user acceptance and rejection of a system.

EASTERN ENERGY

Customer Service Centre:
PO Box 2021, Rayleigh, SS6 9FB

Q
05
32
1

Please let us know if any of these details are incorrect

QRTON/3.37/1

Electricity Bill

Meter Readings Present	Meter Readings Previous	Units Used	Unit Price (Pence)	VAT Code	Amount £
61833	61722	108	6.53	D	7.05
		3	6.13	D	0.18
Standing Charges from 16 Apr 99 to 29 Apr 99				D	0.98
		Total exclusive of VAT			8.21
		VAT on £8.21 at 5.0%			0.41
		Total Amount Due			8.62

Supply Number(s) S 01 801 003 / 10 1308 1030 588

Paying by cheque?
Please make all cheques payable to Eastern Energy for your electricity bills.
Please allow a minimum of 3 working days for your payment to reach us

Please see reverse for further information

Customer Number
86 2579 0020 82

YOU CAN CALL US 24 HOURS a day 7 DAYS a week

Customer Services Advice Line
0181 366 1112

Supply Failure?
0800 7838 838

Date of Bill
4 May 99

Pricing Scheme
Domestic General

Total Amount Now Due
£8.62

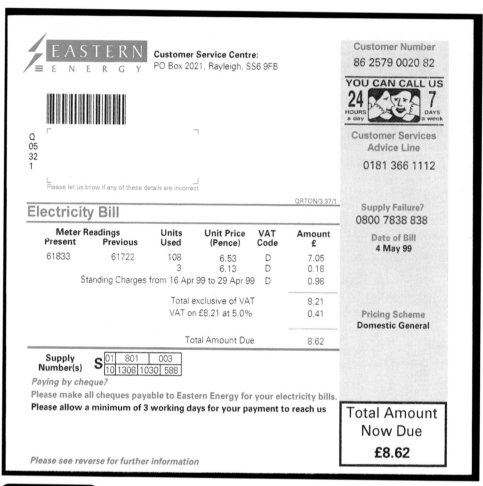

Figure 9.6 A utility bill

Figure 9.7 Diagram of part of the menu hierarchy for a stock control/customer order system

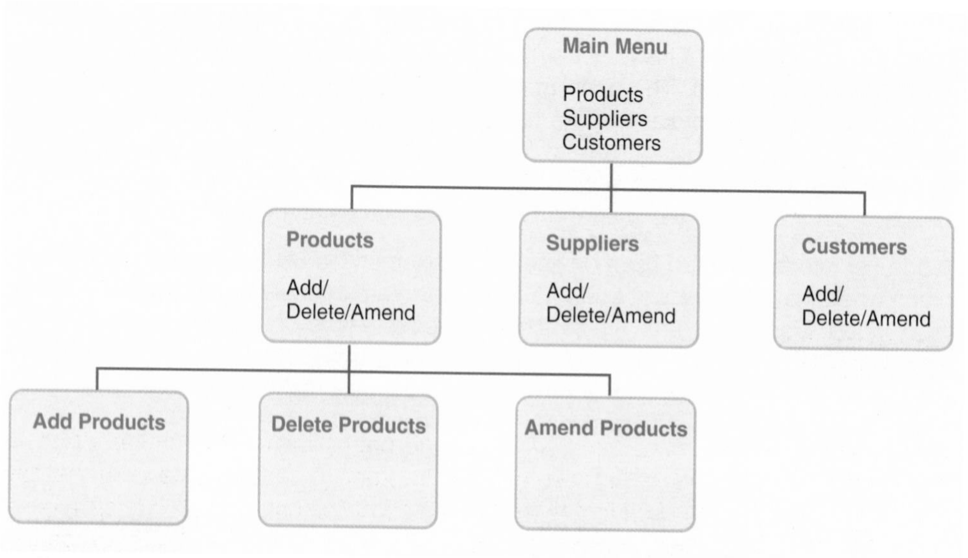

Hierarchical menu systems are a common feature of many user interfaces.

b) *Harmonious colour schemes*. The user will find bright colours which clash. These are very tiring to work with over long periods of time, so restful colours which work in harmony, like pastel colours which are known to work well together are a sensible choice for on-line work.

c) *Clear, consistent pathways through the system screens*. The user can easily become lost if the system is very large. There should be a clear set of pathways to each task-related screen. These pathways should be consistent too. For example if both products and suppliers can be added, deleted and changed in a stock control system, there should be buttons or menu options which when clicked take you (along an imaginary route or pathway) to the right screen. The same method or type of pathway should be constructed for both products and suppliers. To avoid user confusion it is also a good idea to include a 'home' button or icon, which will take the user back to the main introductory screen.

d) *Clear labelling*. The screens and user options should be clearly labelled to avoid any confusion as to which item or task is currently being dealt with.

e) *Uncluttered screens*. If too many items are displayed on the screen at any one time the user may be overwhelmed with the content and not be able to make sense of the display. The rule is *approximately* seven items of information or options on the screen at any one time.

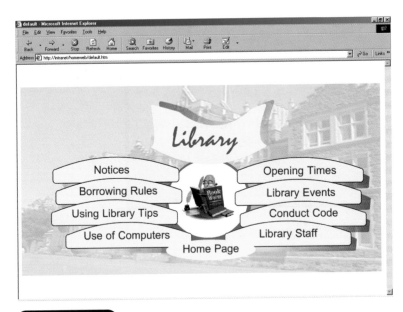

Figure 9.8 A well designed screen

Similar rules apply to both on screen forms and paper forms. Sometimes when we design forms for new computer systems, it is in order to capture data from the data subject. We have already seen that a pupil or the pupil's parent, may fill in a form, which will capture the basic data we need to record on our pupil data file. There are general rules governing the design of forms whether they are on-line forms or paper based forms. It is important to note that where a signature is required for legal reasons, a paper-based version of the form must be completed.

Screen design and form design are important aspects of system design. It is important to ensure that designs are consistent, logically organised and easy to complete.

Rules for designing forms

a) Make sure that the title is clear, prominent and related to the purpose of the form.

b) Make sure that there are clear instructions for filling in the form.

c) Make sure that there is enough space to write what is required for each item of data.

d) Make sure the layout is progressive and logical. For example start with the vital information and make sure that the following item is related in some way. Remember we write left to right and top to bottom as we fill a page.

e) Make sure tick boxes and selections are incorporated in the form where possible to reduce the amount of writing.

f) Use fonts which are easy to read.

g) Split the form into logical sections if possible. In our pupil form example, we might have a separate section for personal details like name, address and date of birth, another section for medical details (perhaps using tick boxes) and another for examination results and achievements.

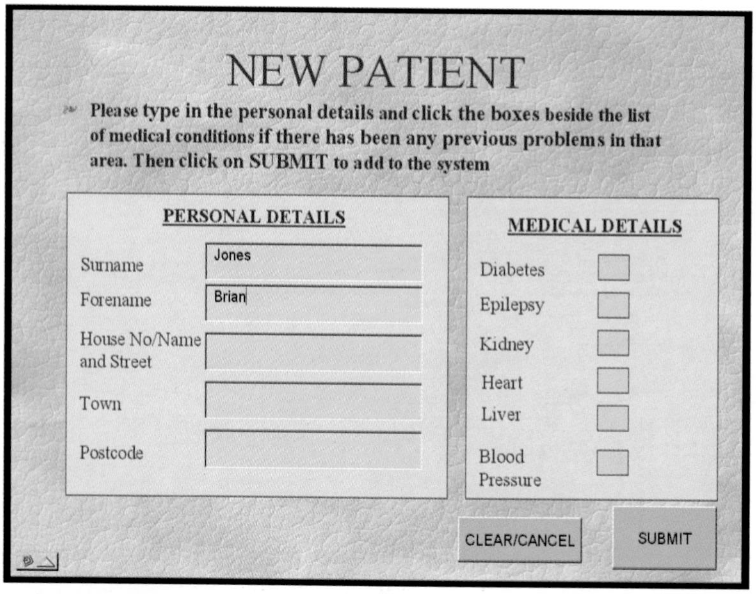

NEW PATIENT

Please type in the personal details and click the boxes beside the list of medical conditions if there has been any previous problems in that area. Then click on SUBMIT to add to the system

PERSONAL DETAILS

Surname	Jones
Forename	Brian
House No/Name and Street	
Town	
Postcode	

MEDICAL DETAILS

Diabetes ☐
Epilepsy ☐
Kidney ☐
Heart ☐
Liver ☐
Blood Pressure ☐

CLEAR/CANCEL　　SUBMIT

Figure 9.9　A well designed form

Data structure design

Files and records are all examples of data structures (or data groups). Good data structure design is extremely important. It involves choosing the relevant data items and putting them together in such a way that it is easy to extract information from the final structures. It should also be easy to combine data from one data structure with another to produce information displayed on screen or printed on reports.

What is important at the design stage is that we make decisions about the fields we wish to include in our files or database, their data type and length (if required). Also data will be grouped logically. We must also allow for modification to our data structures and ensure that it is possible to extract data in such a way that we can present it as useful information for our user. Default values may also be decided upon if they are required. For example any date fields may automatically be filled with today's date from the system if the user leaves them blank at the input stage.

> **Data structure design** involves choosing the correct fields to fulfil the processing requirements, deciding on the data type: e.g. text, numeric, data/time, setting the length of some fields.

Output design

Output can take many forms. Mostly we will choose to design our output so that it can be displayed on screen or as a printed report. The design may be drawn out in rough or may be set up as a part of a *prototype system* (system which is not complete but demonstrates the main features of the final system). Output design should basically follow similar rules to that of form design. The layout should be clear, uncluttered, use fonts which are easy to read, have a clear title and not overload the user with too much information. Any on-screen error messages may have a bold colour scheme to alert the user.

> Output design must also be uncluttered, logical, and consistent in its layout.

Summary

Computor systems: components and types

✓ Archive data is a copy of data which is no longer in regular use but which we may need to look at occasionally. Back-up data is a copy of data in regular use taken for security reasons.

✓ Data security is about the safety of data and data integrity is about the accuracy of data.

✓ Verification is when data on the computer is checked by operators to ensure that it is the same as on that recorded on the source document. Validation checks are carried out by the software to reduce the amount of errors introduced to the system.

✓ Verification may be a visual check by a single operator to ensure that data is transcribed correctly or two operators may be used to check that the data is transcribed in the same way twice.

✓ Typical validation checks carried out by the software are picture check, presence check, range check, comparison check, file look up, check digit check, batch header check.

✓ Parity checks are checks on individual characters as they are transferred from one hardware component to another.

✓ On-line processing is when work is carried out whilst a computer/terminal is connected to the main computer but during off-line work the connection is not used.

✓ Real time systems usually process lower volumes of data than found in batch processing systems. They respond immediately and data on the system is always up to date.

✓ Batch processing is where large volumes of data are verified and validated before they are sorted for processing against a master file. The hit rate is high, which means that most records on the master file will be updated.

✓ Project identification is all about establishing which area in an organisation needs attention.

✓ Fact finding or systems investigation methods often used by consultants are: observation, questionnaires and interviews.

✓ Feasibility studies are carried out to determine whether it is sensible to develop a new system. A cost benefit analysis is an important part of the feasibility study report.

✓ Analysis is where all the details of the current situation are described and analysed to establish any problems and user requirements.

✓ Design is where the new system is specified so that it meets all the requirements of the user. A test strategy should be designed at the same time.

✓ Development is concerned with setting up data structures, input, output and processes using the chosen hardware and software.

✓ A test strategy is designed and during the development of the system, testing is carried out to determine whether the system will work.

✓ Implementation must be planned and includes user training, data conversion and system changeover.

✓ Maintenance of a system is necessary to keep the system operational as user needs change.

✓ The systems cycle has eight stages: project identification, initial fact finding, feasibility study, analysis, design, development and testing, implementation and evaluation, monitoring and maintenance.

✓ A prototype computer system is usually built using several screen designs and reports in order to give users an idea of the way the system will look and feel to use. Its capability to process any data is limited.

✓ A control system is one which uses sensors to detect certain aspects of a situation. The sensor readings are input to the system which then decides on what sort of output to produce to modify the situation.

✓ Feedback is when some aspect of the output is used later as input. It could be used in a control system or using turnaround documents in a data processing system.

✓ Hierarchical menu systems have options for the user to choose from. Further menus may appear on screens as the user makes selections.

✓ Data structure design involves choosing the correct fields to fulfil the processing requirements, deciding on the data type: e.g text, numeric, date, setting the length of some fields.

✓ Form, screen and report designs must be well designed, easy to use, have clear legible fonts, be uncluttered and consistent in the way they are laid out.

? Test and review

1. State the difference between archive and back-up data. _____

_____

2. State the difference between data security and data integrity._____

_____

3. Tick the correct statements about verification:
   a) Verification is when data is on the computer is checked by operators to ensure that it is the same as on that recorded on the source document.
   b) Verification carried out by the software to reduce the amount of errors introduced to the system.
   c) A typical verification check is a range check.

4. Tick which checks are validation checks.
   a) Two operators check that the data is transcribed in the same way twice.
   b) Picture check.
   c) Batch header check.
   d) File look up.
   e) Visual check.

5. What are parity checks and how do they work? _____

_____

6. Describe the difference between on-line and off-line processing._____

_____

7. State the main characteristics of a real time system. _____

_____

8. State the main characteristics of a batch-processing system. _____

_____

9. What do we mean by the term 'file hit rate'. _____

_____

10. Stages in a large scale batch processing system. (fill in the gaps).

    a) Collect together the source documents in batches and prepare a batch header.

    b) _____

    c) Validate the data and create a valid transaction file and list of errors.

    d) _____

    e) Match the sorted transactions against the master file and perform any updates necessary

    f) Produce a list of mismatched data and any other reports.

11. Fact finding or systems investigation methods often used by consultants are O_____, Q_____ and I_____.

12. Describe the contents of a feasibility report._____

_____

13. Which comes first – Analysis or Design? _____

14. Tick the correct items to be included in the design specification.

    a) List of problems found

    b) Screen and report designs

    c) Detailed hardware and software specification

    d) User manual

    e) List of user requirements

    f) Data structure details

    g) Test strategy/Test plan

    h) Details of tests carried out

    i) Details of any processing

15. Describe what happens during the development and testing of a system.

_____

_____

16. Describe two changeover methods that may be used during conversion from the old system to the new system. _____

_____

_____

17. Implementation must be planned and involves user training and two other tasks. What are they?

_____

18. State two tasks we must carry out for maintenance on computerised information systems. _____

_____

_____

19. State in order the main stages (eight) of the systems life cycle _____

_____

_____

20. State three characteristics of a control system. _____

_____

_____

21. Feedback is when some aspect of the output is used later as input. Describe two ways (not example systems) in which feedback is used in computerised information systems. _____

_____

22. State three tasks you must carry out when designing a data structure.

_____

_____

23. Form, screen and report designs must be well designed. State three features of a screen layout, which has a good design.

24. A printed form should include the following features (tick the correct options).
a) A clear title.
b) Correct amount of space for each item to be written.
c) Multiple choice tick lists when appropriate to save writing.
d) Important details at the top of the form.
e) Fancy fonts.
f) Sections to split the type of data to be captured.
g) Lots of pictures.
h) Space for a signature.

Review and thinking tasks

Take a backup copy of your work. Where will you keep it to ensure that it is safe? Think about different types of systems you have seen such a supermarket stock control systems. How many other examples have you seen? What are they? What sort of input, output and processing is involved. List these items? Is there any feedback? How is it used? Do you think the system has a database. If so what type of files will be stored?

When you next enter a car park with an automated barrier system, consider how it works. How is the ticket produced to raise the barrier. How does the system know when to display the FULL or SPACES message. Is there any feedback in this type of system? Is it a closed system?

Networks

This chapter is about networked computers (usually computers connected together by cables). We often talk about the Internet (computers all around the world that are connected together) and most of us will already know that we can logon to the Internet using an Internet Service Provider (ISP – page 116). As soon as we make our connection to the ISP our own computer behaves like another computer or terminal which is part of that network. The Internet is what is known as a common **network environment** or *public network environment*. In this chapter we are going to look at different types of network and the way that computers are connected together so that they can talk to each other. We have already seen in Section A that the Internet is a *Inter*national *net*work of computers but before we look at the Internet and public networks in more detail we are going to look at private networks and how they work.

Local and Wide Area Networks

Networks can be categorised in two ways. There are networks which have computers located quite close together perhaps in the same room or just scattered around a building. When these computers are connected together the network is known as a Local Area Networks (LAN). Sometimes computers are connected together and are located a long way from each other, perhaps even 100 miles apart. For example when a company has offices all over the UK with computers located at each office. If we connect them together in a network this type of network is called a Wide Area Network (WAN).

Local Area Networks (LANs)

A Local Area Network known as a *LAN* is a group of computers which are linked together on the same site or within the same building. You may have a LAN at school. If you have a LAN at your school the computers will most likely be connected together by cables.

How can you tell whether a computer is networked to other computers?

Some standalone computers (computers which are not networked) may be set up for you to logon and use a password as you would with a networked computer. However, there are other ways you can tell if your computer is networked.

a) Usually a networked computer will allow you to send messages to a friend who is working on another computer.

b) You will probably see messages telling you are entering a networked system when you logon.

c) Sometimes you will see shared resources such as files and software.

d) Sometimes you will have a choice of more than one printer to send your printouts to.

e) If you have a file server you are also likely to have some space on the server's disk reserved for you to save your work.

So far we have seen that to logon to the Internet we need a telephone line and a modem or access to a digital telecommunications line. One of the main features of a

> Local Area Networks (LAN) are a group of computers, which are linked together on the same site.

LAN is that it is not necessary to use these telecommunications lines because computers are fairly close together. Even if the site where computers are located is quite large (perhaps even extending across a public road) it is still not necessary to use public telecommunication lines. Instead we can use cable to link the computers together. Different types of cable can be used (page 116) and there are different ways we can join computers together. The way in which computers are connected together gives us different patterns or layouts and these different layouts are *called network topologies*. Network topologies are discussed on page 113.

To make a network usable it is necessary to have the right hardware and software. Network software can watch users who logon and log off. It also looks after other events which happen on the network for example the sharing out resources such as printers, applications (like a word processor) and user work areas. The term '*client-server*' is used to describe networks that have computers or terminals (clients) that are connected to a *network server*. Networks that operate with no main network server are known as '*peer to peer*' networks.

> **To make a network usable we need: computers, cables, connectors, network cards and network software.**

The hardware that is required are the computers themselves, network cards, connectors and cables. Network cards are located in the computer and are small circuit boards. They have connectors to allow the network cables to be plugged into them.

LANs have many advantages over standalone computers.

1. Users can send messages to one another.
2. Data and software can be shared.
3. Printers, hard disk space and other resources may be shared.
4. Backup of all data can be done using the file server.
5. It is possible that the LAN has a facility called a gateway facility, which is the hardware and software allowing users access to computers away from the rest of the computers connected on the LAN.

> **LANs allow users to share data, resources and support e-mail but security must be good.**

LANS main disadvantages over standalone computers.

1. There are additional tasks involved in maintaining the details of all the users able to logon to the network
2. There are added risks of virus infection because people will bring floppy discs and logon to the network. Any infected discs may cause the whole network to be infected.
3. There are additional security problems because data and programs are shared so the risk of hacking is greater.

The characteristics of a LAN are shown below. Note the difference between the Wide Area Network in Figure 10.2

The basic characteristics of a LAN may be summarised.

1. More than one computer connected together using cable on the same site.
2. Computers which are connected in order to share resources and data.
3. Network software controls access and users must logon.
4. There may be a network server which monitors all other computers. In a *client-server* network where there is no network server the LAN is known as '*a peer-to-peer*' LAN.

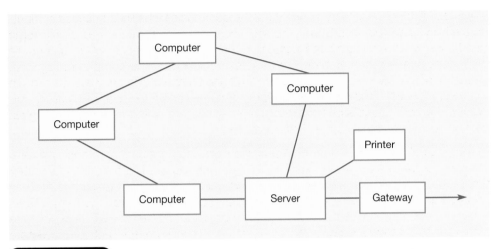

Figure 10.1   A small LAN providing basic facilities

5.   There may be gateway to other networks.
6.   Users are able to communicate with each other.

Wide Area Networks (WANs)

Wide Area Networks are known as WANs. This time the network of computers, which are connected together, is spread over a much wider area perhaps many miles apart. Computers may be scattered all over the U.K and many sites may be involved including those located in other countries.

Large organisations often depend on WANs for exchanging data and communicating with one another. Think about our example of a payroll system (page 97) where all the employees' working hours were transmitted to a London head office for processing. They would use a WAN. WANs are therefore dependent on communication links which are able to carry data long distances. Within the UK the most common communications links that are used are telephone lines. If links are required over very long distances, perhaps to other countries, it is more likely that satellite or radio waves are used. In our payroll example the WAN would look like the diagram in Figure 10.2. Notice that at each site there is also a LAN.

Network topologies

We have already identified that the way the cabling and computers are laid out is known as a network topology. There are three main types of network topology. These are star, ring and bus.

Star

The star topology is appropriately named because it has all the cables for each computer routed directly to the main computer. This is usually the file or network server. The network server is the computer which controls all the other computers and monitors, users' access to work areas and other resources. Because each computer on the network has a direct line to the server, communication is often very fast and should any other computer on the network breakdown no other computer will be affected. It is therefore often a very good layout to choose for a WAN.

It is an expensive topology to install because more cabling is required to give each computer its own dedicated communication link with the network server. A star topology is shown in Figure 10.3. (Notice that because the network server's load is not too heavy the printer is also linked straight to the server. This is not always the case and a separate print server may be installed, or the printer could be attached to one of the

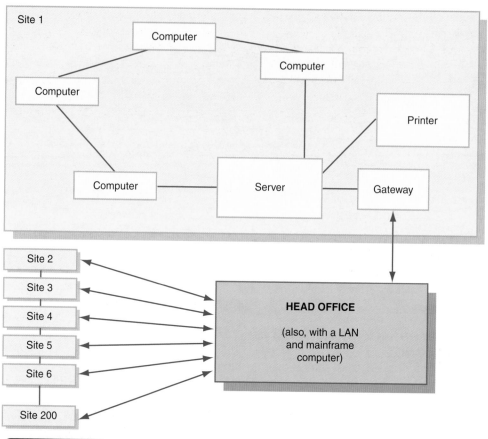

> The star topology provides high speed dedicated communication links to a central computer for each computer terminal, and is the choice for WANs.

Figure 10.2 Wide Area Network (WAN) for the payroll system example

computers. However should the computer or print server be out of service users would not have a print facility.)

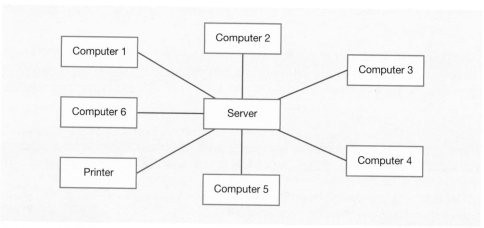

Figure 10.3 Star topology

Ring

The ring topology is also aptly named because the cabling is set out as a ring with a break for each computer. It is not necessary for any computer to have overall control of access to the network although one computer may be allocated this task. For this reason ring topologies are usually LANs, which are known as 'peer-to-peer' (see p112). Messages and data flow around the ring in one direction from computer to computer and is called the 'token ring' system. The advantages of a ring topology is that we save on cabling costs, have high speed simple (one direction only to deal with) communication but unfortunately should any computer breakdown the whole ring circuit is broken and communication between any of the other computers cannot take place. Figure 10.4 illustrates the ring topology.

> The ring topology is ideal for peer to peer networks, being simple and inexpensive to install, although they have the disadvantage that one computer out of action will cause the whole circuit to be out of action.

```
Computer 1 ──── Computer 2 ──── Computer 3
    │                               │
Computer 7                          │
    │                               │
Computer 6 ──── Computer 5 ──── Computer 4
```

Figure 10.4 Ring topology

Bus(line)

In a bus topology or line topology the computers are connected like branches off a single line. There is a file server which looks after the main files and user details and usually one computer is used as a print server. A bus topology is frequently used for a LAN because it is not possibly to use very long lines. Bus topologies are frequently used by small organisations with LANs because it is economical to install and maintain since new computers and other resource can be added without disrupting the other computers. Similarly if one computer breaks down it can be attended to without affecting any of the other computers. The main disadvantage is that the communication can be slow if many computers are added to the same line. The bus topology is shown in Figure 10.5.

> The bus topology is an excellent choice for a LAN with a file server. It offers a low cost solution where each computer linked to the line does not affect any other resources linked to the line. If there are too many users the service could be slow.

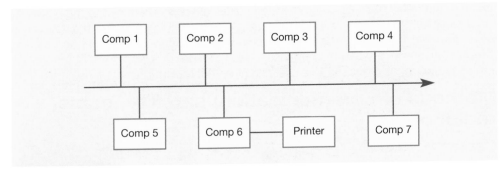

Figure 10.5 The bus topology

Comparing advantages of different network topologies

Star topologies are good for WAN's because we use telephone wires to access a central computer. Star topologies provide a dedicated line to each terminal computer providing high-speed access. If a star topology were to be used for a LAN it would prove to be an expensive option.

The ring topology has the advantage that it is simple to manage but when one computer is out of action it breaks the circuit and all others on the circuit are out of action. This type of topology is sometimes used for small parts of a LAN. For example a small group of users in the same office may be on a ring circuit whilst the rest of the LAN is configured as a bus topology. Ring topologies tend to support peer-to-peer networks better since no file server is required.

The most common topology used for LANs is the bus topology because it is so easy to manage and has the added advantage that one computer out of action is not going to affect the rest. There is also the added security of attaching a network file server to manage user work files and other resources. Network service may be very slow if there are a lot of users logged on at the same time.

Common network environments

Common network environments are networks that are open for use by everyone and thus are known also as public networks. The most well known common network environment is the Internet.

Uses of common network environments

Common network environments like the Internet are used for:

1. searching for information;
2. displaying information;
3. communicating with others via e-mail, discussion forums or chat rooms.

To search for information we use a *search engine*. A search engine is software provided for users so that they can enter key words about a topic they want to find out about. Search engines are also able to automatically follow links to pages of information adding the *address of the page (URL)*, the title of the page and the first paragraph of the text to a database. It is this database, which is indexed, that is searched when you enter a key word to search for. There are many examples of search engines on the Internet.

To display information, users, if creating a web page for transmission over the Internet, need to register with a Internet Service Provider (ISP) so that they can use space on the ISP's server to store their information. Web page addresses can be registered with a particular search engine, so that it is stored on their database.

On public networks like the Internet there are often newsgroups and chat rooms as well as e-mail that allow users to communicate in different ways. There is also the possibility to videoconference. Users can also join mailing lists by sending e-mail to the mail server which provides the facility. This means users have *subscribed* to the mailing list and they can *unsubscribe* when they no longer wish to receive news from that mailing list. There are thousands of mailing lists covering all sort of topical interests.

Methods of communication: satellite, cable, radio, optical

Cable

We have already seen that we can use cables for communication. Digital lines such as ISDN and analogue telecommunications lines are commonly used to transfer data from one computer to another (see page 32). There are basically two categories of telephone line.

- public lines which are paid for depending on how much they are used;
- and private lines for which there is a fixed annual cost and no further charge.

Cabling for LANs are normally well insulated and able to transmit data at high speeds. They are generally *coaxial cables or fibre optic cables*.

Public or common networks like the Internet allow users to exchange information by providing search, display and communication facilities.

Public telephone lines are charged based on the amount of use whilst private telephone lines are charged at a fixed annual rate.

Coaxial and fibre optic cables are often used to cable LANs. Fibre optic cable is a better option for transmitting data, which may be subject to interference (over a roadway or car park), or when there are large volumes of data to transmit at once. It is much more expensive than the cheaper alternative coaxial cable.

Coaxial cables are made up of many wires and are the most inexpensive cable to install. They are often used for LANs.

Fibre optic cables transmit pulses of light in digital format rather than using electrical signals. There is generally less interference and more data can be transferred at any one time, although it is more expensive to install.

Satellite and radio/microwaves

There are hundreds of satellites in orbit around earth, which are used to receive and transmit signals. Signals are coded so that only those people who have a decoder can receive the signals. Satellites are used for transmitting data over very long distances, across continents. Their main advantage is that signals are transmitted at high speed with a low rate of interference.

Microwaves are similar to radio waves. Stations called microwave stations are located no more than 30 miles apart because microwaves travel in straight lines and are unable to travel in curves around the earth. Mobile telephones use microwave radio links and are able to transmit data using one simple device, the Internet ready mobile phone. Their main disadvantage is that there must be many stations set up so their use is limited to within the continents and countries. There are many different networks of stations set up.

Satellites are often used for very long distance data transmission, such as transmitting weather data /pictures. Microwaves, although used for transmitting data over distance, must have many stations to pass messages from one to another.

Summary

Computor systems: components and types

✓ Networks allow users to share data, resources and support e-mail, but security must be good.

✓ To make a network usable we need computers, cables, connectors, network cards and network software.

✓ Networks may have a file server or main computer controlling all network activities. These are called client-server networks, or they may have no file server and are known as peer-to-peer networks.

✓ A LAN is a group of computers connected together to facilitate communication between users on the same site. A WAN facilitates communication between users located a long distance away from each other.

✓ The star network topology provides high speed dedicated communication links to a central computer, for each computer terminal, and is the choice for WANs.

✓ The ring network topology is ideal for peer to peer networks, being simple and inexpensive to install. They have the disadvantage that one computer out of action will cause the whole circuit to be out of action.

✓ The bus network topology is an excellent choice for a LAN with a file server. It offers a low cost solution where each computer linked to the line does not affect any other resources linked to the line. If too many users are on the line the service could be slow.

✓ Public or common networks like the Internet allow users to exchange information by providing search, display and communication facilities.

✓ Public telephone lines are charged based on the amount of use. Private telephone lines are charged at a fixed annual rate.

Coaxial and the more expensive fibre optic cables are often used to cable LANs.
Satellites and microwaves are often used for long distance data transmission.

 Test and review

1. State three advantages of using a network rather than a standalone
   computer. _____

   _____

   _____

2. To make a network usable we need network software and some hardware.
   Name two items of hardware other than computers that are need to set up
   a network. _____

   _____

   _____

3. Describe the difference between a client-server network and a peer-to-peer
   network.

4. Tick the following characteristics which are TRUE about a LAN.
   a) A LAN is a group of computers connected together to facilitate
      communication between users on the same site.
   b) A LAN facilitates communication between users located a long distance
      away from each other, such as in different countries.
   c) A LAN has computers which are connected in order to share resources
      and data.
   d) A LAN is always a peer-to-peer network.
   e) A LAN has network software controls access and users must logon.
   f) There may be gateway to other networks.
   g) Users are not able to communicate with each other over a LAN.
   h) Satellite communication or fibre optic cable is always need for a LAN.

5. Match the statement to the correct network topology by entering the
   correct letter beside the following: RING _____, STAR_____,
   BUS_____.
   a) provides high speed dedicated communication links to a central
      computer, for each computer terminal.
   b) is simple and inexpensive to install, but has the disadvantage that one
      computer out of action will cause the whole circuit to be out of action.
   c) offers a low cost solution where each computer linked to the line does
      not affect any other resources linked to the line, although if too many
      users are on the line the service could be slow.

6. State three uses of a common network environment like the Internet.

_____

7. Describe the main differences between coaxial and fibre optic cables.

_____

_____

_____

8. Name one use for satellite transmissions. _____

9. Name one use for microwave transmissions. _____

Review and thinking tasks

Look at your geography notes about weather. How do you think weather satellites work? How do you think they transmit digital data? Think about satellite digital television. Does this work in the same way?

Look at your computers in school. Are they standalone or networked. If the are networked, try and find out if you have a peer to peer network. You should be able to access your own area on a file server if you have a client-server network.

Section B   Test your knowledge

1. State the main differences between a mainframe computer and a microcomputer.

    _____

    _____

    _____

2. Name one application which is suited to each of the following modes of processing, giving a reason for your choice.

    a) batch processing _____

       _____

       _____

    b) real time processing _____

       _____

       _____

    c) on-line processing _____

       _____

       _____

       _____

       _____

3. Describe the main features of a supermarket stock control system.

    _____

    _____

    _____

4. Compare bar code readers with keyboard input, highlighting their advantages and disadvantages.

    _____

    _____

    _____

    _____

5. Select one choice for backup media from the list below giving a reason for your choice.

    a) CD-R (Compact Disc Recordable)

    b) Zip disc

    c) CD-ROM

    Reason _____

6. Name two ways in which CAL software provides feedback to the user

    _____

7. Describe multimedia. _____

    _____

    _____

8. State four characteristics of a GUI. _____

    _____

    _____

9. The main characteristics of command line interfaces are

_____

_____

10. List three commonly known generic applications packages and their uses.

_____

_____

_____

11. Identify the difference between applications software and systems software.

_____

_____

12. Identify the differences between bespoke systems and off-the-shelf systems.

_____

_____

_____

_____

_____

13. Name three 'Acts' which may affect computers use, stating the purpose of each Act.

_____

_____

_____

_____

_____

14. Describe three ways in which you can prevent unauthorised access to your data.

_____

_____

_____

15. Briefly discuss the following statement: 'ICT has caused massive unemployment both on the factory floor and in the office. Soon there will be no work for anyone!'. Your answer should refer to the capabilities of ICT and the changing pattern of the UK workforce.

_____

_____

_____

_____

_____

_____

_____

16. Describe what happens when you try to obtain cash from an ATM when you use your bank card.

_____

_____

_____

_____

17. State the difference between data security and data integrity.

_____

18. Describe the difference between verification and validation.

_____
_____
_____

19. In a batch processing system the transaction file is sorted. Explain why this is necessary.

_____
_____
_____

20. Describe three methods for finding out the data and processing involved in an existing system and explain the advantages of using each of them.

_____
_____
_____
_____
_____

21. What is a test plan, when is it created and how is it used?

_____
_____
_____
_____

22. Describe what happens when system changeover is direct and explain its disadvantages.

_____
_____
_____

23. Explain why we must carry out maintenance on computerised information systems.

_____
_____
_____

24. Explain how a control system differs from a large scale database system.

_____
_____
_____
_____

25. Explain why most LANs tend to use a bus topology.

_____
_____
_____

26. Working on-line using a WAN, requires a password and user-id for access. Describe the likely topology to support this situation awnd explain the sort of communication hardware a home user is likely to use in this situation.

_____
_____
_____

Section

Practical skills and understanding of the use of ICT applications

This section is all about the applications software you will use to carry out practical tasks, such as word processing, spreadsheets and databases. It also looks at other types software, such as control software. Everyday tasks that you may carry out on your computer such as using the Internet, are also covered in this section.

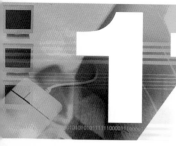

Word processing,
desktop publishing and other presentation software

We need to communicate with others and even from a very early age we learn to speak, read and write, so it is not surprising that beginners choose how to use a word processor on a computer first of all. Once the basic keyboard layout has been learned it is just a matter of typing the words and saving the document.

This sounds simple, but there is much more to a word processor than typing words and pressing the 'enter' key as we shall see in this chapter. Additionally, word processors are not the only software we may choose to use to communicate with others. We may choose to use desktop publishing software or presentation software instead. E-mail is also software we can use to type messages and communicate with one another and it is not uncommon to attach a word-processed document to an e-mail message for the recipient to read.

Word processors and desktop publishers

To be able to word process a document we first need to have the correct software installed on the computer. Also most computers will have a mouse, keyboard, monitor and printer attached to them so that we can see the documents we type and print them when we are satisfied with them.

There are many different brands of software available today. The subject material covered in this chapter is about the general features found in most word processors, desktop publishers and presentation software.

Common features of a word processor and desktop publisher

When typing a document on a word processor (such as a letter) it is possible to *edit* (or change) and ***format*** (or alter the layout) of text. This provides enormous advantages over using typewriters where typists would need to re-type the whole document if an error was made. Editing and formatting features are common to most software and are present in all brands of word processor and some desktop publishers, as well as other presentation software (which we will consider a little later).

It is important to make the distinction between editing and formatting. Editing is when we change the content of the document. For example a mistyped letter may be replaced with the correct letter or we may decide to add some punctuation to a sentence after we finished typing it.

Formatting is when we change the layout of our text. For example we may decide to change the heading so that it is in the centre of the page rather than over to the left-hand side of the page.

Editing features

The following editing features are common to many different types of software but are more particularly found in word processors and desktop publishers.

1) Deleting an unwanted character or inserting a missed character, for example the sentence:

> The main advantage of using word processors rather than typewriters is that we can easily edit (make changes) to our document. There is no need to re-type the whole thing.

> Editing is when we change the content of a document. Formatting is when we change the layout of the document.

> '*The cat licked its lips thinking to himself what a lovely meal a mhouse made.*'

could be edited to read:

> '*The cat licked its lips, thinking to himself, what a lovely meal a mouse made.*'

notice the added punctuation and deleted letter 'h' from 'mouse';

2) Replacing characters or words which have been type incorrectly. For example

> '*The cat started to purr and begun to doze.*'

Could be edited to read:

> '*The cat started to purr and began to doze.*'

Notice the word 'begun' is replaced by 'began'.

3) Re-arranging a sentence. Most word processors and desk top publishing (DTP) packages allow the user to move text by deleting, saving to a temporary area in memory and placing the saved text somewhere else. This technique is known as '*cut and paste*'. For example

> '*The cat started to purr and began to doze*',

may be re-arranged by swapping the phrase 'began to doze' and 'started to purr'. It now reads:

> '*The cat began to doze and started to purr*'.

4) Copying blocks of text or words so that they are repeated elsewhere in the document. This technique is similar to the 'cut and paste' technique except that instead of cutting (deleting) the phrase in question, we highlight the text and copy the phrase before we paste it.

5) We may use a facility called a spellchecker. The word processor will scan the document or selected text that you have typed. It can do this, sometimes automatically, sometimes only if you ask it to do a spelling check. It will detect spelling errors you have made. It may even suggest the correct spelling so that you do not have to look it up in your dictionary. It can only tell you a word is spelled incorrectly if the word is stored in its own dictionary.

6) Thesaurus and Grammar checker are not usually a feature of a DTP package. A thesaurus will suggest other optional words for you to use if you highlight text and select the thesaurus option. It can only do this based on the words it has stored. Similarly the grammar checker will help you write sentences correctly. If you make an error when you construct a sentence the computer will highlight the text that is wrong. Grammar checkers have their limitations because the English language is so complex.

These editing features are the most commonly used. In addition we may choose to insert pictures, tables, headers (a heading which appears at the top of each page), footers (text which may appear at the bottom of each page), page numbers, date and time and a range of other objects (such as other software items like a spreadsheet).

Formatting features

To format a document we change its layout or the way it looks.

Typical formatting activities.

1. Embolden characters: for example we change the look of a character so that it stands out in heavy type such as 'hello' changing to '**hello**'. This is known as making the text bold.

Re-arranging words, replacing characters, inserting and deleting characters are all typical editing activities.

Spellcheckers, Thesaurus and Grammar checkers are all additional tools to help us edit our documents.

2. Make characters italics, for example 'hello' changing to *'hello'*.

3. Underline characters, for example 'hello' changing to '<u>hello</u>'.

4. Changing the font type or font size. This means selecting a different style of writing and changing its size respectively. For example '**hello**' (in Times New Roman 12 point) may be changed to (Arial 14 point) '**hello**'. Both these are commonly used fonts.

5. Changing the spacing between lines. We write close underneath the previous line of writing or we can space it out so that there is a larger gap. Common line spacing are single line spacing and double line spacing.

6. Making the left and right margins bigger or smaller. This means that the blank space down the left and right side of the paper changes size according to what you want.

7. Setting up tabs or indenting text. This means that you start text at different points across the line. In the following example tabs have been set so that neat columns of text are created.

First text	second text	third text
First text2	second text2	third text3

Indenting text means that the text on one line starts at a different point to other text lines. For example

'This first line is indented when compared with the next line of text. Notice that now the line of text is again in line with the previous line of text.'

8. Setting up page breaks which means specifying that a new page should start rather than carrying on to the next line.

9. Text can be left justified, right justified, centred or fully justified. Left justify means all text is lined up on the left margin but not at the right margin. Right justify means that all text is lined up on the right margin but not at the left margin. Centred text has no alignment with margins. Text is evenly balanced around the centre line of the page. Full justification is when text is lined up evenly at both left and right margins. The example below shows centred text and right justified text. More often you may see full justified or left justified text.

This text is centred in comparison with the fully justified text,
which appears on the lines below.

Headings of reports are often centred, whilst main text is usually fully justified. Right justification is more rarely used and left justification is often used for letters or more informal documents.

10. Borders can also be used to make text stand out, for example.

> THIS IS AN EXAMPLE OF A BORDER ARRANGED AROUND TWO LINES OF
> TEXT WHICH IS CENTRED

11. Bullet points and numbers can also be used to itemise our text. The text you are reading has numbering to describe the main formatting and editing features of word processors.

These features are the more common formatting features and may be applied just by clicking on a button on the screen or selected from a range of options on a menu (see figure 11.1). Other formatting features which are not so commonly used, and not found on all word processors, are fancy lettering, different colour choice for text and the use of a highlight tool to draw blocks of colour over important parts of the text (rather like using a highlighter pen).

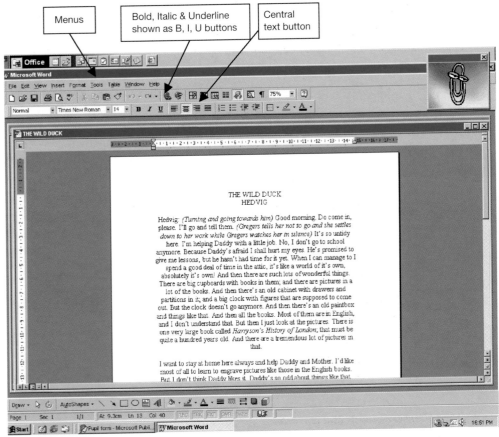

Figure 11.1 Word processor window with some buttons and menus

Not all these formatting features are available when using presentation software or when using a desk top publishing package. The main differences between word processors and desk top publishers are discussed later (page 128).

Remember too that whatever package you are using there is usually a **HELP facility**. This is there to help you locate some of these editing and formatting features, should you not know which menu they belong to or how to use them. Remember that the text will need to be highlighted before you can change the layout of it if you have already typed it.

We have looked at the most common editing and formatting features found on most software but mostly are available on word processors. To summarise here are some other features you may find on word processors.

a) A help facility.

b) Creating and editing tables with rows and columns.

c) Drawing tool so that you can draw your own shapes such as arrows, lines, circles and squares. There is also the facility to group shapes so that the whole drawing becomes one object on your page.

d)   Inserting a variety of objects such as pictures.

e)   Mail merge where a standard document can be prepared and merged with a data source so that many different copies of the standard document are created dependent on the data stored in the data source. For example the data source might contain customer data and a standard letter could be sent to every customer by merging the name and address from the data source.

f)   A feature that will add up the number of words in your document.

Today word processors also have many features which at one time could only be found on desktop publishers. As part of the drawing feature some word processors have the facility to add text to the drawing area.

Desktop publishers have many of the above features except that they have more flexibility in the way text and other objects may be laid out on the page. However they do have many editing and formatting features already described. Additionally they often have an on-line help facility, the facility to create and edit tables and also a drawing tool. They too will allow the addition of pictures and the creation of mail merged documents.

Differences between a word processor and desktop publisher

Desktop publishers and word processors are designed to provide us with a variety of facilities to create documents for us to print out and use to communicate with others. The main differences between today's word processors and desktop publishers.

1.   To create text in a desktop publisher we need to have a text box or frame to write in. In word processors generally we start to type in text straight away. The words we write using a word processor are also never split into two parts because of a facility called word wrap. Desktop publishers will often split a word and insert a hyphen. Some word processors also have text frames.

2.   The spellchecker in a desk top publisher only works for the text frame that your cursor is located in. The whole document may be checked automatically if you wish with a word processor.

3.   Thesaurus and Grammar checkers are found in word processors but not desk top publishers.

4.   Some word processors will automatically correct typing errors whilst this is a facility not normally found on desktop publishers.

5.   Desktop publishers have the flexibility to layer objects, so that text frames can be made transparent (or see through). Perhaps a picture could appear behind the text.

6.   Desktop publishers have the ability to flip and rotate objects, so a text frame can be put onto its side or onto a diagonal. This is not possible at present with most word processors.

7.   Text frames in desktop publishing can be linked so that text automatically flows from one area on the page to another. This is particularly useful when setting out pages with columns or creating documents with multiple pages.

8.   Desktop publishers also have extra features to help you easily design layouts of documents, or select a pre-designed layout of a document.

A typical desktop publisher window showing some features is shown in Figure 11.2.

Basic tasks and uses of word processors and desktop publishers

Word processors are often used for writing essays, reports, memos, letters, books and all kinds of text based documents. They are also becoming more powerful and can assist with the layout of some of these basic documents. However if you wish to create a document which has not so much text but has many different design features, it is often more sensible to choose a desktop publisher.

Desktop publishers commonly produce newsletters, business cards, brochures, flyers and posters because the layout of text, design features and pictures can be more complex with objects rotated or flipped and some objects layered one behind the other.

Presenting information in textual, graphical or multimedia format using presentation software

Presentation software is designed to be interactive, so that whoever is giving or using the presentation can select pathways through material or choose to display or animate

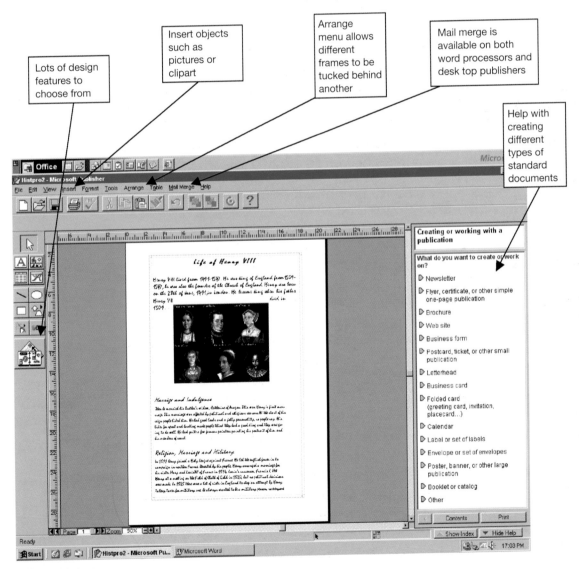

Figure 11.2 Window showing some desktop publishing features

certain objects. Presentation software is more dynamic because presentation features can include text and pictures as with word processing and desktop publishing software but it can also include animation, video and sound.

There are many different types of presentation software available. Some are known as slideshow software, others are known as multimedia publishers, and others are known as multimedia programming tools. People often choose to use software which is easy to use and may not wish to use a complex multimedia programming package. Presentations may also be very complex, for example, when writing CAL material, or they may just be something simple such as providing the computer user with information about sport in your school.

The simpler slideshow software often has all the basic editing and formatting features you would find in word processors and desktop publishers. It is also possible to arrange slides in an order and create a master slide template so that the design of your slideshow is consistent throughout the presentation. As well as being able to check spelling you may check the style of your presentation. This provides comments about the style of presentation, for example, on the number of bullet points per slide.

Presentation software also often has a drawing tool and the facility to insert different objects such as spreadsheets and pictures. Video and sound objects are other objects which in particular can be inserted with this type of software. The timing of the appearance of objects can also be crucial in a presentation and so it is possible to rehearse timings and re-arrange how and when items appear on the screen.

Narration can be added by recording the spoken word. Different animation effects can also be used so that objects may appear on screen from the left side or the right side, one word at a time or even a letter or phrase can appear in one action. Slideshow software also provides users with the facility to jump from screen to screen using buttons. Buttons provide a facility for the user to navigate from screen to screen. It is a feature that is very important in multimedia software or slideshow software. A typical example of a small set of slides under development is shown in Figure 11.3.

> **Presentation** software adds a new dimension to communicating with the user allowing video and sound to be used as well as text and pictures.

A new slide can be inserted

Various tools can be used such as the Stylechecker

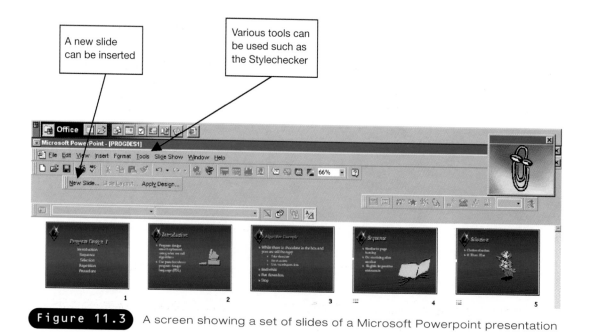

Figure 11.3 A screen showing a set of slides of a Microsoft Powerpoint presentation

To summarise, slideshow software often has multimedia capability. It extends the communicative capability of the printed documents produced by word processors and desktop publishers because it has additional features.

The main features of multimedia presentation software may be summarised as:

1. Most editing and formatting features such as bold, italics, centring text etc. are usually present.
2. A facility for checking the style of presentation, or running animations, rehearsing timing to ensure smooth running of the presentation is also an important feature.
3. Being able to add multimedia objects such as sound and video, so that the user is presented with information in a different way.
4. Control of pathways through screens of information using navigational aids like buttons.

This provides the developer with enormous advantages when developing material, because it is easier to capture audience attention with the powerful, dynamic multimedia presentations in today's competitive world. Multimedia and slideshow software is an ideal choice for developing Computer Aided Learning (CAL) software.

Presentation software is often a popular choice for creating web pages, business presentations and also for CAL.

> Many additional features such as using buttons to jump from one screen to another, rehearsing timing of screens and the appearance of objects on the screen, together with checking the style of layout are available with multimedia presentation software.

Summary

Computer systems:
components
and types

✓ Editing is when the content of the text is changed. Formatting is when we change the way the text is laid out on the page.

✓ Common editing features are using cut and paste to move text, inserting text, deleting text, and changing existing characters.

✓ Common formatting features are bold, italic, underline, centre, justifiy, borders, tabs, change of font style or size and margin adjustment.

✓ Editing and formatting features, on-line help, tables, drawing tools, inserting objects such as pictures, mail merging are common to both word processors and desktop publishers.

✓ Word wrap and Thesaurus are word processing features not desktop publishing features, whilst a spellchecker is common to both types of software, although they work in a slightly different way.

✓ Desktop publishers have much more flexibility than word processors because they can flip, rotate and layer different objects within a document.

✓ Word processors are often used for writing essays, reports, memos, letters, books and all kinds of text based documents.

✓ Newsletters, business cards, brochures, flyers and posters are commonly produced by desktop publishers.

✓ Presentation software adds a new dimension to communicating with the user, allowing video and sound to be used as well as text and pictures.

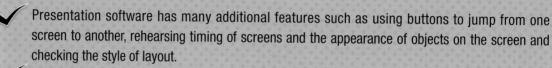

✓ Presentation software has many additional features such as using buttons to jump from one screen to another, rehearsing timing of screens and the appearance of objects on the screen and checking the style of layout.

✓ Presentation software is often a popular choice for creating web pages, business presentations and also for CAL.

? **Test** and review

1. Describe the difference between editing and formatting. _____

   _____

   _____

2. Circle all the editing examples and tick all the formatting examples.
   a) inserting text
   b) emboldening
   c) deleting text
   d) change the font size
   e) centre heading
   f) add a space between two words
   g) add punctuation to a sentence
   h) underline the heading

3. Name two other features commonly found in both word processors and desktop publishers.

   _____

   _____

4. Describe one feature found only in word processing software and one feature found only in desktop publishing software._____

   _____

   _____

5. Circle the tasks you would carry out on a word processor and tick those tasks you would carry out on a desktop publisher.
   a) writing essays
   b) designing a newsletter
   c) writing a report
   d) writing a memo
   e) creating a flyer or brochure
   f) writing letters
   g) creating a business card.

6. State what is meant by the term 'multimedia'. _____

   _____

7. Name two features common to multimedia software. _____

   _____

8. Describe, using an example, what a 'navigational aid is.

_____

_____

9. Name one task you would use presentation software for. _____

Review and thinking tasks

Look at the software on your computer. Is your word processor capable of all the features described in this chapter? Try creating a business card on your word processor. Then do the same task on a desktop publisher. What features of a desktop publisher make the task easier or the design of your business card better?

Make sure you use some presentation software. Try creating three screens which describe your school dining room at lunch time. What can you include on those screens to make your presentation more interesting than it would be if for example, you used a word processor to write text only, or used a desktop publisher to created a poster with a picture of the dining room?

Graphics production and image manipulation

There are all types of different graphics package available. Graphics packages are programs that will allow you to create and change pictures (we call them images).

We have already seen that in word processors, desktop publishers and presentation or slideshow software, that there are facilities to create drawings with lines, circles, rectangles, arrows and sometimes much more. These drawings can be filled with colour, meaning that the shape is coloured in, or we can change the colour of the lines around the edges of shapes.

There are also some graphics packages which provide all these facilities, together with the facility to zoom into small areas of your drawing and also to allow you to draw freely with the pen tool. More sophisticated graphics packages provide many more features.

Common features of basic graphics packages

Here are the most common features you may find in graphics packages.

1. Fill: which means you colour in a shape. The circle below has been drawn with a red line in the first instance and then has been copied and filled with colour completely.

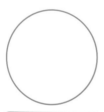

Figure 12.1

2. Shadowing: this is where a shadow is added to the drawn object. A plain rectangle is shown below and a shadow has been selected for the second rectangle.

Figure 12.2

3. Three-dimensional shapes: we can also makes shapes look real by adding depth so that they have a three-dimensional look. The ellipse shape filled with blue colour has been changed to a three-dimensional cylindrical looking object.

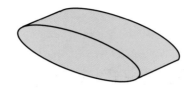

Figure 12.3

4. Layering: is when we put one object on top of another. Below are two filled blue circles with blue lines around the outside edges. They have been placed side by side and the rectangle shape has been layered on top to give a completely different shape. We could then group these layered objects together so that we can move them around as one object.

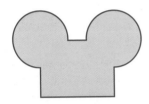

Figure 12.4

5. Change size: To change size, depending on the package you use, it may simply be a case of stretching the drawing out or asking for a magnification of the drawing. Whatever option is available in your own package it can be a very powerful way of changing images, especially when used together with other image manipulation techniques.

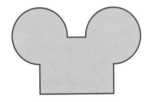

Figure 12.5

6. Change the orientation: this is when a drawing is rotated or flipped over. The rotation could be small or large. The first object below has been rotated just less than 90 degrees whilst the second object has been rotated just less than 180 degrees. Together with layering this is a very powerful technique.

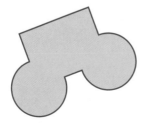

Figure 12.6

7. Repeating pattern: some graphics packages provide a simple one click facility for repeating an object or pattern created a specified number of times. The strange looking object below was created by copying our blue image above (the Mickey Mouse ears!), changing the colour, making it three dimensional and then repeating the pattern many times. The second shape looks entirely different because it has been rotated and had the three-dimensional effect changed.

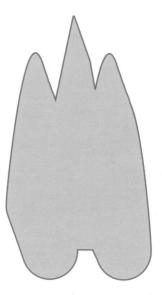

Figure 12.7

Remember that most graphics packages will allow you to add text as well. Some graphics packages will provide a facility to change the type of image you save or even change the size of the file. This is useful if there is a limited amount of computer memory available, for example on a floppy disk. Also, better graphics packages will allow you to carry out more automated image manipulation. These packages allow you to change an image much more readily. You can make an image look clearer or add particular photographic effects to it. Other packages also allow distortion of images in all sorts of ways.

Resolution is a term that you may come across when using graphics software. Resolution is all about the clarity of the picture. If you have a high resolution then the picture will be clearer. It will also be likely to take up more space in computer memory. This is because often to achieve a high resolution we need to store more data about all the little dots that make up the image on the screen. These dots are called pixels. The larger the number of dots, the higher the resolution. Using this technique of storing data about each pixel is known as bit mapped graphics. There is another way to represent images and that is storing details about all the images as equations which are recalculated when the image is resized. The amount of data, which needs to be stored about each image, is very much reduced and less memory is used.

Clipart

Creating images with graphics packages can sometimes be time consuming and often we would like a ready made image that we can use immediately or change a little to fit our requirements. Clipart is a library of images, which have already been created. Clipart libraries sometimes come with a package. For example, word processors can have their own clipart but it is also possible to buy CD-ROMs with clipart libraries.

Scanned images and digital photographs

Sometimes we may have a picture that we would like to use in our documents but it may be a photograph we have taken, or it could be a picture from a magazine or book (always be aware of copyright issues). It is possible, as we have seen in Section A, to scan an image using a scanner and scanning software. Some graphics packages also have built in scanning software. The software records all the data about the image. You will save it to a file for later use or possibly to change it some more using a graphics package.

The main features of scanning software.

1. The ability to preview an image, which means there is a scan of the image presented on screen but nothing has been saved.
2. The ability to select and size the portion of the image we may want to scan. This means that if we do not want the whole item which we have placed in the scanner the software allows us to choose which part of the image we want.
3. The ability to change the resolution of the image so that we can save a smaller file if we want to.
4. The facility to choose the format or file type in which we wish to save the image. It may be as a bit mapped file or vector graphics format (where images are saved as a series of equations).

Remember too that we can obtain images directly in digital format by using a digital camera. Once saved to disk these images can again be manipulated if we wish.

Uses of graphics software

There are many different types of drawing or graphics package. Some are used for photographic work. Glossy magazines sold at newsagents are likely to have images, which have been manipulated in some way. The film industry uses graphical manipulation to create special effects and it is well known that images are created using computer and then animated using animation software when creating a cartoon film.

Additionally there are home users who may want to create and manipulate images for documents they are creating and there are some users who use more sophisticated graphics software for design.

Special Computer Aided (CAD) packages also use graphics to aid the designer. It is easier to draw and manipulate a design drawing using such a package. CAD packages are capable of producing plans of images and three-dimensional images which can be rotated to see what the object looks like in reality (and from different angles).

Computor systems:
components
and types

Summary

- ✓ Although they are primarily for creating and manipulating images, graphics packages also provide a text facility.
- ✓ Common features of graphics package are fill, shadow, 3-D, layering, sizing, orientation and repeating pattern.
- ✓ Some graphics packages provide more sophisticated facilities to sharpen images and add special photographic effects.
- ✓ Resolution refers to the clarity of an image. To have a really clear image we need a higher number of dots per inch to store data.
- ✓ To achieve a high resolution we need a larger memory capacity to store all the data.
- ✓ Clipart is a library of images which may come with the software or separately on a CD-ROM.
- ✓ Scanning software provides previews, the facility to select portions of an image and the facility to ensure that we have the correct file format, size and resolution.
- ✓ CAD has additional features to assist designers when they draw up plans.
- ✓ Graphics and CAD packages have many uses because of the way images are manipulated. Film makers, publishers and designers find them invaluable tools.

? Test and review

1. Briefly describe the common features of graphics packages.

_____

_____

_____

_____

2. Describe what we mean when we talk about the 'resolution of an image'.

_____

_____

3. What is clipart? _____

4. State the features of scanning software. _____

_____

5. What is CAD? _____

6. Who uses CAD and graphics packages? _____

_____

Review and thinking tasks

Which graphics package do you use in school? Think about some of the common features we have covered and list any additional features you can find in the software you have used.

What sort of tasks do you use your graphics software for? Can you think of other tasks you may use graphics software for?

Spreadsheets, modelling and databases

In this chapter we are going to look at spreadsheets and databases. Although they are grouped together in one chapter because of some common features, spreadsheets work in a completely different way to databases and are used for different tasks. It is important that you understand the differences between the two types of software, despite some of their similarities. We are going to look first at the common features found in both types of software and then look at what makes them different and suitable for certain types of task.

Common features of spreadsheets and database software

We have already seen in Chapter 11 that it is possible to edit and format our documents. In the same way we may edit and format spreadsheets and databases. Editing and formatting facilities for any text we put into this type of software are the same as you find in other types of software. The important distinguishing feature that spreadsheets and databases have is that we store data in them. In chapter 5 we looked at some different types of data: text, numeric and date/time. Numeric and date/time data types may also be edited in the same way as we edit text, but we may also format it in different ways.

Numeric data types may be formatted using bold, italic, underline and many other features discussed in Chapter 11 but they may also be formatted in a different way. For example a number may be formatted to contain only whole numbers. These are known as *integers*: 3457. Numbers can also be formatted with a decimal point, and they are then known as *real numbers*: 2345.678. It is also possible to specify whether numbers are allowed to be negative, how many decimal places they should have (the number of numbers after the decimal point) and whether a £ sign is to be used. In some brands of software *currency* and *number* are treated as two different data types. Figure 13.2 shows a window, which allows you to select different types of data for formatting.

Date type data can also be formatted using some of the features we have already discussed. It may also be formatted in various ways so that it looks like some of the examples in figure .

Cells, rows, columns

Spreadsheets and databases must be set out in such a way that there are places to put data. Spreadsheets and many branded databases on the market today display a screen, which looks like a grid so that each part of the grid contains one item. A sample screen is shown in Figure 13.1 Notice that the software is a spreadsheet and each part of the grid is called a cell. For example just underneath the letter A is a highlighted box. This is one cell and in a spreadsheet it has the **cell reference** name 'A1'. Because it is highlighted it is known as the *active cell*. A vertical line of cells is called a column (named by letters A, B, C etc) and a horizontal line of cells is called a row (named by numbers 1,2,3 etc).

Data stored in spreadsheets and databases may be edited and formatted in much the same way as we have seen already in word processing software, but we may format date and numeric data in other ways.

Spreadsheet grids have columns, which are a vertical line of cells each one identified by a letter, and rows which are a horizontal line of cells each one identified by a number. Each cell has a named reference such as A1 or B6.

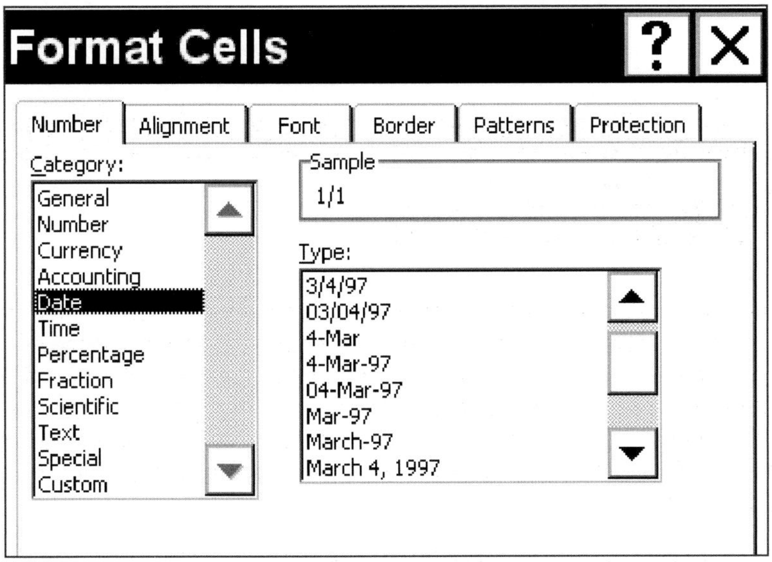

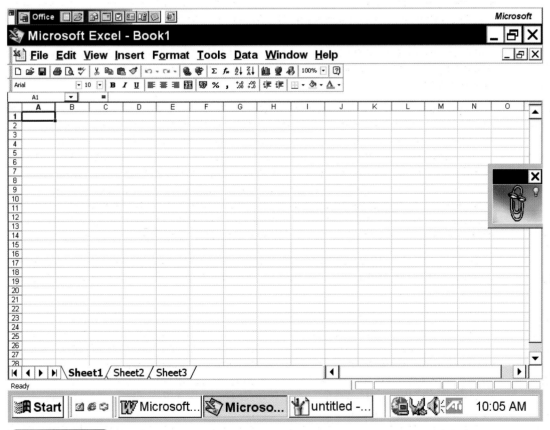

Figure 13.1 Some sample data types showing date type selected and some of its possible formats

Figure 13.2 Cells on a spreadsheet. Notice the similar formatting facilities

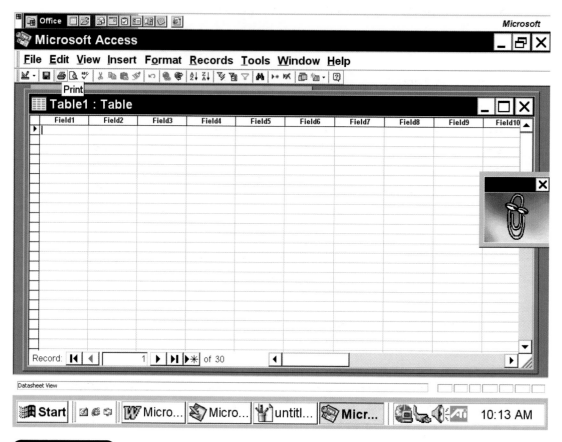

Figure 13.3 A database with fields shown as columns – the fields will usually have names

Although databases have a similar grid with rows and columns they do not have cell references. A typical example of a database layout is shown in figure 13.3. This time you will notice that there are no cell references possible. Instead each column is headed with the name of a field. Several of the fields across the top of the grid are known as a record (see chapter 5). We may then fill our grid with data, row by row, each row of data representing one record.

As we can see, spreadsheets and databases are beginning to look different. There are however one or two other common features. For example because both contain data. It is going to be sensible to put the data into order. We call this sorting. We may sort our data in ascending (e.g. 1,2,3, or A,B, C) or descending (3,2,1 or C,B,A) order. Look for the common sort buttons on the two sample screens in figures 13.2 and 13.3. They have AZ and ZA for ascending and descending sorts.

It is also possible to filter out data we need to look at by using two search features known as AND & OR. AND filters out data in the following way.

I have a set of data representing all the cars in stock in a car dealer's garage. It could be possible to filter out all those cars which are WHITE and are SALOON cars using the criteria.

colour = WHITE <u>AND</u> car type = SALOON.

> Although databases may be displayed as a grid there are no cell references and any columns are headed by field names with rows representing records.

> Sorting is a facility common to both spreadsheets and databases.

On the following car data 2 cars will be selected: 1 and 5

						£
1.	WHITE	SALOON	FORD	ESCORT	1998	£3500
2.	BLUE	SALOON	FORD	ESCORT	1998	£3500
3.	RED	SALOON	FORD	ESCORT	1998	£3500
4.	WHITE	HATCHBACK	VAUXHALL	ASTRA	1999	£4000
5.	WHITE	SALOON	FORD	MONDEO	1999	£6000
6.	RED	HATCHBACK	RENAULT	CLIO	1998	£2500
7.	BLUE	HATCHBACK	RENAULT	CLIO	1998	£2500

If we were to ask for all the blue cars as well as all the red cars, we would need to set up a different type of search using the OR search criteria.

> For example
>
> COLOUR = BLUE **OR** COLOUR = RED.
>
> This would filter out the cars: 2,3,6,7.

Think about what would have happened if we had asked for COLOUR=BLUE <u>AND</u> COLOUR=RED. Would any cars have been selected? To give you a clue ask yourself if there are any cars which have two colours in this database. It is important that you know the difference between AND & OR and when to use them, so take a few moments to study these examples.

There are many other features which are common to spreadsheets and databases. For example it is possible to do calculations (using similar features in both types of software) spellcheck text, import data, write macros (a small set of commands rather like a little program) and create a variety of charts and graphs. In summary here are the common features of spreadsheets and databases.

> **AND & OR** searches are available in both spreadsheets and databases. They select only the data we need. It is important not to get AND & OR confused.

1. Data can be stored.
2. There are rows and columns but only spreadsheets have cell references.
3. Editing facilities are similar to editing facilities found in other software e.g inserting, replacing and deleting characters.
4. Formatting facilities are similar to those found in other types of software e.g. bold, italics, borders, but there are also data formatting facilities.
5. Sorting and searching facilities are available.
6. Graphs and charts may be created.
7. There is usually a spellchecker facility.
8. Calculations may be carried out including the use of **functions** (see page 147).
9. Macros can be written to carry out some tasks automatically.

Databases

We use spreadsheets and databases for different tasks and both types of software were developed with different features to support those tasks. Database software is really a complex set of programs that allow the creation of data structures that allow us to easily and efficiently store, sort, search and retrieve data and is often called a

Database Management System (DBMS)

Database Management Systems also allow us to import data and set up special security measures to stop unauthorised users accessing data that they should not.

We have already discussed fields, records, files and key fields. These items are important when looking at database systems. To store data in a database the data structure must first be designed. This means looking at the sort of fields we need, what the data types should be and which field should be the key field.

Steps in designing a database system.

1. Decide what data is needed. For example if we store details about cars, do we need to now the car type such as SALOON or HATCHBACK.
2. Decide on the order in which we want to list them. For example: Car Model, Make, Type, etc.
3. Decide on the type of data. Is it numeric, text, etc.
4. Some fields will also need to have their length specified particularly text fields. For example, car type may not need to be larger than 10 characters long.
5. We must decide on the key field (sometimes called the Primary Key). In our car database we may choose to use a number or even choose to use the registration number of the car itself.
6. Next we may need to decide whether to include any validation on some of the fields.
7. In some cases we may decide one group of data is not sufficient. For example in our car database we may decide that one file with a number as the key is an inefficient way to store the data. Two files may be needed or even more. Databases are good for storing many files and linking them together. It may also be possible to code certain items. For example SALOON may be coded as SAL, HATCHBACK cold be coded as HCB (notice we use the same length of field – 3 characters for our code). We use codes because they are quicker to enter than the full word and they take up less space in our database.
8. When we are satisfied with our data structure design we can enter our data.

When we have tested our data the next step will be to use the data. We may choose to sort or search the data as we have already mentioned. Many databases today allow us to ask questions or make *queries* of the database. The queries are really a way of retrieving data by stating search and sorting criteria rather like we did when we searched our car database using the AND & OR example.

Queries

Queries allow us to ask questions of our database. We have already seen two examples of queries using AND & OR. When creating a query we are able to choose the fields we wish to display, select certain parts of the data and maybe store the query away for future use. Figure 13.4 shows a query which has been created to find all the pupils in two forms from our pupil database.

A Database Management System (DBMS) allows us to efficiently, store, sort, search, retrieve and import data. It also provides ways to help us secure data.

To design and set up our database the basic steps involve choosing fields and their data type, setting field lengths, coding and validating any fields, choosing a primary key field and entering data.

Many databases today allow us to search for data using questions or queries.

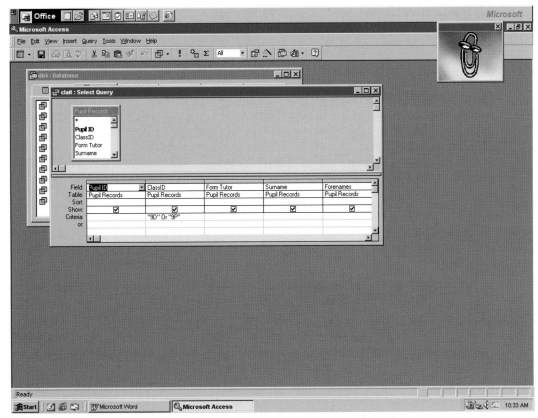

Figure 13.4 A query being designed to find all the pupils in forms 9D and 9P (Note the use of OR.)

We have seen some of the features of databases.

1. The facility to create primary keys.
2. The facility to create queries and maybe save them for future use.

Other facilities

1. To be able to create screens which are easy to use.
2. To be able to **create reports** which are easy to read rather than printing tables of data all the time.
3. To be able to write **small programs** to carry out special tasks.

Uses of DBMS

A typical task which database software might be used for is creating a database of cars, videos, customers, pupils etc that may be searched to answer particular questions we may have about the data. It is therefore often used for data handling applications.

ADVANTAGES

The main advantages to using database software for storing, searching and sorting is that we can

- store data efficiently;
- search and sort easily by asking questions (queries);
- present a user friendly interface because there are good screen design facilities and report creation facilities.

DISADVANTAGE

- The software is a complex suite of programs and can at first be confusing to the first time user. Eventually as user requirements become more complex, some knowledge of programming may be necessary.

Spreadsheets

Although we have seen some features common to both databases and spreadsheets, there are many differences between the two types of software. With spreadsheets it is possible to create many worksheets of data (e.g Sheet1, Sheet2 etc – see figure 13.5) and calculations, with many worksheets of data making up what is known as a work-book.

The idea of a cell reference for each box on the sheet (or grid) has already been introduced (page 166). Cell references are very important because we use them when we make calculations. For example, if we wanted to enter our pocket money for each week of January we may enter the amount in 4 cells across row 3 (see figure 13.5).

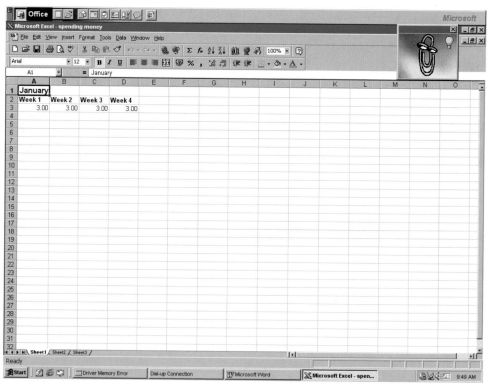

Figure 13.5 Spreadsheet showing four data entries for spending money

Notice that we have entered text 'January' in cell A1, changed its point size to be larger and also made the text bold. Similarly we have text headings in cells A2 to D2. The actual data entry for the spending money on row three has been set up as a formatted decimal number set to two places. To calculate the total spending money in cell E3 we now need to use what is known as a formula. Formulas are used all the time in spreadsheets. They are a very powerful facility. Every time data is used in a formula on a spreadsheet, should the data change, the new result is automatically calculated.

In our example we would say that we wanted to add together cells A3, B3, C3 and D3. So in E3 we may say =A3+B3+C3+D3. This will give us £12 as our result. The 'equals' sign tells the software that there is going to be a formula in the cell and a calculation will be required. Alternatively we can use another powerful facility in spreadsheets, called a *function*. Functions are ready-made calculations, which are named, and we can use them by replacing the whole calculation just by using the name. Two useful functions found in most spreadsheet software are SUM and AVERAGE. There are usually many more. To calculate our monthly spending money using SUM we might say =SUM(A3:D3).

The ability to add, subtract, multiply and divide across rows can also apply to columns and on our sample spreadsheet we may want to add what we spend regularly each week so that we can work out what is left at the end of each week. When we do this we are creating a *data model* of our finances for the month of January (see figure 13.5).

Notice in Figure 13.6 that we have inserted a column for extra text to the left of all our other data and that we have filled up two rows with figures. Another feature of spreadsheets is that we are able to highlight and copy data in one cell then highlight other cells across a row or column and paste identical data into those cells. This was done with the spending for January. Additionally we can do the same thing with formulas and by copying the formula already created in cell F3 to cells F6 and F7. The software automatically changes the row number in the cell reference so that the correct calculation is made. Copying formula like this is called *replication*. When cell references change as a result of replication like this we have used *relative* cell references.

However, it is possible to stop the row numbers (or column letters if we replicate across a row) changing when we do the replication. This is done by using special characters (such as a $) in front to the cell reference. Putting characters in front of the cell reference in a formula makes the cell reference an *absolute* cell reference: e.g. A1 is an absolute cell reference. You do not need to do anything to a cell reference to make it a relative cell reference. Table 13.1 illustrates absolute and relative cell references.

Now when we change any data the whole thing will be recalculated. Look what has happened in figure 13.7 when spending money changes in Week 4 and tuck spending decreases in week 3. The whole spreadsheet is recalculated to give us a different picture or '*scenario*'. We can try out changes on data like this frequently on our data model. These different scenarios are often called '*what-if scenarios*', because we are asking ourselves the question. 'What if I made this change, then what would happen?'.

Functions are named, ready-made calculations which we can use as part of our formulas. An example is SUM which will add up all the cells in a given range e.g. A1 to A10.

A data model is set of data, usually numeric, which represents a real life situation. Spreadsheets are used for creating data models because the data can be used for calculations to show how the model changes or behaves in certain circumstances.

Replication is when we copy the contents of a cell (which contains a formula) to other cells down a row or column.

	A	B	C	D	E
1		No sold today	Price (p)	Formulae for total takings	Profit
2	Mars	5	35	=B2*C2	=D2*B6
3	Twix	7	30	=B3*C3	=D3*B6
4	Bounty	9	32	=B4*C4	=D4*B6
5	Milky way	6	25	=B5*C5	=D5*B6
6	Total				
7	Standard deduction to calc profit	0.60			

Table 13.1 Showing relative cell referencing in column D and a mix of relative and absolute cell referencing in Column E. Note B7 =0.60 and indicates all takings should be multiplied by 0.6 to arrive at final profit figure for each item.

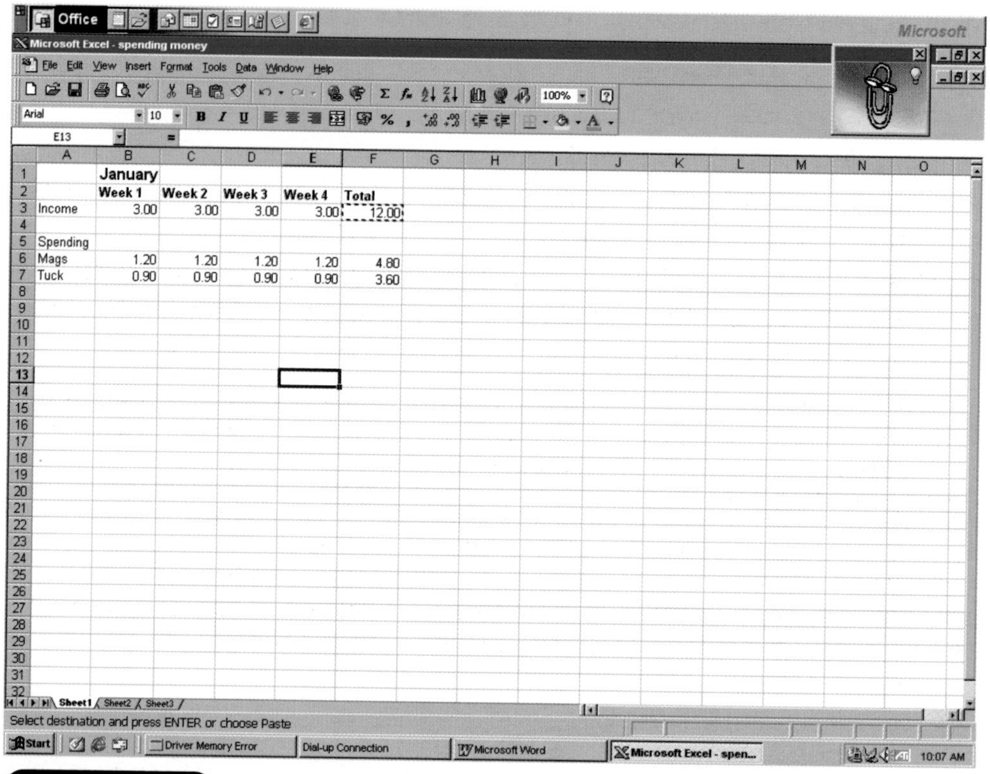

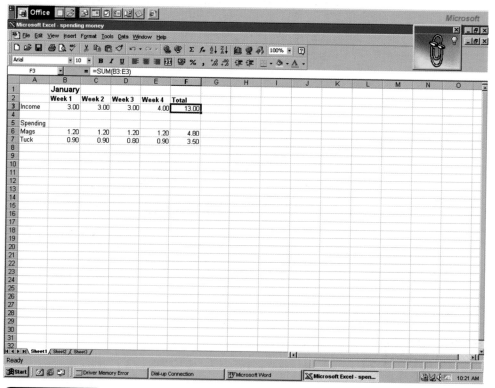

Figure 13.6 Spreadsheet showing column insertion and replication

Figure 13.7 Spreadsheet showing changed data and recalculation of formulas – a 'what if' scenario

We have considered briefly some of the features of spreadsheets.

1. Insertion/Deletion of rows and columns.
2. Copying of data across rows or down columns.
3. Calculation using cell references in formulas.
4. Replication of formulas (using highlight, copy then highlight, paste) where formulas change depending on where the cell is in the spreadsheet.
5. Making cell references absolute so that they will not change as they are replicated.
6. Using the idea of creating 'what-if scenarios', by changing data and watching the formulas on the spreadsheet automatically recalculate.

There are many other facilities of spreadsheets beyond the scope of this book such as referencing data in other worksheets. It is also possible to use lots of other functions and statements which all add to the powerful way spreadsheets allow us to use data to model a real life situation.

There are other types of data modelling software which do not use sheets but may use icons and objects to place items on the screen. Some data modelling software is much easier to work with because of the way the interface is set up. Figure 13.8 shows a data model set up. Notice the graph, picture and labelled data blocks.

> **Recalculation** of formulae when data changes provides us with the capability to ask questions as to how a data model might behave. This is called carrying out a 'what-if scenario'.

> **There are** other data modelling software packages providing a different interface to what we see with spreadsheets.

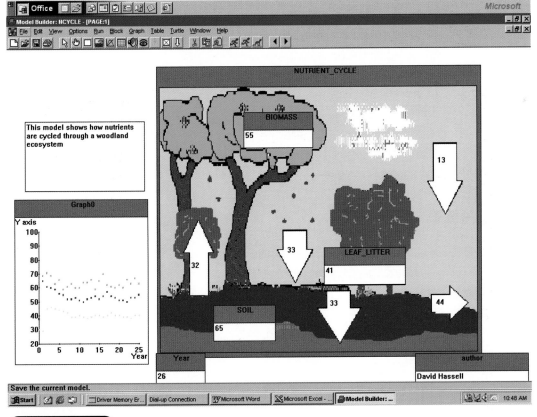

Figure 13.8 A data model

> Spreadsheets are used for data modelling applications such as financial budget sheets because they are very good at supporting the trying out of many different types of data as what-if scenarios. They can look complicated to the first-time user because the interface is not very user friendly.

USES

Spreadsheets are used frequently for data modelling and are a popular choice for financial models such as cash flow statements. There are occasions when you may wish to use a spreadsheet just for storing and sorting the data if a simple single file is all that is required but it is more sensible to use a database for data handling generally.

ADVANTAGES

- Spreadsheets are very good for modelling data and carrying out what-if scenarios because they support calculations and automatically recalculate as the data changes. Functions and replication assist with building the models.

DISADVANTAGES

- Spreadsheets do sometimes look complicated because of all the formulas and data set out as a grid. They do not provide forms to be able to design easy to use screens, but it is possible to **customise a sheet** with buttons and other items.

Computer systems: components and types

Summary

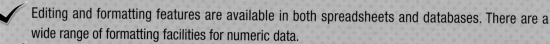

✓ Editing and formatting features are available in both spreadsheets and databases. There are a wide range of formatting facilities for numeric data.

✓ Spreadsheet grids have columns, which are a vertical line of cells, each one identified by a letter, and rows, which are a horizontal line of cells, each one identified by a number. Each cell has a named reference such as A1 or B6.

✓ Databases and spreadsheets both may be displayed as a grid, but in databases there are no cell references and any columns are headed by field names, with rows representing records.

✓ Sorting and searching are facilities common to both spreadsheets and databases.

✓ AND & OR are two different ways of bringing together search criteria, for example display all cars which are red **or** blue.

✓ A primary key field is a field which uniquely identifies a record on a file.

✓ To design and set up our database, the basic steps involve choosing fields and their data type, setting field lengths, coding and validating any fields, choosing a primary key field and finally entering data.

✓ Queries allow us to ask questions of our database such as find all the white saloon cars.

✓ A Database Management System (DBMS) allows us to efficiently, store, sort, search, retrieve and import data. It also provides ways to help us secure data.

✓ A typical data handling task which database software might be used for is creating a database of cars, videos, customers, pupils etc.

✓ Database software may be used for storing, sorting and easily searching for data, but sometimes due to complex user requirements some programming may be necessary.

✓ We can insert and delete rows and columns, use formulas and functions to calculate and replicate cells using spreadsheets.

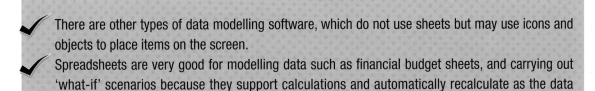

✓ There are other types of data modelling software, which do not use sheets but may use icons and objects to place items on the screen.

✓ Spreadsheets are very good for modelling data such as financial budget sheets, and carrying out 'what-if' scenarios because they support calculations and automatically recalculate as the data changes.

✓ Spreadsheets do sometimes look complicated because of all the formulas and data set out as a grid.

Test and review

1. Spreadsheets have grids of cells. What is:
   a) a cell reference? _____
   b) an active cell? _____
2. In databases the columns on the data sheet are headed by f_____ n_____, whilst rows represent r_____.
3. Editing and formatting are common facilities of spreadsheets and databases. Name two other common facilities. _____
4. AND & OR are two different ways of bringing together search criteria. Describe the difference between AND & OR. _____
   _____
   _____
   _____
5. To design and set up our database there are basic ordered steps. Put the following steps in order.
   a) Set the field lengths.
   b) Choosing fields to include.
   c) Coding and validating any fields.
   d) Choose the field data types.
   e) Enter data.
   f) Choose a primary key field.
   g) Link up any files if we have more than one file.
6. What is a database query? _____
7. List the features of a Database Management System (DBMS). _____
   _____
8. Name a typical task you would carry out on a database and name one task you would use spreadsheet software._____
   _____
9. Database software may be used for storing, sorting and easily searching for data, but it does have a disadvantage. What is it? _____
   _____

10. **Describe how you would replicate a cell down a column.**

_____

_____

11. **Spreadsheets are very good carrying out what-if scenarios because they have the following features (finish the sentence).**

_____

_____

Review and thinking tasks

1. Try creating your own personal budget sheet, showing how you spend your income. Do you have more than one source of income to include? Are there any regular items you buy? How are you going to make the spreadsheet easy to read? Can you use spellchecker? Will you use absolute or relative cell referencing? **Can you create a graph showing how your regular spending is broken down? What will you choose a pie chart, bar or line graph?**

2. Try creating a small database of all the names, addresses and telephone numbers of people you know well. Will you have a key field? What will it be? Can you add any other useful fields to the database? Is there any need to code or validate data? Can you add their birth date and format it?

Data logging, programming and control software

In this chapter we are going to look at collecting data automatically and controlling equipment using computers. This means that we will need to look at hardware devices called *sensors* which will detect some aspect of the environment (for example temperature) and collect data about it. This is known as *data logging*. Then in order to decide what sort of action is necessary because of the data collected, the computer will need some instructions (a program). This is known as *control software*.

Data logging

We have looked at various ways of collecting and inputting data. Many of these methods involve a person. For example a person will either type in data or swipe cards through a reader or maybe scan a bar code. Some methods we have looked at are more automated and machines will recognise marks or characters written on paper, but wouldn't it be useful if we could collect data about all sorts of aspects of our environment without having to detect marks, characters or prepare written text in some way. This is what data logging is all about.

Often data can be collected over a period of time. A common data logging application is to collect data about the weather. You may have a weather station in your school. If you wanted to collect details about how much rain fell yesterday, you would need to measure the rainfall for that day in millimetres using a rain gauge. If you wanted to measure the highest and lowest temperature for the entire day you would need to constantly be taking temperatures at fixed intervals throughout the day, using an ordinary thermometer. There are also many other aspects of the weather you may wish to record such as wind speed and hours of sunshine. Whatever data you collect some different items will be needed to measure each aspect of the data.

Another example of where you might use data logging is when ships enter a harbour or cars enter a car park. By counting the number of cars entering the car park or the ships entering the harbour an attendant would know when the harbour or the car park was full.

Monitoring the temperature and air pressure inside an active volcano, or monitoring weather conditions in the arctic is more dangerous, and the person who will be taking the readings will be at risk.

To save time and take more regular readings in safety we may choose to take our data readings automatically. No attendant needs to be present. A machine will be set up to record readings taken by sensors. There are many different types of sensors available to detect all sorts of conditions. They behave rather like input devices. Here are some typical examples.

A Light sensor detects light and can be used to measure daylight or sense when an object is *not* blocking a light beam. Look at the light sensors on some of the lift doors in department stores. They are used to detect a light beam shining across the door. If a person blocks the light by entering through the door, the door will stay open.

A Temperature sensor detects the current temperature reading and is used in all sorts of situations, such as weather stations, scientific experiments, central heating systems, washing machines and even green houses.

> **Data logging** is about automatically collecting all types of data without the need for a human operator.

> **Data can** be collected over long periods of time at fixed intervals using special sensors.

> **Sensors** are used to detect all sorts of conditions and behave like input devices.

Humidity sensors detect humidity (water content of the air). Again the uses are in weather stations and greenhouses.

Pressure sensors detect the pressure applied by a object as it comes into contact with the sensor. Pressure sensors are used to detect cars as they enter car parks (sensors are put in the road) and people as they enter a department store (pressure sensors are in the mats as they walk in).

Passive InfraRed (PIR) Sensors detect movement and are sometimes used on security lights and burglar alarm systems to detect when someone is present.

A Contact switch detects when the contact is broken between two parts of the switch and is often used on windows and doors in burglar alarms.

The data from all these sensors is known *analogue* data. For example the temperature measurements from a temperature sensor will be a voltage representing degrees centigrade. This must be converted to digital format (0's and 1's) so that computerised equipment can make sense of it. To do this we need an *analogue-to-digital converter*, sometimes known as an ADC.

Data logging can be carried out by equipment which usually looks like a box and has sensors attached to it. It is known as a *data logger*. Data loggers may be set to take readings from the sensors at specific intervals over a specific time period. They have an analogue-to-digital converter built into them. Data loggers can be connected directly to the computer, which after readings have been taken and converted to digital format, are sent directly to the computer. Other data loggers can operate standalone and have the facility for capturing, converting *and* storing the data for later transfer to a computer for analysis. This second type of data logger is often used when remote data logging is required so they also need their own power supply.

ADVANTAGES

- Data logging can be used in remote or dangerous situations
- Data logging can be carried out 24 hours a day, 365 days per year.
- More frequent and regular time intervals can be set up because no-one need to be in attendance.
- Data logging is often more accurate because there is no likelihood of human error.

DISADVANTAGES

- If the data logging breaks down or malfunctions some data could be lost.
- Equipment can be expensive for small tasks. Remember though that labour saved over long periods for big tasks usually balances the cost of the initial outlay.

Computerised control

Data logging, we have seen, is all about recording data over long periods of time for later analysis. Sometimes though, instead of capturing and recording the data for analysis, it may be necessary to respond to certain changes in the data.

This immediate response gives us an element of control of the situation we are monitoring. It is important not to confuse data logging and computerised control. Both use sensors to monitor a situation but different things happen once the data is captured. When we are controlling the situation, there are programmed instructions, which tell other hardware devices to do something. A typical example of computerised control is when we control a greenhouse environment. Based on readings from temperature and humidity sensors, the programmed instructions (software) in the computer can make motors open and close windows, or turn on water sprinklers. The hardware devices which respond to the output signals the computer produces are known as *actuators*.

Temperature, pressure, humidity, PIR, and light sensors are all valid types of sensor. Contact switches are sometimes used in certain situations when we are gathering data as well.

An analogue-to-digital converter is used to transform the analogue data collected from sensors to the digital format the computer understands.

A data logger is the device which can be connected to a computer or work on its own. It can be set up to record data from sensors at specific time intervals. It has an ADC built into it.

Automatic data logging is more advantageous than manual data logging because it is less prone to error and will work 24 hours per day.

Another example of computerised control would be when we respond to data collected about cars coming into the car park. Instead of just logging the number of cars we could stop more cars coming into the car park until some of the parked cars have left. Robots are also examples of computerised control. All these situations require sensors, actuators and a computer. We will look at some example applications in more detail at the end of this chapter.

Responding to data from sensors

To respond to data captured from sensors it is necessary to write an instruction, which detects when a certain condition has been met. We can do this by using a particular type of instruction called a *conditional* statement. Some software packages allow us to write conditional statements by using the word IF, others use the word WHEN. Whatever the language or software package you will be using, a conditional statement always has a condition (such as A<20 or B=35) which must be met. It is followed by the action you wish to be carried out if the condition is true. Notice that we have to have a named item to compare against in our condition. This named item is known as a *variable* (in the example below this is temperature) because it can contain a variety of values.

Conditional operators we might use in a conditional statement are:

= or equals,

< or less than,

> or greater than,

<> or NOT =,

NOT < or not less than

NOT > or not more than

For example:

IF temperature > 60 MOTOR Forward.

This example shows that when a temperature sensor installed in a greenhouse reads any value above 60 degrees, the MOTOR is switched on. The MOTOR must move in a particular direction to open a window. In this case we say Forward. Somewhere else in our program we will also need to check for the temperature falling below a particular value. This might be 50 degrees. The statement may then be:

IF temperature < 50 MOTOR Back.

Of course it would not be sufficient to just switch the MOTOR on. After a while the MOTOR will need to stop because the window will be opened sufficiently. To stop the MOTOR we might say MOTOR stop after waiting a specified period of time. Now instead of just saying MOTOR Forward and having a single action we actually will have three things to do when our condition is true.

IF temperature > 60

    MOTOR Forward

    WAIT 10

    MOTOR Stop

The same will apply to our other conditional statement. Finish off the instruction for closing the window in our greenhouse example.

An actuator is a hardware device which responds to signals which are output by the computer. An example might be a motor.

Computerised control is when software responds to data captured from sensors and makes another device work so that the situation remains under control.

A variable is named data which can contain many different values such as temperature.

IF temperature < 50

   MOTOR _____

   WAIT _____

   _____

It is important that the WAIT and MOTOR Stop instructions are only carried out as part of the conditional statement. There are a variety of ways that different software packages make sure which statements belong to the conditional statement and which statements are carried out anyway no matter what happens.

To start a program we usually have a START statement and to stop a program we usually have a STOP statement. Both these statements will be carried out at the beginning and end of a program whatever the conditions are in other statements. Sometimes these are referred to as *sequence* statements because they follow one after another and are carried out in the order in which they are written. Other typical sequence statements are often READ, DISPLAY, and WRITE type of statements known as input and output statements. We could have for example:

START

READ temperature

IF temperature > 60

   (MOTOR Forward

   WAIT 10

   MOTOR Stop)

Etc.......

....

STOP

Note that the brackets mean that all the actions are part of the IF statement. In a real control program to control our greenhouse environment there will be more readings from other sensors, more conditions and more actions to carry out. It will also be important not to keep starting and stopping the program so we may want to check conditions over and over again. To do this we use *looping* statements. You may see REPEAT, WHILE, LOOP and many other variations, which means that the instructions which follow the looping statements will be carried out over and over again. Sometimes the looping goes on forever and sometimes it stops when a condition is met. Again it is important to recognise where the loop begins and ends. In our example below brackets are used but particular software packages which allow you to write this type of program may use other methods.

LOOP forever

   (READ temperature

   IF temperature > 60

   (MOTOR Forward

   WAIT 10

   MOTOR Stop)

Etc.......

........)

Or we could write:

    LOOP

    (READ temperature

    UNTIL temperature > 60)

    IF temperature > 60

        (MOTOR Forward

        WAIT 10

        MOTOR Stop)

    Etc....

        ....

Both of these methods use different types of looping statement and tackle the program writing in a different way.

So far we have been able to write basic instructions to control our greenhouse environment. There are other devices we may wish to control besides motors. We may wish to sound alarms or switch on lights. Other examples of control programs allow us to control a robot or a floor turtle.

Most control software provides facilities to write *macros or procedures* which are basically mini programs which carry out a small but common tasks. Common tasks which are written as macros or procedures have the advantage that they can be used in different situations over and over again because they are given a name and stored for regular use. All that is required when you want to execute a macro or procedure is that you use its name in your program. For example we may have a macro that sounds a buzzer and flashes a red light as a warning:

    Start Macro WARNING

    LOOP for 4 secs

        (SOUND 99

        SWITCH ON 1

        WAIT 2

        SWITCH OFF 1)

    END Macro

Sound 99 is the buzzer sound for a fixed period of time and switch 1 the red light.

Now when we want this warning to happen we just use the macro name.

    START

    READ temperature

    IF temperature > 60

        (MOTOR Forward

        WARNING

        WAIT 6

        MOTOR Stop)

Looping statements provide the programmer with the facility to instruct the computer to carry out the same instructions more than once.

Output devices which we may control are sound, light, parts of a robot, floor turtles and motors.

> **Macros or procedures are mini programs which carry out small but common tasks that can be used in different situations over and over again.**

This means that the warning will sound as the MOTOR in our greenhouse opens the windows. We could use the same warning macro when the temperature falls below our specified value and the windows close.

This example is very much simplified and perhaps it is not entirely sensible to sound a warning every time the temperature changes beyond our very artificial choice of temperature range. However it does illustrate the concept of program construction and macros. In turtle graphics programs procedures are used instead of macros. Below is an extract from a sample program followed by an extract from a sample flowchart program.

```
TO SQUARELOOP
RT 90
REPEAT 4 [FD 30 RT 90]
squareloop
END
```

Figure 14.1 An example of a turtle graphics program

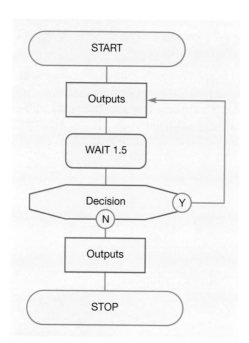

Figure 14.2 Extract from a sample flowchart

Description of typical applications involving the use of control software or data logging

The following applications are described in terms of input, outputs and processing.

Controlling the opening and closing a department store door

Inputs: Pressure pad in front of the door to sense the presence of a person.

Outputs: Motor turns and moves the doors.

Processing: When the pressure pad senses someone wishes to enter or leave the store the computer sends a signal to the motors to open the doors. While there is still pressure on the pad the doors will remain open. If no pressure has been sensed within a certain period of time the motors are activated to close the doors.

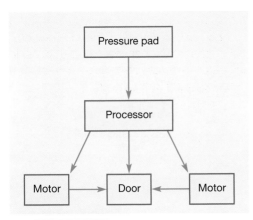

Figure 14.3 Controlling automatic doors in a department store

Controlling a set of traffic lights

Inputs: Pressure pads in the road to detect the cars waiting.

Outputs: Red, Amber and Green lights.

Processing: When the pressure pad detects a car a signal is sent to change the traffic lights. A time delay will operate so that a minimum fixed amount of time is set to allow cars through in the opposite direction before the lights change. This will stop the lights changing too frequently. A maximum amount of wait time will also be set so those cars waiting do not wait too long.

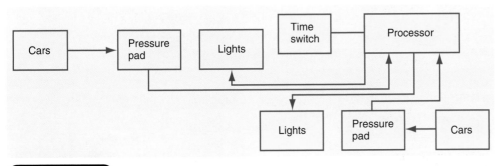

Figure 14.4 Controlling traffic lights

Data Logging the number customers entering a department store

Sensors: Light sensor is used to detect the number of people crossing a beam of light as they enter.

Processing: Every time the light sensor has the light blocked one is added to the customer total.

Think about what will happen if there is a constant stream of people coming through the entrance. How we improve the situation so that it is more accurate?

Summary

✓ Data logging is about automatically collecting all types of data, without the need for a human operator. We use sensors to gather the data.

✓ Sensors are used to gather data by detecting all sorts of conditions. They behave like input devices.

✓ Examples of sensors are light, sound, pressure, temperature and humidity sensors.

✓ An analogue-to-digital converter is used to transform the analogue data collected from sensors to the digital format the computer understands.

✓ Data can be collected over long or short periods of time at fixed intervals using special sensors.

✓ A data logger is a device which can be connected to a computer or work on its own. It can be set up to record data from sensors at specific time intervals. It has an ADC built into it.

✓ Automatic data logging is more advantageous than manual data logging because it is less prone to error and will work 24 hours per day.

✓ An actuator is a hardware device which responds to signals which are output by the computer. An example might be a motor.

✓ Computerised control is when software responds to data captured from sensors and makes another device work so that the situation remains under control.

✓ A variable is a named item of storage in which we can store different values.

✓ Conditional operators allow us to compare a value with the contents of a variable, Conditional operators are =,<,> etc.

✓ The outcome of a condition when tested may be true or false.

✓ Conditional statements allow us to ask questions about incoming data so that certain actions can be taken by the computer system when the data meets a particular condition.

✓ Looping statements provide the programmer with the facility to instruct the computer to carry out the same instructions more than once.

✓ Macros or procedures are mini programs which carry out small but common tasks that can be used in different situations over and over again.

Test and review

1. **Give three examples of different types of sensor.** _____
   _____

2. **Sensors are used in data logging applications. Explain why an analogue-to-digital converter is needed to transform the data collected by the sensors.**
   _____
   _____

3. **State three advantages of automatic data logging when compared with manually gathering data.**_____
   _____

4. **What is an actuator? Use an example to illustrate your answer.** _____
   _____

5. **Name three computerised control applications.**_____
   _____

6. **Describe the difference between data logging and computerised control.**
   _____
   _____

7. **Explain how variables are used in conditional statements.**_____
   _____
   _____

8. **Tick the correct answers.**
   The outcome of a condition when tested may be.
   a) true b) false c) Yes d) No e) None.

9. **Why do programmers use looping statements?** _____
   _____

10. **What is a macro or procedure?** _____
    _____

Review and thinking tasks

Look at pedestrian crossing systems. How do you think they work? Identify the input, output and processing?

How do you think weather-forecasting works?

Write a simple program on your computer. Try writing a program to draw a variety of shapes. How does an automatic washing machine work? Identify its input, output and processing.

General IT tasks

Basic features of good user interface software

We have looked at the features of a Graphical User Interface (GUI) (page 71). A user interface can be the software which sits between the user and the operating system or for example, an interface can be designed to sit between the data stored in a database and the user (such as screen designs with buttons).

Features of a good user interface.

1. It is easy to use: for example a GUI has a point and click facility.
2. It has a good layout with items placed in similar positions from screen to screen. For example an exit button may be in the bottom right hand corner of the every screen or pull down menus may be placed in the same position and order on the screen.
3. Colour schemes do not clash and restful colours such a pastel shades are used, although warning messages should draw the attention of the user.
4. On line help should be available.
5. Screens should be uncluttered and not contain too much information.
6. It should be easy for users to navigate from screen to screen or easily work out where in the system they are positioned
7. There should be an escape route (exit) from every screen display
8. It should be interesting and pleasant to use perhaps with graphics included.

A GUI should have a good layout which is consistently designed and has good navigational aids.

Software which has a graphical interface

Software is an interface which runs different tasks within a rectangular area which is called a window (figure 15.1).

A window can be made smaller or larger and often windows will overlap each other. It is also possible to move a window around and position it somewhere else on the screen. Windows software is available to run on personal computers and on mini computers.

Basic features of an electronic mail package

Electronic mail provides many facilities as we have already seen on page 35. In summary these allow you to send messages, reply to messages, forward messages, attach files to messages and send multiple copies to a large number of recipients. There are additional features that some e-mail software provides, such as:

1. providing a help system;
2. providing a facility to store regularly used addresses;
3. customising messages with a personal signature or special stationery;
4. sending messages which are coded so that they are secure;
5. informing the sender when the recipient reads the mail;
6. storing a copy of all messages sent;
7. automatically forwarding selected messages to another address.

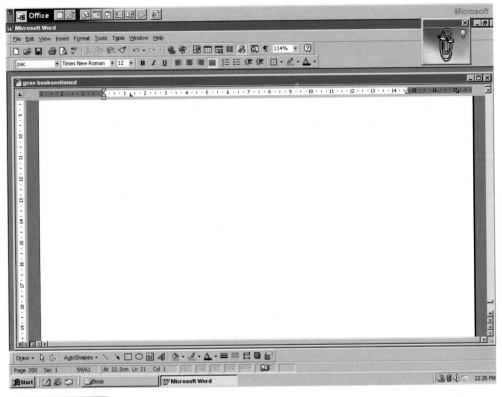

Figure 15.1 A typical window

It is also possible to set up your email interface so that it appears on screen as you wish.

A typical example of e-mail software can be seen in Figure 15.2.

Note that the message bar at the bottom of the screen states that the user is working offline. On the left of the screen in the folders area there is an inbox which shows incoming mail, an outbox which shows outgoing mail, sent items which records copies of all items sent, drafts which show messages currently partly constructed. The outbox is selected and there are no messages waiting to be sent.

There are pull down menus and an address book facility shown as an icon along the toolbar. The address book is also accessible when the new mail icon is clicked to send a new message as shown below. The small icon beside the To: where the recipient's address goes may be clicked to show the contents of the address book and then the recipient can be selected directly from the list of addresses stored there. The 'CC' slot underneath the 'To:' area also has an icon beside it which will display the address book again so that you may select recipients who should receive a copy of the message. The 'subject' space provides a space for you to write a title about the content of the message. This gives the recipient an idea of what the message is about before it is opened.

Notice the paperclip with the word attach on an icon on the toolbar of the new message window. Clicking on attach will display your directories, folders and files so that you can select which file you wish to attach to send with your message. It is also possible to check the spelling of your message and give it a high priority so that it is delivered quickly before you click on the send button. The main part of the window is where you write your message.

> **E-mail software has many features such as an address book, a facility for encoding messages, a facility for forwarding messages as well as the usual send, receive and attach documents.**

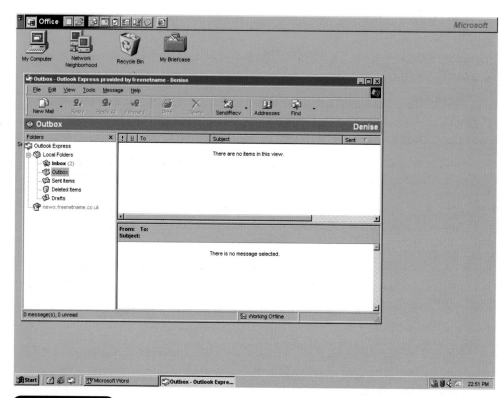

Figure 15.2 An e-mail window

Basic features of an internet browser

An Internet browser is a program, which allows you to move from site to site on the Internet. There are a number of different Internet browsers available. Some people call these programs web browsers because you can browse not only from web site to web site but also from page to page on the same web site or across many different web sites. A typical example is shown below. It illustrates some common features of browser software:

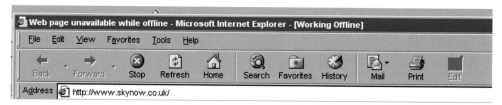

Figure 15.3 Browser software

1. Notice that there is a 'Favorites' menu where it is possible to easily add and retrieve the addresses of your favourite web pages.
2. The address of the web page is displayed in the address area.
3. There is a facility to revisit past pages using the 'Back' icon and to browse forward again using the 'Forward' icon.
4. The 'Stop' icon stops the transition from one page to the next if it has been requested.

5. 'Refresh' renews the page display and is useful if there is a problem accessing the web page initially.
6. 'Home' takes you back to your usual start up page. This can be set to whatever you would like it to be using the Tools menu and selecting Options from the menu.
7. There is also a search facility and a facility called 'History' which records the pages you have visited.
8. It is also possible to initiate your e-mail facility from the Browser window.

Browser software is also useful for browsing your own Intranet if you have one. An Intranet is a web site, which is viewed by only the users on the site. The site users own the content of the pages. It contains local information. Your Intranet at school may contain details of different departments, the school calendar, learning resources, the school's recent achievements, news, events and exhibitions etc within the school.

Managing directories and files
Many computer systems today have what is known as a directory structure. Directories are usually hierarchical and could contain other directories and other files or documents.

The top level of the tree structure is often the letter name of the drive. For example you may have a floppy disk which has the letter 'A' assigned to it. On your 'A' drive you may have three folders: homework, assessments, notes. In the homework folder you may have different subject folders such as Maths, English, etc. In assessments, possibly there will be school assessments, external assessments and so on. The directory structure could look like the diagram in figure 15.4.

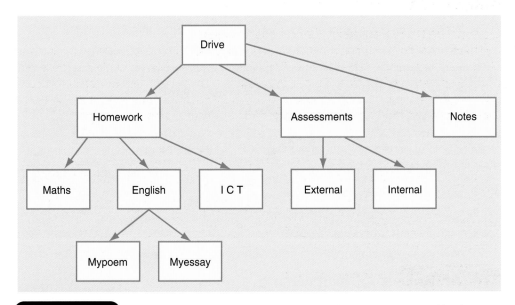

Figure 15.4 A directory structure showing two documents stored in the English directory

To access MYPOEM in the English directory we would need to know that it is stored there. It is possible to browse around directories or search through directories to find a document if we know its name. Although we may regard the document name as MYPOEM, the system needs to know exactly where in the directory structure the document is stored. The full name giving the path from the root down to the document at the

> **An intranet** is a collection of web pages with information which is all about the internal activities of an organisation.

> **A directory** structure is a bit like an upside down tree with many sub directories which have documents stored in them. The root (or start) of the tree is usually the drive.

bottom of the tree is called the **pathname**. In this example the full pathname would be: Assessments/English/Mypoem.

Computers use this type of directory structure. Note that documents are always stored at the bottom of the tree and that the drive name is always at the top of the tree. The top of the tree is known as the 'root directory'.

Basic troubleshooting activities

Sometimes when using computer systems the tasks we are working on do not always go according to plan. In these situations we have to be able to work out what has gone wrong and try and sort out the problem. This is called **troubleshooting**.

For every problem there are basic questions you need to ask yourself, find the answer to them and then put the situation right if the answer is not what you expect. Here are some typical troubleshooting tasks you may have to do, just to illustrate this process:

Solving why a print instruction produced no printout

1. Is the printer switched on? If the answer is 'No' switch it on.
2. Is the printer cable connected correctly? If the answer is 'No' make sure the connections are secure.
3. Is there any paper in the printer? If the answer is 'No' load the paper.
4. Is there enough ink in the cartridge? If the answer is 'No' change the cartridge.
5. Is the printer driver software installed? If the answer is 'No' install the correct software.

Solving why a file cannot be read from your floppy disk

1. Is the floppy disk inserted correctly? If the answer is 'No' re-insert the disk.
2. Is the file required stored on the disk? Check by looking at the disk content and if the answer is 'No' check another floppy disk.
3. Is the correct version of software available to read the file stored on the disk? If the answer is 'No' convert the file or Install the correct software.
4. Is the disk faulty? If this is likely run a software check to diagnose and fix simple errors.

Sometimes the problems you may have to resolve may be software related. There are four possible ways that you could get help with troubleshooting software problems and even some hardware problems.

1. A user manual may be provided with a troubleshooting guide.
2. An on-line help system may be provided.
3. There may be a telephone help line.
4. There may be direct access to a troubleshooting web page via the Internet.

Other types of software

Design packages

The most common type of design package is a Computer Aided Design (CAD) package. Designers often use CAD for drawing up plans and artistic impressions of various views (called elevations) of buildings, cars and other objects. They have special features, which mathematically calculate what different views of the design object will look like once basic measurements and other data have been entered.

CAD software has the following advantages.

The pathname of a document is the full address from the top (or root) of the tree to the bottom of the tree where the document is stored. Each directory which has to be entered to get to the document must be included in the pathname: e.g. Assessments/ English/Mypoem.

Troubleshooting is when we try to work out what is going wrong, why it has gone wrong and taking action to remedy the fault.

User manuals, on-line help, telephone help lines and web pages can assist with trouble shooting or providing general help..

1. It saves time because there is no need to keep re-drawing plans. They are easily edited and the software re-draws new designs.
2. Drawings can be easily edited and manipulated on the screen. For example rotating to see different views, and viewing in three dimensions rather than two dimensions.
3. Drawings can be easily scaled up or down.

Garden design software is also a well-known type of design software. A plan of the garden can be drawn and then viewed in three dimensions. It is even possible to take an imaginary walk through the garden, displaying different views on the screen.

Computer Aided Manufacture (CAM) software is often closely linked to CAD software because the designs can be manufactured using numerically controlled machine tools on the factory floor. A design which is specified in numerical terms can therefore be passed straight onto the manufacturing process. A big advantage of CAM is that product changes can be made very quickly with little cost.

> **CAD/CAM** software provides the facility to specify a design numerically and pass it to computerised control equipment to manufacture on the factory floor.

Simulation software

Simulation software is used in all sorts of applications such as the sciences and the military. Chemistry experiments and airline training are two very typical examples and in fact the most common application that people think of is the flight simulator. Special hardware is available with a flight deck just like that found on an aeroplane. Software then simulations the conditions a pilot may encounter during take-off, flight and landing.

The main advantages of using simulations are:

1. It is safer to use a computer simulation and study the effects.
2. It is much cheaper to build a simulation than it is to build and carry out the real tasks.
3. Computer simulation often allows simulations to be carried out where it is impossible to do this with a real model.

> **Simulation** software allows users to experience conditions that they may experience in a real situation.

> **Simulation** software allows users to experience conditions that they may experience in a real situation.

Expert Systems

An expert system is a program, which aims to bring together human expertise in one knowledge base (set of data and rules). Expert systems are sometimes known as knowledge based systems or information knowledge based systems (IKBS).

The main features of an expert system are:

1. Only one specialised area is covered by the expert system.
2. There are many rules specified. For example if patient has spots and a temperature then Measles is a probable diagnosis (strength 50%). Many rules similar to this with different probabilities (strength of belief) could be specified.
3. The user is often asked to respond to questions, which cause certain rules to be triggered. The user can provide 'don't know' responses and give the degree of uncertainty attached to the answer.
4. Advice and diagnosis may be given.
5. Explanations may be provided.
6. Reasoning is part of the processing to be carried out.

> **Expert systems** have a knowledge base, inference engine and the capability to offer advice or make a diagnosis.

An expert system has a knowledge base (facts and rules provided by the experts) and an inference engine which is the computer program which works out the diagnosis or advice by checking the rules, knowledge base and the input from the user.

Typical examples of expert systems application are:

- medical diagnosis
- car engine fault diagnosis
- geological surveys

Steps in creating an expert system

1. Interview experts and use other expert sources such as text books to gather as many facts and rules as possible.
2. Design the knowledge base.
3. Select software to use. This may be an expert system shell (already built inference engine) or a computer language appropriate for building the knowledge base and an inference engine.
4. Implement the design making sure the interface is easy to use.
5. Test the design.
6. Document the system and create a user manual.
7. Check the system with the experts to make sure it produces sensible advice or diagnosis.

Creating an expert system is very time consuming and the fact finding stage is often very difficult because the systems consultant often finds it difficult to understand the area of expertise due to its complexity.

CD-ROM packages

CD-ROM software is now a common commodity. There are many different CD-ROM packages available. Some of the most common CD-ROM packages are multimedia encyclopaedia. They provide a large amount of information in different formats such as text, pictures, and videos in a small amount of space. A variety of indexes are provided so that it is possible to search for items alphabetically, by topic and by using keywords.

Other CD-ROM packages which are becoming more commonly available are CAL applications. Foreign Languages, Mathematics, Science and many other titles are now available as a CD-ROM, with all the information catalogued and various pathways provided through the material.

Creating an expert system is time consuming because there are so many facts and rules to find out about and store in a knowledge base.

CD-ROM packages provide a concise source of information with indexes to enable the user to search using different methods.

Summary

✓ A GUI should have a good layout which is consistently designed and has good navigational aids.

✓ E-mail software has many features such as an address book, a facility for encoding messages, a facility for forwarding messages and attaching documents.

✓ Internet browser software allows the users to search, store favourite web page address, keep a history of web pages visited, browse backwards or forwards amongst the pages visited and return to the HOME page easily.

✓ An intranet contains web pages which contain information about the organisation such as dates of events, recent activities carried out, management structure, plan of buildings and other internal news and information.

✓ A directory structure is a bit like an upside down tree with many sub directories which have documents stored in them.

✓ When encountering problems as we use computer systems, we have to be able to work out what has gone wrong and try and sort out the problem. This is called *troubleshooting.*

✓ User manuals, on-line help, telephone help lines and web pages can assist with trouble shooting or providing general help.

✓ CAD/CAM software provides the facility to specify a design numerically and pass it to computerised control equipment to manufacture on the factory floor.

✓ Simulation software is used in all sorts of applications, such as the sciences and the military.

✓ Expert systems have a knowledge base, inference engine and the capability to offer advice or make a diagnosis.

✓ The early stages of expert systems development is time consuming because all the facts and rules must be gathered from experts.

✓ CD-ROM packages provide a concise source of information with indexes to enable the user to search using different methods

Test and review

1. Name three features of a well designed graphical user interface. _____
   _____

2. Name five features of e-mail software. _____
   _____

3. Name five features of an Internet browser. _____
   _____

4. Explain the difference between the Internet and an Intranet. _____
   _____

5. Draw a diagram of a typical directory structure, showing a root directory
   with two sub directories A and B and one document called **MYDOC** in
   directory A. Then write down the pathname from the root to **MYDOC**.
   _____

6. What is troubleshooting? _____

7. CAD/CAM software provides the facility to specify a design numerically.
   How does this help when using CAM software? _____
   _____

8. What are he benefits of use a flight simulator? _____
   _____

9. Describe
   a) a knowledge base _____
   b) an inference engine _____
   c) an expert system _____

10. CD-ROM packages provide a concise source of information with I_____
    to enable the user to search using different methods.

Review and thinking tasks

Try using the Internet to find details about well-known expert systems. When were they
written? What do they do?

Section C   Test your knowledge

1. Explain the difference between word-processing software and desktop publishing software, illustrating your answer by describing three different features.

   _____
   _____
   _____
   _____
   _____
   _____

2. Explain the difference between desktop publishing software and slideshow software illustrating your answer by describing three different features.

   _____
   _____
   _____
   _____
   _____
   _____
   _____

3. Name and describe the features of one multimedia system you have used.

   _____
   _____
   _____
   _____

4. What sort of software package would you use to develop a multimedia system?

   _____

5. What is CAL?_____

6. Briefly describe the common features of graphics packages?

   _____
   _____
   _____
   _____

7. What do we mean by the term 'resolution'?

   _____
   _____

8. What is clipart? _____

9. Explain why we use scanning software _____

10. Describe one task which you would use spreadsheet software for giving a reason for your choice.

   _____
   _____

11. Describe one task you would use database software for giving a reason for your choice.

_____

_____

12. AND & OR are two different ways of bringing together search criteria. Describe the difference between AND & OR, illustrating your answer with examples. _____

_____

_____

_____

13. Describe the stages necessary to design and set up a database.

_____

_____

_____

_____

_____

_____

14. Give three examples of different types of sensor. _____

_____

15. Explain why an analogue-to-digital converter is needed to transform the data collected by sensors.

_____

16. State three advantages of automatic data logging when compared with manually gathering data.

_____

17. What is an actuator? Use an example to illustrate your answer. _____

18. Describe how an automatic car park control application works. _____

_____

_____

_____

_____

19. Name one data logging application and explain how it works.

_____

_____

_____

_____

_____

20. Why do programmers use macros and procedures?

_____

21. Explain the difference between a sequentially organised file and a randomly organised file?

_____

22. Describe the difference between the World Wide Web and the Internet.

_____

_____

_____

_____

23. Describe why it may be better to look on the Internet for information rather than look on a CD-ROM.

_____

_____

_____

_____

Section D

Aproaching GCSE coursework for the short course

Coursework is the single most important element of the GCSE ICT assessment. Whether you are doing the short or full course, it makes up 60% of the final mark. It is important to plan and carry out your coursework carefully. You will record details of your coursework deadlines so make sure you keep a diary/planner. Coursework is much more manageable if it is broken down into small tasks, each with its own date for completion. Later in this section there is an example of coursework planning to help you.

All the guidance in this book refers to the OCR syllabus A for GCSE ICT.

There are two courses – the full course and the short course. The short course requires you to complete two pieces of work called Project 1A and Project 1B. The full course has the same requirements but in addition to Projects 1A and 1B there is another project, which has to be submitted, called Project 2. Advice on this piece of coursework is given in Section D because there is a need to analyse and design a problem as well as show that you can use IT for different purposes. The mark allocations for the three different pieces of coursework are:

- Project 1A : 28 marks
- Project 1B : 28 marks
- Project 2 : 56 marks.

The marks for Project 1A and 1B are added together to give a total of 56 marks. Up to 4 additional marks are then awarded for how clearly you have written up your work, which gives a total of 60. This is also done for Project 2.

What do I need to do for each short course project?

One piece of work (Project 1A) will be mainly about communicating information. You will need to show your skills at word processing, desktop publishing, building a web-site or creating a multimedia presentation, and how good you are at collecting information from newspapers, magazines and through the Internet. You may choose to use several pieces of software to create your new piece of work. As well as being used for your GCSE ICT coursework, this piece of work can be used to help you get your key skills certificate in IT. The total number of marks available for each short course project (1A and 1B) is 28. For Project 1A the first 12 marks are set out so that they match the criteria for keys skills in IT for level 1 and the rest of the marks are concerned with key skills in IT for level 2. Remember though that if you achieve full course GCSE IT with a minimum grade of C, you will automatically have the achieved the equivalent of level 2 IT key skill and so will not need to worry about how to use your coursework and build up a portfolio of work for a separate qualification.

The second piece of work is called Project 1B. For this, you will have to produce a piece of work for which you will have to use a particular type of software. You have a choice of using:

a) database software,

b) modelling software (usually a spreadsheet),

Coursework is worth 60% of the final award for both the short or full course so planning and setting yourself deadlines for different portions of the work is very important.

Meeting the Project 1A mark criteria can help you achieve either level 1 or level 2 IT key skills but you do not have to worry about this, especially if you are entering for full course GCSE in IT.

c) measuring software, or

d) control software.

In Project 1B the 28 marks are divided up into a number of mark ranges. What you have to do to gain higher marks gradually builds up, as the marks get higher. Each mark range has a set of requirements. When you match every one of these requirements (you are not allowed to miss even one!) you will get a mark in that range. You will get a mark at the start of the range if you have met all the requirements. You will get a higher mark if you have met all the requirements in great detail.

Only people who are doing the full GCSE course will have to do Project 2. When you are doing Project 2 (rather like Project 1B) you must look at what is required for the first mark before you start. Because you must score the lower marks in order to progress up through the mark range you cannot miss out any steps in your work.

A second piece of coursework called Project 1B is required to fulfil short course requirements.

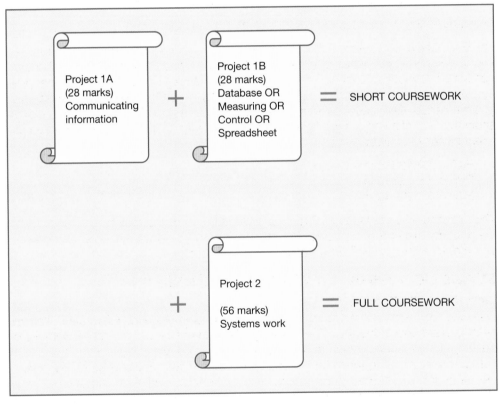

Coursework requirements

How to plan your work

The illustration on page 177 shows an example of a coursework planner or diary. The actual dates have not been included since most schools and teachers work to different deadlines. You would need to fill in the actual dates yourself if you were using a planner like this. The example used is based on the data-handling (database) strand for Project 1B. At the moment, it is not important for you to understand the requirements for this piece of coursework. It will be explained later. The planner makes assumptions about the number of lessons you have and a number of other things. Remember this is just a guide and you will need to set out your own planner to suit yourself.

Things to remember when producing your planner

a) Aim to finish your work one week before your teacher has asked you to hand it in. This will give you a little time to go back and check that you are happy with everything and also builds in a bit of time in case anything goes wrong.

b) Produce a separate planner for each Project you do (1A and 1B for the short course, 1A, 1B and 2 for the full course).

c) Set sensible targets for yourself. The planner shown on page 177 assumes that you want to achieve full marks. Not everybody is capable of achieving this and you will need to remember to cover **all** the requirements in the mark range that you are targeting.

d) Always talk to your teacher first, before starting your plan of work. S/he will know what you are capable of and can help you structure your work so that you achieve the maximum mark you can.

Academic Year 2001/2002
ICT coursework planner

Date	Syllabus requirement	What I have to do
Week 1 Lesson 1	Identify the required output for a given task;	Write down the task. Write down what use the database will be put to. Write down some of the questions the database will need to answer.
Week 1 Lesson 2	Construct a method of collecting data based on this output;	From the list of questions written down last week, make a list of the fields which will go in the database. Draw a data capture form with these fields on (perhaps use a spreadsheet layout).
Week 2 Lesson 1	Collect a range of data;	Collect cuttings from magazines, newspapers, catalogues or from a real source. (If the database is a cars database, collect the data from a real car showroom).
Week 2 Lesson 2	Give reasons for the relevance of their choice of software to the required output;	When the database is finished, write down all the reasons why the software used is the best. Refer back to what was written about the task and compare two alternative database programs. Appropriate reasons need to be made. If the task requires a lot of graphs choose the better graph-producing package. If it requires a lot of searches choose the simpler searching package.
Week 3 Lesson 1	Give reasons for the relevance of their choice of fields, field types and lengths to the required output;	Refer back to what was done on Week 2 lesson 2. The reasons will more or less refer to the data collected on the data capture form. For example if the longest car manufacturer is 15 characters long then that should be the size of the manufacturer field. If all the data collected in one particular field is numeric then that field should be numeric. Write this down even if it is stating the obvious.
Week 3 Lesson 2	Create a database using selected pieces of this data;	This will probably take two or three weeks. Create the database structure. Make sure the fields are the right type and size. Use the data capture form to check that the fields will be long enough.
Week 4 Lesson 1		Type in the data. Not every field on the data capture form will have data in it for every record. (If it's a cars database and the data has come from newspapers etc. there may not be all the details for every car.) Make a note of the fields which have had to be left out.
Week 4 Lesson 2		If there is more than one newspaper, magazine, catalogue etc. some records may be on the data capture form twice. Make a note of this and don't type them in twice.
Week 5 Lesson 1	Visually check the database for accuracy;	Check through the database for mistakes. (It is essential that you can prove that you understand what verification is.) If there are no errors, put some in. Print the database out and highlight all the mistakes.
Week 5 Lesson 2	Check the database for accuracy using validation routines;	There should have been validation checks built into the database. If they have not, search the database for numbers or prices outside a given range. Also search for invalid characters in any 'y/n' fields.
Week 6 Lesson 1	Edit the database in light of the mistakes found;	Correct any data errors in the database. Print out the corrected version.
Week 6 Lesson 2	Using more than one condition, search the database to produce the required output;	Answer the questions listed on Week 1 lesson 1. Make sure that AND and OR conditions are used in the searches and that they are used at least twice.
Week 7 Lesson 1	Comment upon how easy it is to use the software to produce the required output;	Write about how the software was used to search the database. Make it like a user guide. Write an evaluation section about how easy it was to do the searches. Say how hard it was to do certain types of search.
Week 7 Lesson 2	Comment upon how easy it is to produce the required output in different forms of tables and graphs.	Write about how the software was used to produce different types of outputs, reports etc. and how it was used to produce graphs. This could be added on to the user guide produced last week. Writing about how easy or difficult it was this can be added on to the evaluation section produced last week.
Week 8 Lesson 1		Finish off everything

16 Meeting the syllabus requirements for projects 1A

Writing the introduction

Before you start your work for this project, you will need to write an introduction. In the introduction, describe the task you are going to do and how you intend to save it. In particular make sure you state the purpose (objective) of your work.

For example if you consider the task in the OCR syllabus booklet which talks about creating an A4 poster advertising a school event, you could choose an event such as a Sports Day. There must be at least one purpose identified. For example, **one purpose will be to produce a poster advertising the event,** in order to attract visitors from outside. **Another purpose will be to produce handouts giving the results of each event,** together with the running totals of points for each house or year (depending on how your school organises the day). You may want to produce lists of pupils/students who are going to be competing for form/house tutors. All these details must be stated at the beginning of your work. **It is important that you make the purpose of your work clear. One purpose only is required.**

> **Before you start work, write a clear description of the task, identifying at least two purposes (which effectively are two different types of printout for use in different circumstances) and how you intend to to carry out the work.**

Structuring Project 1A for presentation

It is a big advantage if you set out the structure of the work you are planning to hand in. By deciding on headings for certain parts of your work and writing little targets for what you are going to write under each heading, you are providing yourself with an invaluable guide. Here are some suggested headings (in bold) with content targets (in italics) for Project 1A. The structure assumes you are aiming for full marks.

1. **Introduction** – (see above).
2. **Collecting information to suit my purpose:** identify and briefly describe how you collected information from – Internet, CD-ROMs, databases, material to be scanned, files on disks, newspapers and other non IT sources.
3. **Selecting information for my purposes:** describe which sources of information are relevant and useful for your purpose, making sure you choose a variety of different sources.
4. **Developing information to present to my audience(s):** a) show use of copy and paste, tables or frames etc and describe how you brought together information from your chosen range of sources (including text, images and data sources); b) describe and show how you explored the effects of changing information; c) organise the information in your developed documents under headings, include charts/graphs; d) show how you derived new information – NOTE remember to describe the development of your work.
5. **Presenting information: show** a) design and use a consistent and appropriate layout for your newly developed documents e.g margins, borders, font sizes & styles; b) highlight information and show that it meets your identified purpose; c) check work for accuracy and get feedback from others, describing how you did it – include evidence

of feedback obtained; d) show you have saved your work properly in a folder with a set of sensible names for all documents created (use printouts which have been annotated).

6. Advantages and disadvantages of using IT for this task
7. The importance of copyright and confidentiality
8. Error handling and virus protection
9. Health and safety matters

Note that headings 6–9 should include descriptions which show your general understanding of ICT.

Making sure that you get the marks

The most important thing to remember is that you will need to structure your work so that it is easy to see that you have met the mark criteria. You may be able to see this easily from the suggested outline structure already presented. However, to help you even more there are details about what you will need to do to meet the mark criteria or mark targets. For each target achieved your evidence should be included with a description under the appropriate heading. Recommendations of where material should be placed within your coursework are indicated at the end of each mark target description. You will realise as you work through these mark targets that some of the marks higher up the range are concerned with expanding work you have done for lower mark targets. It may help to check ahead and work through which mark targets you wish to achieve and how they all relate to each other. The headings will also help with this.

Remember for this project if you do not achieve a mark target it does not always mean that you cannot achieve the next mark target on the list. *NOTE that mark targets are worth one mark each and are equivalent to the 28 sub skills for IT key skills.

●MARK TARGET 1

The first thing you must do is **collect information from IT sources and non-IT sources.** You will need to do a little bit of investigation and find information you need to use to do your task, such as pictures you are going to include in your poster. Include with your work examples of things you have found on the computer and things, which were found in newspapers, magazines etc. Make sure you **collect text, images and numbers. Some of the information must be from non-IT sources.**

If you were doing the example task, you might need to collect details of which events to include. The PE staff might have details. You could find a list of the events and when they are taking place and find some pictures to go with them. Say where the pictures you have found come from. At this point you only need to prove that you have collected this information. You do not have to do anything with it. You will need to have printouts of the computer-based work as well as the hand-written pieces included in your work. (Put this work under heading 2.)

●MARK TARGET 2

You have to **decide which of the information you collected is relevant.** You simply need to mention which of the information collected so far is relevant to your purpose. You will have collected newspapers, photographs, printouts of a variety of clip art etc. You need to write why you chose the information you used instead of the rest. In other words, why do you think this information is relevant? (Put this work under heading 3.)

●MARK TARGET 3

You will need to show that you can:

develop & format your documents;

use copy and paste;

import images.

You can do this by writing on printouts of documents you have developed or by writing a few lines saying where you copied the text /image from or where you imported the image from. (Put this under heading 4.)

MARK TARGET 4

This is simply exploring different layouts. You can move the text and pictures around the page saying which is the best way of setting out your poster.

MARK TARGET 5

Now you have to show development in your work. To do this it is best to get a print-out of the text you used followed by the same text and a graphic. You then might have a further printout of the graphic positioned correctly. You will also need to include numbers in your work so you might wish to import some data from a spreadsheet which is being used to store results. The end product must be a document, which is neatly laid out. (Put this under heading 4.)

MARK TARGET 6

You need to show that you have chosen appropriate layouts. This means that you have to show that you have used a different layout for certain parts of your work than for others. You may need to produce different documents for this. A list of pupils for the form tutor or house tutor will be set out in a more formal way than a poster advertising the sports day. Consequently, you will need to provide two separate layouts for these documents. These must be appropriate to what you are displaying. In other words, just producing two different layouts will not get you the mark. They need to be set out in a manner which is sensible for what you are producing. (Put this under heading 5.)

MARK TARGET 7

To be awarded this mark you need to show that you have been consistent in your approach to the layout. For example, if you have produced pupil lists you must have used the same format each time they occur in your documents. Each name will start in exactly the same place on a line. The indentation, the font and size will be the same for each name. However the font could be different for the headings. You may have tried to do something special such as using a different font, size or colour for the winner of each event. If so, then the winner of every event will need to be highlighted in a similar way. (Put this under heading 5.)

MARK TARGET 8

You must show you have developed your work to meet your purpose. This is a follow on from the development in your work required for mark 5. The difference here is to show how you have changed some of the text or moved it around, using cut and paste. You must say why you have done this to meet your purpose. You will need to annotate your work in order to say how the development matches your purpose. For example, a poster advertising Sports Day may need to have a photograph of the school and its address so that visitors know where it is. (Put this under heading 4.)

MARK TARGET 9

You need to show you have checked your work for accuracy by producing 'before and after' printouts.

You will need to:

- print out what you think is your final effort;
- use a spellchecker and correct your spelling mistakes;

> **To gain** these first 5 marks you must find different types of information, deciding which information is relevant for your purpose and develop a document by combining the information. Then you must explore and organise the information.

- print out the corrected version;
- get somebody to read through your work who will write comments about how you could improve it (this is called proof-reading);
- improve it;
- print it out.

This mark can be achieved by just doing this for one document. Put this under heading 5.

MARK TARGET 10

You need to show you can save and find your work easily. Hopefully, you will have created a folder called 'ICT GCSE coursework'. Inside this folder you will have created a new folder called 'Project 1A'. Finally, inside this folder you will have saved your document with an appropriate name such as 'Sports day poster'.

You will not get this mark if you have called your work 'Man Utd', 'Arsenal', 'Spice girls', 'Britanny' etc.

You will need printouts of the screen showing your folders and the name of the document you have saved. (Put this under heading 5.)

MARK TARGET 11

You must write a description of how you have used IT to produce your work and compare it to using other methods for producing the work. It does not have to be too detailed but you must mention the way IT has made it easier, for example, to produce your pupil lists, result sheets or poster. You will need to mention how it would have been done without a computer. You only need to do this for one document you have produced. (Put this under heading 6.)

MARK TARGET 12

You must provide evidence that you are aware of safe practice in the computer room and know how to look after your work. You will need to write a list of do's and don'ts about working in the computer room. For example, 'never eat in the computer room' is a don't. 'Always save your work and log off at the end of a session' is a do. You will also need to describe the methods you use to make sure you don't lose your work, including making backups and knowing how to ask for help when you see error messages (either by using the on-line help or asking a teacher/technician). (Put this under heading 9.)

To gain mark targets 1–12 you only need to have 'collected' information together. To gain mark targets 13 and upwards you will need to provide evidence that you have searched a database to get information. This database can be the Internet.

MARK TARGET 13

To gain this mark you will need to use the Internet or a database. If you search for information on the Internet you must print out what you find and mention the address of the site you have been looking at – unless it is already printed on your printout. In addition to this you will need to include material to be scanned such as photographs of athletes. (Put this under heading 2.)

MARK TARGET 14

You will need to collect outputs from searches to a database/spreadsheet. Some spreadsheet software these days let you create filters for searching. You will need to show that you can use operators such as 'AND' as well as operators like 'greater than i.e. >', with the database. One search you could do would be to search the Internet for school AND sports AND day.

To gain 6-12 marks you need to present information in a consistent way to meet your purpose, showing you can select appropriate layouts for different types of document, check for accuracy, save work and compare using IT to develop the work in comparison to manual methods. You must also describe how to work safely, take care of equipment, avoid losing information and get help when dealing with errors.

To gain mark targets 13–15 you need to identify suitable sources of information, search using operators such as 'AND' and interpret information, selecting what is appropriate for your purpose. As you can see this is more in depth work based on the very first few mark targets.

MARK TARGET 15

For this mark you will need to produce a document that makes use of the information you collected for marks 13 and 14. You might want to produce a poster combining a list of events with the graphics downloaded from the Internet and a scanned image.

MARK TARGET 16

Bring together information using formats that help development, for example you could use tables or frames. You can do this by taking the text and where appropriate and convert it to a table. If your software does not allow you to do this you will need to draw a grid and copy your text and paste it little by little into your table. Make sure you use a sensible spacing so it is easy for the reader to understand the information. Print out your work and annotate it (i.e. write notes on your printout saying what you did). (Put this under heading 4.)

MARK TARGET 17

You need to explore information relevant to your purpose. You outlined your purpose at the beginning of your work. You need to write down reasons why these searches of the Internet suit this purpose.

MARK TARGET 18

You will need to include the results of searches in your work showing how you develop information in the form of text, pictures etc. You have already done this for mark 15. Show how you developed the work showing printouts of the stages your work has gone through. (Put this under heading 4.)

MARK TARGET 19

You have to say how you have compared two pieces of information which you searched for and why you chose one above the other and develop new information from your sources. They might be two images which you considered including in your work. They will be from different sources. You will say why you chose one over the other. (Put this under heading 4.)

MARK TARGET 20

You have to show that you have chosen appropriate layouts. Although you have done this before, the difference this time is that it refers to how you have combined information. You must show that you have set your work out in a sensible way. You will have used:

- a sensible width for your margins;
- subheadings where it is appropriate to do so;
- borders around the images in your posters, handouts etc.
- tables with the rows and columns not too wide or too narrow.

You will have to write about your layout saying all this. This is the difference between gaining a mark for layout and this mark. Because the reference this time is to combined information, you must write about your pages which include combined information i.e. not just text or graphics on their own. In addition, you will need to write a sentence about each one saying why you think the layout is appropriate in each case. (Put this under heading 5.)

MARK TARGET 21

You will need to produce two printouts of each document you have created. That is to say, if you have produced pupil lists and results handouts you will need to have two printouts of each one showing that you have been consistent with your layouts. (Put this under heading 5.)

Mark targets 16–19 are about developing information by for example: using tables, making predictions, organising information from your searches, for example under headings or in graphs. You will also need to describe how you developed your work and compare information you have found stating why you chose one source rather than another.

Mark targets 20-23 are about presenting information and you will need to show consistency of layout over several documents. Work must be checked for accuracy and you must obtain the views of others.

MARK TARGET 22

You need to develop the presentation to include text, graphics and numbers and show it meets your chosen purpose. You will need to reposition a graphic or show how you changed your mind about the graphic and used another one. You should include numbers i.e. the points scores for the forms/houses and show how you moved them to a different position to where you originally put them. For each change or development you must say how it meets your purpose. This can be the same as saying why you think the people you were presenting this to would prefer it. (Put this under heading 5.)

MARK TARGET 23

You will need to spell check your work and have it proof-read by someone. Also you will need to show you have saved your work properly. Produce evidence of checking work for accuracy using before and after printouts and as described previously, show you have created a folder called 'ICT GCSE coursework'. Inside this folder you will have created a new folder called 'Project 1A'. Inside this folder you should have saved all your work with appropriate names such as 'form lists', 'result handouts', 'Sports day poster'. As has already been said you will not get this mark if you have given your files silly names. You will show your organisation by producing printouts of the screen showing your folders and what you have saved within them. (Put this under heading 5.)

MARK TARGET 24

You need to write down some of the advantages and disadvantages of using IT. You will need to include examples of both. One big advantage is the way that you can change information in a word processed document without having to write or type it all out again. A disadvantage might be that if someone gains access to your work they could delete it all. With a manual method this is less likely to be the case. You never keep all your folders, exercise books in the same place at the same time but on a computer you do keep all your work together. You will need to list benefits and disadvantages. (Put this under heading 6.)

MARK TARGET 25

For this you will need to write about how it is necessary to observe copyright and confidentiality. You will write about the fact that it is illegal to use copyright material without the owner's permission. You will also write about how personal information should not be made public. You will need to give examples of each. (Put this under heading 7.)

MARK TARGET 26

You will explain how to identify errors and their causes. This could be a description of the error messages you have encountered in your work. You will also say how they could have been avoided in the first place. One such error might have been the fact that you got an error message when you typed in an address on the Internet. You will need to describe how you used the on-line help provided with the software package. You will describe exactly what you got wrong and how you were helped to correct it. (Put this under heading 8.)

MARK TARGET 27

You need to talk about virus prevention such as: not using other disks when you don't know where they come from. You could write about not downloading software from the Internet, being careful about downloading attachments to your e-mails and using virus checkers and killers. (Put this under heading 8.)

MARK TARGET 28

You will need to describe safety and health issues related to I.T., for example, what people need to do generally and what you do yourself to maintain health when using a

> **Mark targets 24–28 are basically descriptions about your knowledge of the advantages and disadvantages of IT, copyright, error handling, minimising the risk of viruses and how to work safely and healthily in a computer room.**

computer. You will talk about sitting properly to minimise backache. The need for taking breaks every so often to reduce eyestrain can be mentioned. This description could be an extension to your description of how to work safely in a computer room. (Put this under heading 9.)

Don't forget – you get one mark for each mark target you achieve, so it does not matter if you fail to get two or three, you will still get a very high mark.

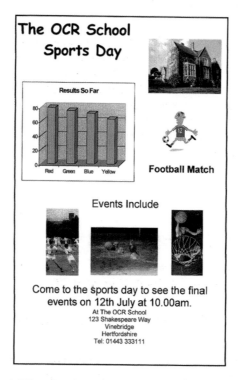

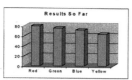

Figure 16.1   Examples of finished documents for Project 1A

Meeting the syllabus requirements for projects 1B

For Project 1B you may choose from one of 4 strands – Modelling, Handling Data, Measuring or Control. Marks are organised in such a way that when you meet a set of requirements you get a mark. However unlike the requirements for Project 1A where you get a mark for one mark target, Project 1B is set out slightly differently. When you meet a set of requirements you are given a mark within a range of marks. Higher mark ranges have more demanding requirements. When marking your work, your teacher will decide which mark range you fit into and whether your work is worth the top, middle or bottom mark in the range. For example, you may be doing a project on data handling and you have:

- developed a method of collecting data;
- created a database using this data;
- visually checked the database for accuracy;
- searched the database for answers to specific questions.

This would mean that you were entitled to a mark of between 11 and 13. Your teacher would decide whether your work was good enough for 13 marks to be awarded, 12 or even 11.

In order to gain a mark within any mark range, your work will need to match *all the statements in that mark range*.

There may be a temptation to just aim your work at one of the higher mark ranges but this approach can lead to disaster. There is very little point in attempting to produce a piece of work which matches all the statements in one of the higher mark ranges without first making sure that the lower mark ranges have been satisfied.

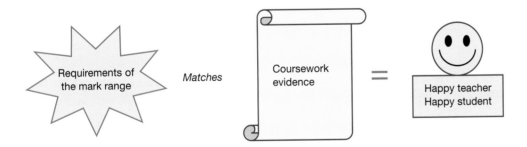

Make sure you can provide evidence that you have met all the requirements in a given mark bracket before tackling the next mark bracket. If you fail to provide evidence that you can do the simpler tasks, you will not be able to gain marks for more complicated tasks.

For example, if you look at the criteria for the Handling Data strand you can see that the statement 'visually check the database for accuracy' occurs in every mark range from 11–13 to 26–28. What would happen if you aimed for full marks and achieved everything but this one statement from the 26–28 range? You wouldn't just miss out on 28 marks. In fact you wouldn't be able to get any more than 10 marks, because the first time this statement appears is in the mark range 11–13 so your teacher must go to the set of requirements where this statement does not appear! This is because you have failed to provide evidence for just one statement.

The rest of this chapter is divided into advice on what to do for each of the four strands, one of which you will choose to satisfy the syllabus requirement for Project 1B. Mark requirements are different for each strand so there is no sample structure for your section headings in your work. Ask your teacher for help with this.

We start here with advice about the Handling Data strand which usually involves developing a database.

Handling Data

This strand is all about identifying a need for storing data and designing a database which you can use to provide different outputs and views of data (see Chapter 13). In order to get a mark higher than 10 out of 28 for this strand you will need to create your own database. Your teacher will tell you if they want you to do this. They may instead produce a simple database for you to use. You will need to use a database like the one in the following example or devise a method for collecting data and then create and use your own database. Checking for accuracy and justifying the choice of software for the task is also an important aspect of this work.

Here is a simple example of a 10 record database of some houses on an estate agent's selling list:

Area	House type	Price (£)	Bedrooms	Garage
Heaton Mersey	Detached	80 000	3	Y
Heaton Norris	Semi-detached	65 000	3	Y
Heaton Mersey	Bungalow	75 000	2	Y
Heaton Moor	Semi-detached	66 000	3	N
Heaton Moor	Semi-detached	72 000	4	N
Heaton Mersey	Detached	95 000	4	Y
Heaton Norris	Detached	73 000	3	Y
Heaton Norris	Detached	74 500	3	Y
Heaton Moor	Town house	56 000	3	N
Heaton Mersey	Semi-detached	78 000	3	Y
Heaton Mersey	Bungalow	77 000	2	Y

Your teacher will need to give you a list of 3 or 4 questions to answer using the database. If you were using the database above these might be:

* find all the houses which are detached;
* find all the houses which cost less than £75 000;
* find all the houses with 4 bedrooms.

And so on.

You could use this database in order to get at least 10 marks

Below are the mark ranges together with an explanation of what you have to do to meet each requirement.

Remember, you have to meet the requirements for the mark range above before you can get the marks for the next range.

Mark Range	What you need to do:
1–2	• Load the database so that you can see all the records.
	• Search the database to find the answers to the questions your teacher gave you. Print out the matching records.
3–4	• Print out the whole database.
	• Choose a field such as Area and sort the database into ascending order.
	• Print out the whole database again to prove that you have sorted it.
5–7	• Show that you are able to edit data in the database appropriately by changing the details of a house which, for example, should have a Y in the garage column instead of an N. You could, perhaps, change the number of bedrooms from 3 to 4. The statement says 'when appropriate' so don't make silly changes.
8–10	• Create a data capture form or questionnaire to add more information.
	• Use the column headings given above and collect details of 2 or 3 houses from newspapers or estate agents.
	• Put this completed data capture form in with the rest of your work.
	• Load the database.
	• Print out the whole database.
	• Add these new records.
	• Print out the new version of the database. These two print outs will be your evidence that you have added the records.

If you did everything above you would be entitled to a mark in the range 8–10.

> **If you use a database already created for you the maximum mark you can gain is 10 out of a possible 28 marks.**

In order to gain a higher mark than 10 you will need to create your own database.

In the OCR syllabus there is a list of suitable tasks for you to tackle. Here is one of them:

Compile a database of second-hand vehicles using current information from local garage advertisements, leaflets and newspapers. This database will act as a vehicle location service for someone wishing to obtain details on the availability of certain models.

To include:

A data capture sheet;

Collection and input of data;

Sorting and searching of data;

Presentation of results;

Written conclusion;

An instruction sheet to enable another person to use the system to search for information on a specific type of vehicle.

Below is a list of things you will need to do to gain the marks indicated. Each mark range has been included together with what is needed.

Remember, if you miss **just one** statement out in any mark range you will not be given a mark in that range.

It is essential to match **all the statements** in a lower mark range before moving on to a higher mark range.

> To achieve marks 11–28 you will need to devise a way of collecting data, collect a range of data, create a database using selected items of data, visually check the database for accuracy, use validation routines, using more than one condition to search the database, edit the database comment upon how easy it was to use the software and produce different forms of tables and graphs.

Mark Range	What you need to do:
11–13	• Create a data capture form. In its simplest form it would consist of a table drawn on paper with column headings matching the information you needed. Make, model etc.
	• Fill in the data capture form by collecting information about cars from magazines, newspapers, car showroom forecourts etc.
	• Describe how you created the database using the data from the data capture form
	• Provide a printout of the database as evidence. The data in the database must obviously match the data on the data capture form or you will not be eligible for the award of a mark in this mark range.
	• Look through the database and check for any mistakes you have made. It is not sufficient to say that you have checked your database and made no mistakes (this is called verification).
	• Print out your first attempt at the database highlighting any errors, which you have made.
	• Write down a list of searches that you are going to find the answers to from the database. One such search might be to find the details of all the Fords. Write that down.
	• Create your query on the database and print out the results. Do this for four or five searches.
14–16	• Use a range of sources of data. This could be a selection of magazines or a selection of newspapers or details from two car showrooms or a combination of these.
	• Say where the data has come from.
	• Make a decision over what data is to be included in your database. (In transferring the data to the data capture form you may have noticed information which is unnecessary and so you have not copied it down. You may have noticed the same car in different magazines/

newspapers and so you have not used it a second time. You need to point this out in your description of how you collected the data.

- Print out your database with all the errors (which were noticed after verification) removed.

- Make a search for information using the data you have already searched for. i.e. having found all the Fords for 11–13 marks, you now search these for all the Mondeos. Do this for two or three of the searches you have already made.

17–19 • Check the database for accuracy using validation routines. You will need to:

1. Include validation routines when you create the structure of the database. On most database software you can build these routines into the structure of your database. Possible checks to make are a range check on the price field, a format check on the registration number or a logical check on whether the car has air conditioning or not.

2. Print out the structure showing your validation routines. (When you are typing in data you will need to enter some invalid data to show that your validation routines work.)

3. Print out a screen dump of the resulting error messages. (This will show your teacher and the moderator that your validation routines do actually work.)

- Using more than one condition, search the database for answers to specific questions. Complete this aspect of your work exactly as if you were aiming to achieve 11-13 marks but write out questions, which search using information in at least two fields. Search the database for specific records by using the logical operators AND, OR and NOT. Use at least two of these operators.

20–22 • Give reasons for your choice of software. You can not write down answers like:

> 'I chose this software because it's the only one the school has got'.
> 'I chose this software because it's the one I'm most familiar with'
> 'I chose this software because it's easier to use'

Instead, say why you feel that this is the best piece of software for the task. You will find it easier to explain and easier to get high marks if you have two pieces of database software to choose from. If you have not, then you will have to compare it with spreadsheet software.

- Refer back to your introduction to the task or problem you are undertaking. Use the plan of everything you said you would be doing to solve the problem. Refer to the features of the software you said you would be using. For example, you may have said you would be doing lots of searches but not many graphs.

In our car database example, you may say that the car showroom problem requires the use of a database to find the results of mainly complex queries. Therefore choose a package which could do these. You may know of an alternative package but it is more difficult to use when it comes to performing complex searches although it has wonderful graph drawing capabilities. Say that this is a reason for not choosing the second package. This second package would not be considered appropriate for the solution, as little graph output may be required.

- Give at least two reasons.

23–25
- Give reasons why you have chosen the fields you have included in your database.
- Explain why you have chosen certain fields but left out others. (It may be that after you had collected information about the cars you found that there was certain data missing. You have now decided to only include the fields which you have information on all the cars.)
- Give reasons for your choice of field types. (You may well have decided to make certain fields logical because this would make them easier to search and validate than if they were left as text.)
- Explain your choice of field lengths (refer to your completed data capture forms. Say how long the longest 'Make' is and then say this is why you have used this for your field length.
- Do this for each of your fields.

26–28
- Make a list of likely questions from customers who want to look at certain types of car. At least 7 or 8 would be a reasonable expectation. The **required output** is the answers to these questions. Say this is the case.

  Questions could be:

  1. A customer cannot spend more than £10 000 but wants a 4-door saloon car. What makes and models are available?
  2. A customer wants an economical car i.e. engine size less than 1500 cc but it must have air-conditioning and be blue.

  And so on.

- Describe the format of the output which will be needed.

  Will it be in tabular form, lists, single line output or individual fields printed out? Will graphs be needed and if so what type of graphs?

- Make sure that your data capture form is based on the required output (that is, the answers to your list of questions you made above).

  Using the two questions above you would design a data capture form which would collect information about Make, Model, Number of doors, Price (question 1), Engine size, Features and Colour (question 2).

- Explain how you built your data capture form using all the customer questions you wrote down.
- Give reasons why your chosen software is the best one to produce the required output.

  Above, you have said what type and form your output will have. You might have mentioned the types of graph which might be needed. Some database software has a greater range of graph types than others. As was mentioned above it is possible to use different layouts for printing results. You may have said you wanted certain layouts which only your choice of software can provide.

- Give reasons why your chosen fields, field types and field lengths are the best ones to produce the required output.

  This will be a more detailed follow on from the reasons for the data capture form. It will explain the reasons for the field types based on the required output as well as the reasons given for 23–25. When making a choice between, say, text or logical field types, the need to produce output in a readable form may prove more important than the need to use particular validation routines.

- Evaluate your use of the software.
- Having given reasons for choosing the software to produce the required output, say whether your reasons turned out to be justified.
- Having used various features of the software such as searching; searching using more than one field; sorting; producing graphs and probably more. Say how easy or difficult it was to do all these things to produce the required output.
- Say how easy or difficult it is to produce the different forms of output and graphs.

If you did all the above you would be entitled to a mark in the range 26–28.

Modelling

The modelling strand is concerned with using or designing a computer model. Most people use a spreadsheet to do this (see Chapter 13). It is important that you make predictions and try out different data in your model to see if your predictions are correct. In order to get a mark higher than 19 out of 28 for this strand you will need to design and create your own model. Your teacher may decide that you need to get some practice with spreadsheets first. This still means that you can get a mark up to 19. Here is an example of a model set up on a spreadsheet showing weekly sales in a sports shop.

Item	Number sold per week	Cost price	Selling price	Profit per item	Profit per week
Kino trainers	124	£44.00	£49.99	£5.99	£742.76
Sadman trainers	99	£39.00	£43.99	£4.99	£494.01
Kino tracksuits	27	£24.50	£31.99	£7.49	£202.23
Sadman tracksuits	31	£22.00	£29.99	£7.99	£247.69
Footballs	48	£5.00	£8.99	£3.99	£191.52
Goalagame boots	32	£22.00	£27.99	£5.99	£191.68
Nevermiss boots	41	£19.00	£24.99	£5.99	£245.59
Shinpads	26	£14.00	£19.99	£5.99	£155.74
football shirts	132	£25.00	£49.99	£24.99	£3,298.68
Football shorts	128	£12.00	£17.99	£5.99	£766.72
Tennis rackets	12	£49.00	£69.99	£20.99	£251.88
Tennis balls x 6	47	£15.00	£19.99	£4.99	£234.53
Badminton rackets	15	£39.00	£44.99	£5.99	£89.85
Shuttlecocks tubes	47	£24.00	£29.99	£5.99	£281.53

Total profit per week	£7,394.41

Below are the mark ranges together with an explanation of what you have to do to meet each requirement.

Remember, you have to meet the requirements for the mark range above before you can get the marks for the next range.

Mark Range	What you need to do:
0–2	• Print out the spreadsheet.
	• Write down what it does.
	• Write about what each column represents. (If a number in a column depends on the numbers in another column, say how. For example

you will write about how the profit column is the selling price column subtract the cost price column.)

3–4
- Write about how you changed some numbers in one column.
- Write about how other columns changed as a result.
- Write on a printout of the spreadsheet about these changes.

5–7
- Change some things about the spreadsheet. For example, increase the profit margin on some items as they are selling well and decrease the profit margins on some items which are not selling well.
- Write down what you intend to do.
- Change the variables (numbers) in the appropriate columns.
- Write about the effects of your changes.
- Write on a printout of the spreadsheet about these changes.

8–10
- Experiment with the model and write exactly what happens within the spreadsheet.
- Change some numbers.
- Write down what happens as a result.
- Change numbers in all the columns which containing variables.
- Write what happens as a result, to the columns and cells containing formulae.
- Write about how when you increase certain numbers other numbers increase as well (or go down).
- Write about how the model works.
- Be specific about what the formulae do. Mention how addition, subtraction, multiplication and division are being used. Mention some general formulae such as column E= column D – column C
- Write on a printout of the spreadsheet about this
- Make some simple predictions. (One could be that if you increase the Selling Price of football shirts by £1 the profit will go up by £132.) Make four or five predictions. (At this stage you do not have to prove if you are right or not.)

11–13
- Get printouts of the spreadsheet showing how changing some numbers makes other numbers change.
- Make simple predictions about some of the effects of these changes.
- Having made some simple predictions, show if you were right. Get printouts of the changes you made and comment on them saying if you were proved correct.

> **Up to mark 13** you will only need to use a model, which has already been created for you. It may be a fairly simple model.

> **For all the mark ranges higher than 13** you will need to use a complex model. A complex model is one that contains at least two columns with formulae in them. The formulae must use at least two and at least two worksheet functions supplied with the software.

For all the mark ranges higher than 13 you will need to use a complex model. A complex model is one that contains at least **two** columns with formulae in them. The formulae must use **at least two** operators (that is, addition, subtraction, multiplication or division) and **at least two** worksheet functions supplied with the software. The spreadsheet you have been using so far has only used one worksheet function (SUM). Here is one that uses two (SUM and IF).

Item	Number sold Per week	Cost price	Selling price	Profit per item	Profit per week	Stock at start of week	Stock at end of week	Re-order level	Re-order Yes/No
Kino trainers	124	£44.00	£49.99	£5.99	£742.76	198	74	100	Yes
Sadman trainers	99	£39.00	£43.99	£4.99	£494.01	186	87	100	Yes
Kino tracksuits	27	£24.50	£31.99	£7.49	£202.23	88	61	75	Yes
Sadman tracksuits	31	£22.00	£29.99	£7.99	£247.69	106	75	75	No
Footballs	48	£5.00	£8.99	£3.99	£191.52	124	76	75	No
Goalagame boots	32	£22.00	£27.99	£5.99	£191.68	112	80	50	No
Nevermiss boots	41	£19.00	£24.99	£5.99	£245.59	101	60	75	Yes
Shinpads	26	£14.00	£19.99	£5.99	£155.74	88	62	50	No
Football shirts	132	£25.00	£49.99	£24.99	£3,298.68	211	79	150	Yes
Football shorts	128	£12.00	£17.99	£5.99	£766.72	201	73	150	Yes
Tennis rackets	12	£49.00	£69.99	£20.99	£251.88	52	40	25	No
Tennis balls x 6	47	£15.00	£19.99	£4.99	£234.53	121	74	100	Yes
Badminton rackets	15	£39.00	£44.99	£5.99	£89.85	56	41	25	No
Shuttlecocks tubes	47	£24.00	£29.99	£5.99	£281.53	152	105	75	No

Total profit per week   £7,394.41

To gain up to 19 marks you will need to use a complex model and develop it further.

Mark Range	What you need to do:
14–16	• Repeat everything done to get 8–10 marks using a complex model like the one above.
	• Repeat everything done to get 11–13 marks using a complex model like the one above.
	• Alter some of the formulae in the spreadsheet.
	One easy formula to change might be the re-order (yes/no) column. At the moment stock is only re-ordered when the amount in stock falls below the re-order number. You might want to change it so that as soon as it equals the re-order number stock is re-ordered. You will need to print out the spreadsheet showing the original formulae and a printout showing the changed formulae.
	• Make some predictions about what will happen when you change the data.
	• Having made some simple predictions, show if you were right. Get printouts of the changes you made and comment on them saying if you were proved correct.
	• Write a description of how well this model represents a real business situation. Would it be possible to use a version of it in a real business?
17–19	• Develop the model by changing the formulae to solve a given task.

Your teacher will give you a scenario to modify this model. It could be that you are asked to imagine that the shop is having a sale. Prices will be reduced by 10%. You will need to insert a column calculating the SALE selling price. You will also need to change the profit formula to use the new selling price.

- Write a description of how well the new model works, including the successes and failures. (Your teacher will have already told you what your amended model would have to be able to do. Write about how well it does this.)

In order to get a mark above 19 you will need to produce your own model – you can no longer rely on your teacher to do it for you.

Your teacher can, however, give you ideas for the task you will do. A suitable task to undertake might be to use a spreadsheet to model the payroll system of a small business. You could make changes to items such as the hours worked, overtime rates and tax rates. You could write about how these changes affect the profits made by the business and how they affect the wages of workers.

You would have to include in your work:

- A detailed description of how the model was designed and created;
- A printout of the spreadsheet showing values and formulae;
- Predictions about the likely effect of reducing or increasing hours worked, removing overtime and increasing the workforce;
- The results of these changes;
- An evaluation of the model and its effectiveness.

Below is a list of things you will need to do to gain the marks indicated.

20–22
- Write out a full description of the task.
- List all the things which will be needed to do to fulfil the task requirements.
- Design the spreadsheet.
- Sketch the structures of the spreadsheet, showing how you developed the design.
- Include columns for names, hourly rate, hours worked, overtime, taxes etc. (As columns are added and formulae developed, draw a new sketch of the spreadsheet, explaining the developments made since the previous version.)
- Use at least two operators (that is, addition, subtraction, multiplication or division) and **at least two** worksheet functions supplied with the software.
- Choose an appropriate piece of software.
- Refer to your task description and list what the software is required to do.
- Compare your choice of software to another type of software saying why your choice will fulfil these requirements.

To gain up to 28 marks you will need to design a complex model, choose software, use the software chosen to create the model, answer some 'what-if' questions, write about how valid the software was for the task, describe how the model was created and how it was suitable for this purpose.

- Construct the computer model using this software

  Load the software and create the model. Do this by creating all the relevant columns and using the formulae that you have already said you will. Include at least two columns which contain formulae. Include two functions supplied with the software. The two most obvious ones are the SUM and IF functions. Use SUM to find the total of a particular column. If there is a column for tax allowance some workers will not pay tax if they earn less than this amount. Use the IF function to find out if they do pay tax or not.

- Use the software to provide the answers required to solve the problem.

  In your introduction to the task you should have said that your model will be able to provide answers to some 'what if' questions. Having created the spreadsheet you must use it to do all the things you said it would. This will involve changing some of the variables such as hours worked, overtime and income tax rate. You should compare the cost to the company of employing another worker and getting rid of overtime. How many hours of overtime does there have to be before it is worth employing a new worker? You must make some predictions about the likely effects of changing these variables.

- Write a description of how well the model works, including the successes and failures.

  You have already made a list of things your model would have to be able to do. To finish up with you must write a description of how well you think it does these things. Try to imagine it being used in a business situation. Would it be possible to use a version of it in a real business? It would probably have to be modified to do so. You need to say what modifications would be needed.

23–25
- Give a step-by-step account of how the model was created.
- Include a list of all the features of the software used.
- Write about how you loaded the software how you typed in column headings, how you typed in formulae and how you used the replication function.
- Write about how to insert columns.
- Include everything that you did.

26–28
- Evaluate the software and how easy it was to create the model using the software.
- Write about anything which worked out to be more complicated than at first thought.

  Some types of spreadsheet software have quite complicated ways of doing replication, for instance. Some have different names for functions to others such as AVERAGE in one package might be AVE in another. Did this cause problems?

If you did all the above you would be entitled to a mark in the range 26-28.

Measuring

For the measuring strand you will be required to design and create an experiment where you can collect data over a period of time using sensors (see Chapter 14). In order to get a mark higher than 19 out of 28 for this strand you will need to design and create your experiment. If you use an experiment which has been set up for you, it will only be possible to score lower marks.

Below are the mark ranges together with an explanation of what you have to do to meet each requirement.

Remember, you have to meet the requirements for the mark range above before you can get the marks for the next range.

Mark Range	What you need to do:
0–2	• Write about two devices that you know about, which measure physical variables like temperature, sound, pressure etc. This means that the devices must use some sensors and timing devices. The sensors could be pressure sensors, temperature sensors, light sensors, sound sensors, moisture sensors etc. You could write about speed cameras and how they work. You could write about how weather stations use sensors to monitor weather conditions.
3–4	• Repeat your description for the 0–2 mark range for another two devices.
5–7	• Write about how you have connected computers to equipment which uses sensors to measure physical variables in an experiment or monitors them over a period of time. (Your teacher will have done some work with you on measuring. All you have to do is to write about what you did in that lesson).
8–10	• Print out the results of your measuring experiment. • Write about the things you had to do to get the computer to do the measuring. • Write about what else you had to do to get the results displayed. (How you used the software to get the computer to take the results in and how you used the software to produce tables or graphs.)
11–13	• Explain what your results mean. • Use your graphs or tables to point out what you are writing about. • Write about any trends you have noticed. (You may be measuring how quickly different liquids cool. It may be that the temperature always drops quickly to begin with and then more slowly after a period of time.)
14–16	• Describe how you have used computers to measure physical variables in an experiment or to monitor the variables over a period of time. • Write about what the purpose of the experiment is. • Write about what you set out to find. • Write about how the system changes analogue variables into digital signals so that the computer can deal with them.

The measuring strand is concerned with collecting data from an experiment using sensors.

Marks up to 19 can be gained by carrying out tasks on an experiment set up for you, but to get a mark above 19 you will need to produce your own experiment.

17–19
- Write about the reasons why you felt you needed to use a computer.
- Write about how accurate a computer is when it comes to reading data. If you had not used a computer you would have had to take the readings yourself. That would involve you either

  (i) sitting down for long periods of time taking the readings

  or

  (ii) having to keep coming back at regular intervals to take readings.

  You might get tired and make mistakes. You might forget the time and miss taking a reading. What you have to ask yourself is whether a computer would get tired or forget?

- Write about the sensors you have used and how accurate they are. Think about the alternatives you could use and why these might not be so accurate or dependable.

  In order to get a mark above 19 you will need to produce your own experiment. You can no longer rely on your teacher to do it for you. Your teacher can, however, give you ideas for the task you will do.

Use suitable data logging equipment with a variety of sensors to conduct an investigation into weather conditions in your area over a period of time. Trends and patterns should be identified.

To include:

- a detailed description of how the investigation was carried out;
- a printout of the results;
- a conclusion supported by graphs and charts;
- an evaluation of the investigation.

Remember – to meet all the criteria you will need to provide evidence that you have done the work.

Below is a list of things you will need to do to gain the marks indicated. The list is written in such a way that you do not need to have achieved everything for 17–19 before you start on the 20–22 mark range. You must, however, match all the statements or you may get no marks at all, unless you have worked your way through the previous mark ranges. To get higher than 22 marks it is essential to match **all the statements** in a lower mark range before moving on to a higher mark range.

20–22
- Write about four devices that you know about, which measure physical variables like temperature, sound, pressure etc. This means that the devices must use some sensors and timing devices. The sensors could be pressure sensors, temperature sensors, light sensors, sound sensors, moisture sensors etc. You could write about speed cameras and how they work. You could write about how weather stations use sensors to monitor weather conditions.
- Write down the task for which you are going to do your experiment.
- State the main problems that will need solving.
- Write down the things that you are going to have to measure. (These might be the amount of sunlight and rainfall, the atmospheric pressure, the temperature, wind speed etc.)
- Write down the type of computer system required.
- Write down the sensors which will be needed.
- Write down the form of output which will be used.
- Draw a diagram of how the various components will be set out.
- Design the output format which will be used i.e. design the form of graphical output or design a spreadsheet or both.
- Construct the experiment and measure more than two physical variables.
- Write about how you connected the equipment together, making use of at least three different types of sensor.
- Take a photograph of the constructed equipment and include it in your write up.
- Provide printouts and write about how you got the computer to display the results of the measurements.
- Get a printout of your results.
- Write about how you produced them using the various features of the software (Did the results go straight into a spreadsheet? Describe, step by step, how you produced graphs to show your results.)
- Explain the meaning of the displayed results.
- Explain the trends shown by the results. (If one of the parts of the experiment was monitoring temperature in a weather station you could explain the peaks and troughs by comparing these to the time of day. You would explain how temperature falls at night and rises during the day.)
- Write about how you saved your results as a file of data. (This could be using the software built in to the system or how the data was exported to a spreadsheet or similar file format.)
- Write down some reasons why computers provide reliable measurements. (You could write about the fact that alternative methods may be more unreliable and are possibly less accurate. You will need to give reasons why this is the case.)

23–25   • Name each of the sensors and describe what they are measuring.
         • Store the displayed results using more than one file format. (You will need to describe how you have saved the displayed results. One of the ways will perhaps have been how you saved the data in the internal format of the software used. The other will be how you exported the data to a spreadsheet or database package and then saved it in that format.)

26–28   • Give reasons for your choice of hardware and software.
         • Describe the hardware system you have used.
         • Describe the software you have used as well.
         • Compare the hardware and software you have used to other alternatives. (You will need to say why the hardware and software you used is better for your task than the alternatives. Saying things like 'it's the only hardware/software the school has got will not be sufficient).

         If you did all the above you would be entitled to a mark in th range 26–28.

Figure 17.1   A remote weather station

Control

The control strand is all about using sensors, writing instructions to respond to data from sensors so that the experiment or equipment can be controlled. For examples of control systems see chapter 14. In order to get a mark higher than 19 out of 28 for this strand you will need to design and create your own control system. In order to get a mark up to 19 you only need to be able to **use** a control programming language, such as Logo, which allows you to control a screen turtle or image. You will need to write programs, which either produce shapes on the screen, control the movements of a robot around an obstacle course or control other types of equipment. All the examples below refer to a screen image. If you are using a robot or buggy the requirements are still the same.

Below are the mark ranges together with an explanation of what you have to do to meet each requirement.

Remember, you have to meet the requirements for the mark range above before you can get the marks for the next range.

> **For the control** work you will need to use sensors and write instructions to control equipment.

Mark Range	What you need to do:
0–2	• Write down a list of devices which you know about which can control the way things work. (They must involve the use of sensors and timing. Examples such as traffic lights, which use pressure sensors to detect a car approaching the traffic lights, need to be given. You could mention washing machines, which use temperature sensors and heaters to make sure the water is at the right temperature. A list of 3 or 4 together with what they do would be enough.)
3–4	• Use a programming language such as Logo.
	• Write down what you are attempting to do with the screen turtle. (You may be moving it around a maze on the screen. You may be drawing some shapes on the screen. Whatever it is, you will need to make it very clear to anybody who is looking at your work what you are doing.)
	• Draw a diagram showing this together with a few lines of writing. (This should say in words what the diagram is showing.)
	• Write down how you controlled a screen turtle or robot to achieve this outcome. (You will need to write down a few lines describing how you did this. At this point you do not need to print out the instructions you used.)
	• Print out the pattern or shapes you created.
5–7	• Write down the instructions used together with what they did. (This can be done by writing on a computer printout of the instructions but it doesn't have to be.)
	• Print out the pattern or shapes.
	• On the printout write some of the instructions next to the part of the shape or pattern where they were used.
8–10	• Save the instructions as a program.

- Write down, step by step, how you saved the instructions.
- Print out the program. (It is now not enough for you to write down the instructions. You must get the computer to print them out.)
- On the printout write down what each group of instructions does. (For example, you might have drawn an equilateral triangle as part of your work. That part of your annotated program might look like this:

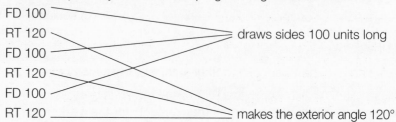

FD 100
RT 120   draws sides 100 units long
FD 100
RT 120
FD 100
RT 120   makes the exterior angle 120°

11–13
- Annotate your program making it quite clear that you understand how important it is to be precise in forming your instructions. (You must not be afraid of stating the obvious. Using the equilateral triangle as an example, it is obvious that if you make the angles 130° then you will not get the shape you intended as the last two lines will not meet at a point.)
- Illustrate this by getting a printout of a mistake.
- Write about how you used precision in sequencing instructions. (This is more about the need to be precise about where you put certain instructions within a program.)

    This is when you may be drawing a series of triangles. You might be using instructions to move the screen turtle across the screen to draw the next shape. You must write down what would happen if you typed the instructions in the wrong order. One of the shapes might appear in the wrong part of the screen. You should now print out a picture to show what happens when things happen in the wrong order.

14–16
- Take some of the patterns you have already drawn and combine them into a pattern which is more complex. (Suppose you were drawing a house. You would start off by drawing individual windows, a door and a roof. A complex shape would be formed by combining them to make a house.)
- Write about how you used precision in sequencing instructions. (You have to do the same as what you did for 11–13 but for this more complex shape. It will probably be easier to explain using the house as an example. If the roof were drawn out of sequence it might appear in the wrong place on the screen. A printout of this would explain the problem.)
- Write about how you tested the program.
- Produce printouts at different stages in the writing of the program.
- Show how the instructions might not have worked properly. (This will need to be done showing your mistakes at all stages. It needs to be done for each of the simple shapes you have combined to make the complex shape. If you were drawing a house you would need to show your initial attempts at drawing windows, doors and a roof perhaps.)

- Write about how you changed the program to make it work better.
- Show the points at which you had to improve the programs for each of the simple shapes and your attempts at combining them.

17–19
- Write down any loops and procedures that you have used in your program.
- Explain what the program would have looked like if you had not used loops or procedures.

To get up to 19 marks you need to use a control system. To score higher marks you will need to design a control system such as a burglar alarm.

In order to get a mark above 19 you will need to produce your own control system. You can no longer rely on your teacher to do it for you. Your teacher can, however, give you ideas for the task you will do. For this strand the sort of task you might want to undertake is:

Create a burglar alarm system, which can be used in a house.

To include:

- sensors to detect movement;
- sensors to detect if a window has been opened;
- sensors to detect if someone has walked on the floor;
- an audio alert for output;
- an emergency button to set of the alarm immediately;
- an off button to switch off the alarm;
- documentation of the system.

Below is a list of things you will need to do to gain the marks indicated. The list is written in such a way that you do not need to have achieved everything for 17–19 before you start on the 20–22 mark range. You must, however, match all the statements or you may get no marks at all, unless you have worked your way through the previous mark ranges. To get higher than 22 marks it is essential to match **all the statements** in a lower mark range before moving on to a higher mark range.

20–22
- Write down the requirements of the task as above.
- Describe how you intend to approach the task.
- Draw some designs of the burglar alarm system including the sensors you propose using.
- Write about your designs.
- Construct the system and use at least two different sensors. Examples are heat, light and sound sensors.
- Connect them up to the interface you intend using and connect that to the computer.
- Write about how you connected all the equipment to a computer. (Write a description telling the reader how you connected the sensors to the control box/interface and the box/interface to the computer.)
- Provide diagrams or photographs showing the constructed equipment. Either draw a detailed diagram of the layout of the equipment or take photographs of it. Label the diagrams or photograph to show

what each part is. Include these diagrams or photographs with your written description.

- Print out the program. (You will have written a program of instructions to get the equipment to do what you want it to do. You will need to print this out.)
- Annotate the program. (Write next to each statement or groups of statements what they mean. Make it clear for anyone to understand exactly what each part of the program does.)
- Save the instructions as a program. (Just indicate on a printout of them the name you have given to the program.)
- Write about how you trialled the program.

    You will have probably started off by making a few mistakes. You need to show your initial efforts at writing the program and you need to describe what was wrong with them. Write about what things went wrong with the burglar alarm system.

- Write about the instructions you changed, or added, to make the program work.
- Write about how you used precision in forming instructions. (Say how the instructions had to be used without misspelling them. This description will need to include how the numbers used in the instructions had to be written exactly.)
- Comment on what would have happened if you had used the wrong numbers.
- Write about how you used precision in sequencing instructions.

    In order to get the program to work in the correct order you will have needed to make sure that all the instructions were in the right order. This is the part of your written description where you give examples of how you were careful to make the instructions occur in the right order. You may also give examples of what might happen or what did happen if you did not put them in the right order.

- Write about how you used loops and procedures.
- Indicate on the printout where these occur.
- Refer to these and explain what the program would look like without the loops and procedures.
- Write about how much longer and difficult to understand it would be without the loops and procedures.

23–25
- Write a few lines about the sensors you are using.
- For each one write down which physical variable you are using them to detect.
- Making use of your description of the task, compare alternative software packages.
- Give reasons for why you chose the package you did. (These reasons must relate to the requirements of the task.)

To gain maximum marks for control you will need to, design the control system using two different sensors, write instructions, refine and save as a program, write about how feedback is used by the system, provide evidence of how the system was developed and give reasons for the choice of software.

- Write about how you tested the program.
- Explain how you made sure you tested all aspects of the program.

26–28
- Annotate the program indicating exactly where feedback takes place. (Write next to the group of statements where there is a feedback loop. Make it clear for anyone to understand exactly what feedback is.)
- Write about how you used feedback in their program. (Explain what you understand feedback to be and then describe it was used it to make your system work better.)

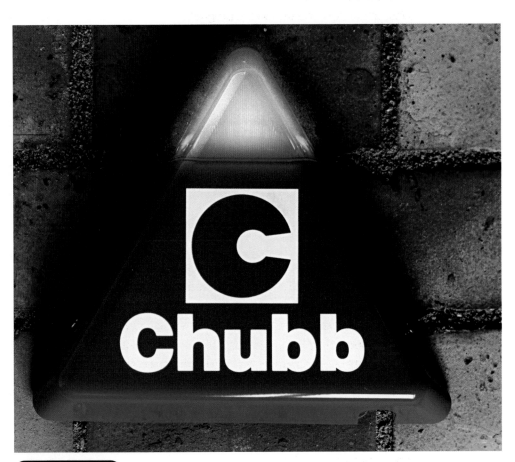

Figure 17.2 A typical control system

Section E

Problem solving using computers

This section is all about the work that *systems consultants* do in order to solve problems and improve inefficiencies in all sorts of business areas (e.g customer order processing, stock control). A systems consultant is the person who will analyse the way that data is collected and used by the business. Sometimes you will hear people talk about a 'systems analyst' or a 'systems designer' and the work they do to help create useful systems using IT. The systems analyst is the person who looks at old systems and works out how the business uses collects and uses data, whilst the systems designer is the person who will design a new system for collecting and using data. Often the same person does the analysis work and the design work and this is why we call them a systems consultant. Whenever you see the term systems consultant throughout the book remember that it means systems analyst or systems designer depending on whether the person is working on the analysis part of the systems life cycle or whether they are working on the design part of the systems life cycle. The systems consultant may also be involved in developing and testing the new system but often someone else such as a computer programmer or database developer may do the work. Again for consistency we will refer to this person as the systems consultant.

The systems cycle is a useful guide for the systems consultant and it was covered earlier in this book in Section B. However, for convenience, Chapter 18 summarises the systems cycle again for you. Chapter 19 uses an example company to illustrate how to carry out the tasks of investigation, analysis, design, development and implementation and Chapter 20 covers how to tackle the major coursework element (called Project 2) which is required for the full course GCSE.

> The job title 'Systems Consultant' is a generalised job title covering many other specific job titles in IT such as: Systems Analyst, Systems Designer, Programmer, Database Developer and many more.

18 System cycle in outline

In Section B we have seen that the systems life cycle in ICT, refers to the course events from project initiation to completion of the project.

The stages of the systems life cycle are:

- Project Identification
- Fact Finding
- Feasibility Study
- Analysis
- Design
- Development and Testing
- Implementation
- Monitoring and Evaluation.

The first three stages of the cycle are crucial in determining whether further work will go ahead.

Figure 18.1 shows the different stages in the life cycle of an IT system. We start at Project Identification.

The stages of the systems life cycle are:

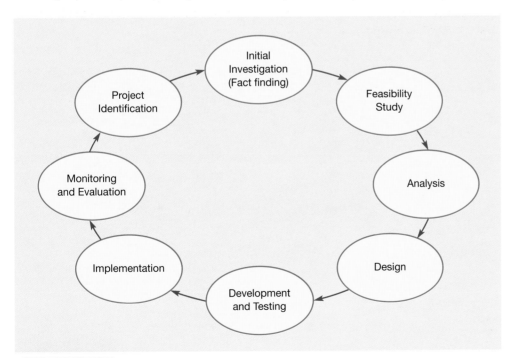

Figure 18.1 Systems Life Cycle diagram

The Systems
Life Cycle covers all the stages in the development of a new IT system.

We have already seen that from time to time there is often a need for organisations to put in a new computer system. These organisations are often businesses, big or small. There may be several reasons for this need, but usually it is because the old system cannot cope with the business increasing. The new computer system will cope with lots of data, storing it and processing it to produce information for many different users. For this reason it is often called an Information System or more frequently these days an IT system.

Whenever a new IT System has been put into a business it is usually after several stages of development have taken place. The business will have identified a number of reasons why they think they need an IT System. They will usually get in touch with an expert (the systems consultant) to ask for a feasibility study to be done. A feasibility report will say be written at the end of the feasibility study to tell the business managers if it is sensible to go ahead and develop a new system (see page 101 Section B).

To illustrate the stages of the systems life cycle in Chapter 17 we will look at a company that wants to speed up its operations.

The process of system analysis,
design development and implementation

W&W Steelstock is a small company in the West Midlands which deals with buying and selling steel. It is owned and run by Winifred Habberley and Keith White. The company employs a number of manual workers, office staff , an engineer and the owners, who themselves are involved in various aspects of the business. The company currently uses a computer for recording invoices and for producing payslips. Most operations carried out in the office are manual or a mix of operations carried out manually and on the computer. Apart from the payroll system no aspect of the business is fully computerised.

Feasibility study

This is a study to see if an organisation does in fact need to computerise its operations. There are several things which the feasibility of a project can be measured against. One of these is whether a particular solution in terms of the necessary software is available and is it capable of meeting the users' needs. Another is whether the organisation can afford the cost of the project in terms of the Systems Consultant's time as well as the cost of the hardware and software. Will it be successful in reducing errors and improving the accuracy of the input? Will it improve customer service? Will it speed up the system in terms of input and data processing time? If the answer to most of these questions is yes then the next stage of Systems Analysis can proceed.

> **A feasibility study is carried out to check whether it will be cost effective and sensible to go ahead and analyse the business problem identified more fully.**

Analysis

W&W Steelstock decided as a result of the feasibility study that they will go ahead and have a new IT System to help them run their business. The job of the Systems Consultant is now to produce an IT system which will solve particular problems in the organisation. In order to do this the consultant must identify what the new system is required to do.

There are three possible types of system, which may be studied by a Systems Consultant. These are:

(i)   a manual system;

(ii)   a system which is a mixture of manual and computerised parts;

(iii) a fully computerised system.

⬤ MANUAL SYSTEM

A manual system relies totally on paper filing systems. Records are kept on paper, which is put into folders and kept in filing cabinets. People who have this type of system probably use some sort of card index system to keep track of where everything is kept.

⬤ MIXTURE OF SYSTEMS

A system, which is part manual and part computerised, uses both paper and computerised records. A company might keep invoices and correspondence on paper but may have other aspects like payroll done in a computerised format. W&W Steelstock have a system like this. They have a computer but perhaps do not use it to its full potential. For example, when they sell some steel the person who has made the sale writes down the details on an invoice form using information on prices kept in a card index system (see

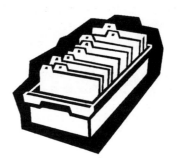

above) and a calculator to work out the price. This is then passed to an office junior who uses a typewriter to type the details of the sale. One copy is sent to the customer and the other is given to the person who is responsible for keeping details of accounts. They then key the information into the computer and these details are stored on a database. Other aspects of the business are dealt with in a similar fashion.

COMPUTERISED SYSTEM

A computerised system is one where all parts of the business are computerised. Payroll, stock control, invoices, employee and customer records and correspondence are all done using the computer.

Problems which may be faced by companies
Whichever system is being used there may, however, be problems.

A manual system will be difficult to organise because it is difficult to find information quickly. In order to find a particular customer record somebody in the office will need to find information from the card index system before looking in the correct drawer of a filing cabinet.

A mixed system will be frustrating to use. Imagine how annoying it would be if the customer records were on paper and employee records were on the computer. You would soon discover that to find the record of one of the workers would be very much quicker than trying to find a particular customer record.

With a computerised system the problems may be different. It is very easy to get used to the fact that everything seems to be quicker using this type of system. After a while, however, this type of system may seem to be fairly slow, which could be because the software or the hardware or both are old. It may be more economical to replace the whole system with a new system rather than try and upgrade the existing system. Another problem could be that although all the different parts of the business are computerised they might not be linked together.

Whichever type of system is currently in use, it is very likely that the users are still quite happy with it. It has probably evolved to match their needs over the years and they will be used to it. What usually happens is that a business has grown or it now does different things from those it used to. The system, which the users are currently using, is no longer capable of coping with this expansion or change of business.

User requirements
The most important feature of any information system is that it must meet the needs of the people who will be using it. The Systems Consultant needs to talk to these people and find out what they require. Most organisations that need new information systems already have ways of working which have developed over the years. It will be essential when talking to the users to find out exactly what jobs the employees have to do and how they do them. There must be problems and shortcomings with the existing system

otherwise there would not be a need for a new system. It is important to discover what these problems are. When a new information system is developed its success depends on involving the users of the existing system. Even the cleverest Systems Consultants, designers and programmers on their own cannot design a successful system without involving the people **who will be using the system**. Although all the workers within a company will, to a certain degree, be users of the system, it is the management who will be involved at most stages in the development of the new system. In our example the management are Winifred and Keith. They will be interviewed so that their requirements are identified. It will be their job to test various parts of the new system. They will be asked for their views on the new system. When the new system is put in place they will be trained to use it and they will then become the users of the system. Before all this happens, information has to be collected from them and the other workers. Fortunately, there are many methods for doing this.

Identifying and using methods of collecting information

Methods for collecting information (fact finding) have been discussed initially in Section B. These are Interviewing, Observation and Questionnaires. Using these different methods it is almost certain that you will collect sample documents that are already in use.

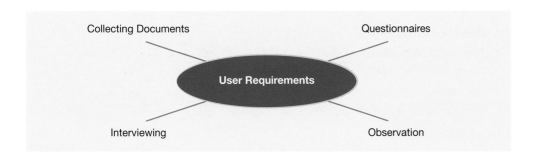

Interviewing

This is the most common method of fact finding used by Systems Consultants. In order to make sure that interviews will produce accurate and useful information several things need to be considered. The first is to identify who will be interviewed and when.

Systems Consultants have to put a great deal of planning into the questions they are going to ask. They have to write them down and use them like a script. They might leave spaces after the questions to make notes about the answers they receive. After the interview they need to write up the results of the interview into a report.

Observation

Watching people doing their normal day-to-day work can often be better than interviewing them formally. Because the workers are relaxed they may provide the analysts with more relevant information. The analysts might see some unusual situations or problems that the worker may forget to mention in an interview. Watching people also gives a clear idea of what documents people need to use. It also becomes very clear how efficient the system is.

There are a number of questions which can be answered as a result of observation. Do people have to get up out of their seat to get the documents they need? Do they have to wait for documents to arrive at their desks? The time taken to complete a task can be accurately recorded, rather than relying on people's memories. Where a task may involve a number of different people, observation gives a broader view of the system

The most important feature of any information system is that it must meet the needs of the people who will be using it. It is important to be accurate in establishing use requirements.

than relying on each individual's description of their role in the process. For example, the W&W system for dealing with invoices (outlined above under the heading 'mixture of systems') involved three different people. All three would have to be interviewed to identify this problem. Each person would describe their particular role. This would take a long time. The reports from all three interviews would have to be examined carefully in order to understand the system, which again would take a lot of time. Observation would allow the Systems Consultant to see all three people dealing with their part in the invoice process. This would make it easier to understand the whole process and the Systems Consultant's job would be done a lot more quickly.

Collecting documents

During the course of the observations and interviews Systems Consultants collect blank and completed documents. These will help in working out the inputs, the processing and the outputs of the system. They then carry out analysis of the documents. This will help to identify the amount of data on different documents as well as how much data there is in total. The Systems Consultant will work out the volume of data going into and out of the system. This will prove very helpful when the type and size of storage media is being decided upon. The number of lines of data on a document and the number of documents are used to calculate how much data there is. In our example the Systems Consultant would collect documents such as invoices, examples of customer records, examples of employee records and so on.

ADVANTAGES

- They can be used to accurately calculate the amount of data in the system.
- The rate at which errors are made can be calculated.
- The nature of the input data can be easily identified.
- The nature of the outputs can be easily identified.

DISADVANTAGES

- It is difficult to see how long the current process takes.
- It is difficult to work out who is responsible for doing what when you are just looking at pieces of paper.

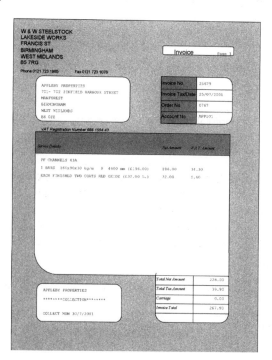

Questionnaires

This is a form of interview where the questions are written on a form. Members of the workforce answer these questions and their answers are analysed. A great deal of planning has to go into the creation of a questionnaire.

1. Questions can be framed so that they are open-ended. This means that the person filling in the questionnaire can write a sentence or two in answer to the question. A typical question might be:

   What outputs would you require from the system?

2. Questions can be multi-choice. This means that the analyst has tried to predict the answers which people might come up with. They have to choose from a list of possible answers. The previous question, if it was used with the W&W Steelstock office staff might have been set out as:

   Which of the following outputs do you require?
   a) invoices;
   b) re-order forms;
   c) warnings when stock is running low;
   d) standard letters to customers;
   e) standard letters to employees;
   f) standard letters to suppliers;
   g) balance sheets;
   h) payslip information.

   The users would tick some or all of these.

3. Questions can be asked so that the people filling in the questionnaire have to put their answers in order. This is virtually the same as multi choice. The only difference is that instead of ticking their choices they put them in order of preference i.e. 1 is the most important, 2 for the next important and so on.

4. Other types are yes/no questions. For example:

   Do you use a computer for any current aspect of your business?

   Yes ☐   No ☐

Questionnaires are most useful where the views of a large number of people have to be obtained.

Whereas it would take a lot of time to organise and then interview a large number of people, it would not be as time consuming or difficult to organise the distribution and collection of a large number of questionnaires. Another situation where it would be difficult to interview people is when they are so busy that they cannot spare the time. The use of questionnaires would be a better way of getting information from employees as it would be where people do not all work in the same office or even in the same building.

ADVANTAGES

- It is a relatively quick way of collecting information from members of an organisation.
- Responses can usually be analysed easily by computer.

- Some workers, though by no means all, find it easier to give answers which are accurate and honest as they feel no pressure due to personal contact with the interviewer.

DISADVANTAGES

- Good questionnaires are very difficult to construct. Systems Consultants have to know exactly what information they want so that they can ask the right questions.
- The answers cannot be examined in more detail by asking another question as can be done in an interview.

W&W Steelstock only have 13 employees and so interviewing is a possibility as a method of collecting information. The Systems Consultant would need to produce scripts for interviews. There would need to be a fairly fixed set of questions asked of the workers but there would need to be a degree of flexibility built in to the interview. This would be so that the different requirements of each person (in terms of what they would need from an information system) could be taken into account.

Three of the workers are involved in driving lorries, delivering the steel to customers, so it would be difficult to organise interviews for them. As they work mainly off site, it would be unlikely that they would be interviewed. A questionnaire might be more appropriate for them.

For most of the workers it will be possible to observe them at work, seeing what situations arise. The office staff will be observed to determine how information is put into the existing system. This observation will also show how the information is dealt with or processed. The manual workers will be observed to see what instructions they receive and in what form they receive them.

Fact finding can be carried out using, Interviews, Questionnaires and Observation. It is also important to collect sample documents currently in use.

Analysing the collected information

Having collected a great deal of information, Systems Consultants are able to clearly identify the problems, which exist with the current way of doing things. The way this is done is to analyse the results of all the activities which they have carried out such as observation, interviews, collecting documents and so on. Using the W&W Steelstock example, a Systems Consultant would soon realise when reading the interview notes, the observation notes and looking at an invoice, that the current way of dealing with invoices is not satisfactory. The result of looking at all the problems, which have been identified this way, is to produce a **system requirements specification**. This will include recommendations/requirements for specific hardware and software as well as ways of using them. The whole point of the Analysis stage in the Systems Design cycle is to look at the results of your research to decide exactly what sort of system you have to produce.

Writing up the system requirements specification

The final part of the Analysis phase is the writing up of a report, which will contain recommendations. They are often called the user requirements because the needs of the user have been identified. The typical contents of a systems requirements specification are:

- the type of information which needs to be produced from the new system;
- the type of hardware which should be considered;
- the type of software to be considered;
- the type of user interface;
- whether or not on-line help will need to be available;
- the type and helpfulness of error messages.

This report will need to contain all the recommendations in a straightforward style with a minimum of technical jargon. It will need to be to the point and easy to understand, if the users are to agree to the recommendations.

Design

The next phase of the systems lifecycle is *Design*. This is when the solutions to all the identified problems begin to take shape. There are many aspects within the design phase. During the design stage the Systems Consultant will decide what sort of system should be developed.

Specifying hardware and software

After all the existing data and its uses have been analysed the next stage is to decide what hardware and software are needed. The Systems Consultant will have already identified the hardware and software (if any), which is already being used by the organisation. The Systems Consultant will calculate how long this equipment is likely to last, given the recommendations stated in the system requirements specification. The consultant will also need to identify a supplier based on their reliability and the hardware and software support they can offer. The amount and level of training they can provide will also influence this decision. The software recommended may well be the existing software, which will then be adapted to the users needs. This is more than likely to be the case with W&W Steelstock because of their small size. Big organisations would probably require the software to be especially written for them.

The next thing that Systems Consultants have to do is to actually design the information system. They will need to design:

- the outputs from the system;
- the files and/or databases needed to store the data;
- the inputs to the system;
- any validation checks which will be needed;
- the processing required to produce the outputs;
- the data needed to test the system.

Design of outputs

When Systems Consultants start to design the outputs from the system they have to consider:

1. Layout:
   The way the output is set out is important. This could be in the form of:
   - tables
   - lists
   - single records from a database
   - graphs
2. Form:
   The way the output is produced has to be taken into consideration. This could be:
   - hard copy (on paper)
   - a screen display
   - sound output.

When Systems Consultants design the output they have to have the user firmly in mind. What the user wants in terms of style and layout must be taken into consideration.

> **When problems** have been identified and use requirements have been established a system requirements specification I produced. This forms the basis for the design specification created in the next phase – Design.

> **An important** part of the design stage is specifying the hardware and software needed to meet the requirements.

The Systems Consultant will decide on what outputs are required having looked at documents and examined the results of the interviews which have taken place.

The style will have also been decided upon using the same methods.

When designing invoices, for example, the Systems Consultant will give careful thought to who will need to see them. The style and content of the invoice will have to match the needs of the user.

Systems Consultants have to take many points into consideration when designing outputs.

When designing printed output, for example, they must take style of output into consideration. Some of the output will go to customers or clients. The right impression must be given to these people so style of output becomes very important. It is important to involve the user in the design phase. Some examples of output can be produced and the user can comment on its suitability. In addition it is important to make the design of the output flexible. In other words, the user should be able to adapt the printed output to suit their needs.

Screen output must be kept simple

The results of the output must be clear to the user and not cluttered up with irrelevant material.

Screen output should have a consistent layout so that it is easy to use (see page 128). On screen instructions should be designed in order to help the user move from one screen to another or back to previous screens. There are many different types of screen output such as: individual record printout, output in the form of tables, output in the form of graphs. The screen needs to be designed taking into account the purpose of the output and the needs of the user.

At this point the Systems Consultant will choose the output devices which will be required. The type of monitors and printers will need to be identified. These will be dependent on the type and form of output to be displayed. High volume output will obviously require a printer that can cope with this. In our example the volume of output will not be too great and so a fairly basic laser printer would probably be sufficient, as it would provide the quality of presentation required.

Design of files

Another part of the design process for our example is to design the database and the file or files within it. The volume of data, and therefore the number of records, will have already been worked out. The next stage will be to decide on the number of fields and the names of each of these fields. Each field will have a name and a description. As well as this the analyst will need to decide on the type of data it will contain. Decisions will need to be made on whether the type of data is alphanumeric (i.e. a text field, able to contain any type of character), an integer (a whole number), a decimal number, a yes/no piece of data, a date etc. The size of each field will also have to be decided. For a text field this means deciding how long each field will be. For a numeric field it means deciding the range of values the field could hold. If the field contains decimal numbers the format will have to be given i.e. how many decimal places. If the field is numeric the units used will need to be decided upon e.g. £ for currency, metres for distance, hours for time etc. The medium to be used to store the file will also be a decided by the consultant. The choice will be from floppy disks, hard disks, magnetic tapes and optical disks.

> Designing inputs, outputs and how the data is to be stored are three important aspects of design.

Minimising data entry errors

One other aspect of design is to ensure that the data entered into the database is sensible. To achieve this the database structure must include the design of validation routines.

One way of minimising data entry errors can be achieved in some fields by the use of effective coding. Where data is shortened this reduces the number of errors. The use of the single character 'F' in a GENDER field will result in fewer errors than if the person typing in the data had to type in 'Female' every time. The advantage of using coding is that simpler validation checks can be used. An appropriate method of data entry has to be chosen. This can result in fewer data entry errors. Direct data entry methods such as bar-code reading and optical mark reading cause far fewer errors than manual typing.

Where possible there should be a validation check on data being entered into each field. For numeric fields it is usual to have a range check. Using our example it would be highly unusual for a customer to order more than £20 000 worth of steel. A check could be put on the COST field to make sure it was not more than 20 000. For some text fields it is possible to have length checks. The Order Number has 4 figures and cannot be more or less than this. There are other validation checks which can be used such as invalid character checks (no letters in the Order Number) and existence checks (customer name).

Let us look at the simple problem that W&W were having with their recording of invoices. The Systems Consultant will need to design a database structure for this part of the system. This database could be called the Order file.

Some method of uniquely identifying the customer would be one field. The name of the customer would be another. Their address, phone number and fax number would be needed to contact them. The cost of the order, the VAT charged and what was ordered would have to be included. The invoice number would be included as would the date of the invoice, and the order number.

The details of the order, the customer's name and address would be text fields and no validation checks would be placed on these.

The Customer reference would be a six character text field. A validation check which could be used would be a length check to make sure it was no more or less than 6 characters long. Another check could be a format check which would check that the first 3 characters were letters of the alphabet and the other three were digits.

A length check could be used with the phone and fax numbers as they must be either 11 or 12 digits.

The cost field would be numeric with 2 decimal places as would the VAT field. The maximum value of the cost is set at £99999.99 because the company never have orders greater than this amount.

The invoice number is a 5 figure number but would be designed as a text field. A length check could be used on this.

The date of the invoice would be a date field.

The order number is a 4 digit number but would be a text field. A length check could be used to ensure that 4 digits were entered.

All this information could be set out in a table like this:

> **Specifying** the validation checks required is part of the design process and is often considered when the data structure (possibly a file or database) is designed.

Field name	Field description	Data type	Length or maximum value	Units	Validation Check
Account Number	Reference number of each customer	Alphanumeric	8 characters		length <8 OR length >8
Customer name	Name of the customer	Alphanumeric	20 characters		
Invoice number	Number of the invoice	Alphanumeric	5 characters		length <5 OR length >5
Invoice Date	Date of the invoice	Date	Maximum value = today's date		
Order Number	Number of the order	Alphanumeric	4 characters		length <4 OR length >4
Description of order	The details of the order in terms of amount and type of steel ordered	Alphanumeric	50 characters		
Cost	The price which the customer is being charged	Fixed point, decimal or currency	99999.99	£ before the value	Value >= £100 000
VAT	Value Added Tax on the order	Fixed point, decimal or currency	99999.99	£ before the value	Value >= £17 500
Address	The address to which the invoices should be sent	Alphanumeric	40 characters		
Phone	The phone number of the customer	Alphanumeric	12 characters		length <11 OR length >12
Fax	The fax number of the customer	Alphanumeric	12 characters		Length <11 OR length >12

Design of data capture forms and input screen layouts

Whether a form or an input screen is being designed several factors need to be taken into consideration. The layout must make it easy to use. The layout will have to be attractive and it must ensure accurate entry of data. The layout must be simple. Complicated layouts with many colours and font styles will only confuse the user, possibly leading to inaccurate data entry.

Data capture forms must be easy to fill in by the user and easily read afterwards. The use of boxes for each character of input will help to make sure that there are fewer errors when typing in the data. There needs to be a clear layout. In other words headings for each section of the form should help the user identify these different sections. The Systems Consultant will need to design the form so that there are instructions provided with, or on, the form. This will help the user to know how to fill it in.

Screen designs must:

- be kept simple and consistent from one screen to the next;
- have clear prompts on the screen should be provided on how to complete the form;
- allow the user to move from one screen to the next fairly easily;
- provide opportunities for editing the input.

Screen displays allow the use of a variety of different icons and buttons. The consultant, when designing these, should ensure that these are not overused. Too many icons and buttons could confuse the user leading to inaccurate data entry.

Data capture forms must:

- be easy to fill in by the user;
- ensure accurate data entry. The use of boxes for each character of input helps with this;
- have a clear layout. For example, headings for each section of the form should help the user identify these different sections;
- have instructions provided with, or on, the form. These should make it clear to the user how the form is to be completed.

Input devices will also be chosen when considering input layouts. For example in our example system for stocktaking it might be decided that each piece of metal in stock has a bar code. This would therefore require software and hardware capable of reading barcodes. It may be that all input will be dealt with using keyboards. All decisions regarding the type of input devices will be taken at this stage.

Design of overall processing

The Systems Consultant will now have to produce some diagrams to give an overall view of how the system will operate and what processing will take place.

Using the above example, the new system will involve the person taking the order for steel typing in the details onto a screen. The bill will be calculated and the details will be stored and copies of the invoice will be printed. One copy will go to the customer, one will go to the person who will deliver the steel and another copy will go to sales person.

A simple flow diagram showing this would be:

Existing Order file loaded
↓
Input screen loaded
↓
New order typed in
↓
Bill calculated
↓
New record added to Order file
↓
Invoices printed

Designing the computer processing is sometimes as simple as deciding the order of tasks.

There are many different types of diagrams used by Systems Consultants to show the processing involved in any part of the system. The processing involved in all parts of the new system would need to be described using diagrams.

This design process will produce the final *design*, which it is then possible to put onto the computer. Putting the design onto the computer is known as the 'Development' stage. This is when we are using the hardware and software to develop our final system.

It is also important during the design or development stage to draw up a test plan, which can be used during the development of the system to test whether the computer processes work. One possible framework for a test plan is shown below:

CUSTOMER RECORD:

Purpose of test	Test data	Expected Outcome	Actual outcome
To check the Customer No. is valid	Invalid Cust No. = 3456 Valid Cust No. = 133	Error message for 3456 Cust 133 added	{left blank for later test}

The first column identifies the purpose of the test. The second column identifies the set of test data with the expected outcomes for each data item listed in column three. The last column is left blank for details of what happens during development and testing later on.

During development and testing any amendments necessary are noted and details of any evidence shown in printed outputs can be entered in this final column, so it is important to leave plenty of space for later comments.

The first thing the Systems Consultant will have to do is to create the file structure. All the fields will be defined for each file. In our example, there will be separate files for the customer records, orders, payroll and employee records.

If we just look at the Order file we can see that each field will need to be defined. The structure as given in the design section will be used.

- Systems Consultants will give each field a name.
- They will define the type of data for each field. Most of the fields on the Order file are text. The only exceptions are the Invoice date field and the cost and VAT fields.
- They will type in the length of each field if it is text or the maximum value expected if the field is a numeric field.
- If the field is numeric the units need to be given i.e. a £ sign if it is an amount of money.
- They will type in the validation rules which each field will use.
- They will type in a description of each field.

The next step will be to create the output formats. These, again, will be based on those produced for the design section.

An example report is shown here.

The final part of the development of the system will be the creation of the input screens.

Again the Systems Consultant will create these screens and they will be based on the designs already produced. An example of an input screen is shown on page 221.

> **Before the development work begins it is a good idea to decide on how to test the system. This could be a general strategy but often a more detailed test plan is written up, specifying the expected outcome for each test purpose. Sometimes the test plan is developed during the development of the system.**

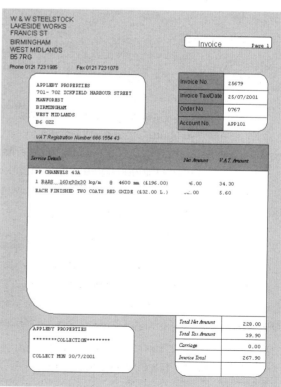

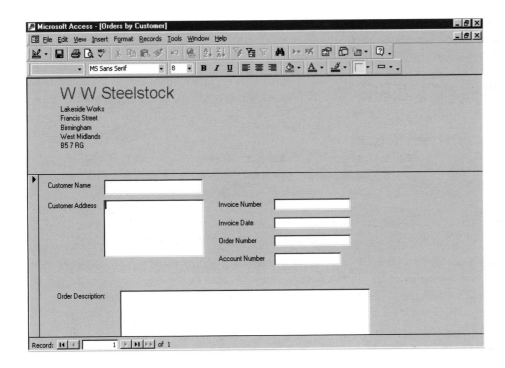

Testing

During the development of the information system there is a certain amount of testing as the system develops. There will also be some involvement of the users of the system. However, before the users test the system, the Systems Consultant will have to test it. Each part of the system is tested using specially selected test data. Putting data into the system, which tests the validation rules will test the file structure.

For example at W&W:

- Seven and nine character Account numbers will be entered. This should produce an error message that there are not enough or there are too many characters. However, most software packages will not allow you to type in more characters than the length of the field.
- Four and six figure Invoice numbers will try to be entered. Again this should produce an error message warning the user that this data is invalid.
- Three and five figure Order numbers will try to be entered.
- Costs greater than £100 000 will try to be entered.
- A ten figure and a thirteen figure phone number will be entered.
- A ten figure and a thirteen figure fax number will be entered.

Performing searches on the files will also test the database system.

The Systems Consultant will perform various searches:

- The addresses of a range of companies by typing in their names.
- The names of a range of companies by typing in their account number.
- The value of a certain order by typing in the order number.

This is just a small selection of tests which the Systems Consultant could carry out.

The Systems Consultant will test that the input forms and outputs work correctly. Getting the users to test these aspects of the system is a good way of doing this. As a result, they will comment on the ease of use of the system.

Finally the whole system should be tested with real data. This means that data that has been used in the old system should be used on the new system. In all these examples, the expected results will have been recorded and these will be compared with the actual results.

When the new system has been developed and tested, the next stage of the project is to implement the new system.

Implementation

As we saw in Chapter 9 suddenly moving over to a new system using the method of *direct changeover* can cause major disruption in a company. There are three main methods used to try to ease this problem.

Parallel running

This is when the new system is run together with the old system. The same data will be input to both systems. There then follows a detailed comparison of the outputs produced by each system. This is done to make sure that the new system is working properly. If there are any errors being produced by the new system the new system will have to be modified. The major advantage of this system is that all faults with the new system can be ironed out with no effect on overall performance of the business. The main disadvantage with this system is that twice as much work has to be done by the same number of workers. This delays the date at which the new system can finally replace the old system.

Phased implementation

This is where the new system gradually replaces the old system. First of all one part of the old system is replaced and when that is working properly the next part is replaced and so on. This approach has two advantages. Any initial problems with the new system can be sorted out and there is less likelihood of disruption to the business if things start to go wrong. The major disadvantage with this method is that it may take too long before the new system is fully in place.

Direct changeover

A third method is less widely used and is called the direct changeover approach. This is when the old system is discarded and the new system is introduced overnight. This is the least popular method. It is obviously the fastest way to introduce the new system. There are big risks involved, however, since once the old system has gone it cannot be brought back. It can only be successful if extensive testing has been carried out beforehand. Users must be able to adapt because the old system will no longer be available.

Monitoring and maintenance

It is a good idea to monitor the system by checking to see that it is still working well. It is likely that problems with a new system may not show themselves in the early days. This can be because parts of the system such as payroll may only be needed every month. It may well be that problems are only seen at this point. The other possibility is that the users get used to the system and start to adapt it to suit themselves. They may not realise it at the time but they may be adapting it in a way, which was never intended by the developer of the system. It is a good idea to get the developer of the system to come back and look at the system to check on any problems, which may have developed. Any errors or bugs, which are found in the system, have to be removed or corrected. This means that the system is constantly being maintained. Other reasons for maintenance could be changes which have occurred outside the control of the Systems Consultant. Such an example was the year 2000 bug. Systems had to be changed all over the world to cope with this problem. The need for constant monitoring and maintenance of a system was highlighted by this problem. As new hardware and versions of software (eg Windows 2000) become available the system will need to be upgraded.

Testing is carried out by the systems consultant and by users.

Monitoring and maintenance is necessary to prolong the life cycle of the system.

Documentation

Documentation comes in two main forms. Both are meant to be guides to how the system works. Both are meant to help the reader to understand the workings of the system. One is called User Documentation and is written for users and is designed to help them operate the system. The other is Technical Documentation and is written for people who are either maintaining the system or are going to develop the system. Both will contain information about the purpose of the system and the limitations of the system but from a different point of view.

User documentation

This documentation is produced to help a user of the system. It does not go into the technical details of the system. It is a guide showing how to use the various aspects of the system. It will show you how to:

- Log on to the system.
- Load the software.
- Save any changes to files you might make or new files which have been created.
- Get printouts from the system.
- Enter data into the system.
- Edit data.
- Search the database.
- Sort the database.
- Produce graphs.

There will be a troubleshooting guide on how to avoid errors and what to do if any are encountered.

Technical documentation

This is used for those systems for which the Systems Consultant has either written new software or has adapted existing software.. It is essential for the maintenance and development of the system when the Systems Consultant cannot be reached. Technical Documentation is designed to help a technical expert who may be called in to fix a known problem or asked to develop the system. It is necessary at all stages of the systems design cycle. However, documentation of the final system can also help with the training of people to use the system. One of the problems with most systems is that not enough systems or Technical Documentation is produced. This is mainly because there is generally no additional payment to the Systems Consultant for documenting the system. Systems are constantly changing but, in the meantime, the Systems Consultant has moved on to another project so there is nobody available to update the documentation.

For small systems this will contain very detailed information on **how** the input forms, file structures, output forms were created.

Evaluation

This normally takes the form of a written report to the management of the organisation. There will be a description of the purpose of the system and the limitations of the system from a user's point of view. There will be a description of the hardware and software being used. Evidence that the system works, as it was required to do by the management, will be provided.

The evaluation will be based on the results of the testing carried out by the Systems Consultant. In addition, users will be given questionnaires to complete. The Systems Consultant, in his final report, will use their responses. Evaluation is a comparison of the final system, which has been produced, with the list of user's requirements as outlined at the beginning of the project.

Project 2

For this part of the coursework you will use a computer to solve a problem. First you will identify a problem. This must involve an existing system which people are using at the moment.

A system is a way of doing things. A system is any method where information comes in to an organisation (Input). This information is processed and then new information comes out of it (Output). A simple form of system is one you might use to find somebody's phone number. Someone has asked you for a friend's phone number. The information going into the system is the name of the person whose phone number you want, let us say it is somebody called 'Sandhu'. You search through the pages in your address book until you find the one with the Surnames beginning with the letter S. You look down the page until you find Sandhu. You then write down the number on a piece of paper and give it to the person who asked for it.

To sum up:

- the input is the person's name.
- The processing is the searching through the address book.
- The output is the person's phone number.

The system you will be looking at will be much bigger than this and will involve lots of inputs, different types of processing and lots of outputs. It will also involve a lot of people using the system.

The existing system you have identified will be one which is not working as well as it might. Then you will provide a solution to this problem. This will consist of a computer system, which will take the place of the system in current use. These types of systems are often referred to as information technology systems. Whilst you are producing your solution you will need to write descriptions of what you have done. You will use various headings:

- Analysis
- Design
- Implementation (putting your design onto the computer – sometimes called development)
- Testing
- Documentation
- Evaluation.

Each section is divided into further sub-sections each one worth a number of marks. These are made up of 1, 2, 3 or 4 marks. The way that it works is that if you do a certain amount of work you get 1 mark, if you add some more to it you get 2 marks. For those sub sections where 3 marks are available you have to add a little more and describe possible alternatives to the way you have done things. Where there is 4 marks, as a rule, you have to give reasons why you used the method you did and why you didn't use the alternatives. You always have to build on what you have done for 1 mark to get 2 marks. It is never the case that you have to do something totally different to get the next mark up. In other words, when you are doing your project you must look at what is required for 1 mark before you start. You cannot miss out any steps in your work.

As this piece of work has to be a realistic problem that requires an information technology system to be produced, you should try and choose a problem of your own. Many students choose clothes shops, computer games shops, sports shops etc. It stands to reason that if you choose a problem related to something that you are interested in, you will tend to work harder to produce a solution. If you find it difficult to choose a problem your teacher will give you a list of problems you can choose from. You will need to include this list of problems in your write up.

Work experience

Many students find that the best way of selecting a problem is to use their own experience of work. If you go on work experience, it is a good idea to look at the company or business and see what aspects of the work could be computerised. It may be that they already use a computer. You could perhaps identify aspects of the work, which they don't use a computer for and see if these could be computerised. An alternative might be to try and improve the existing system, if you think you can.

Using your own experience of work as a basis for Project 2 is good for several reasons.

- You will have several opportunities to talk to the owner, manager or supervisor.
- You will be able to examine the current system quite closely because you will actually be using it.
- You will be able to collect paperwork which will help you in the analysis of the problem.

What type of problem?

One of the Project 2 example tasks in the OCR syllabus is:

Devise a system, which would help the owner of a video rental shop to organise his business. There are several aspects to the business, which he needs help with.

- A record of all the videos has to be kept so that if a customer comes in and make enquiries about a specific video, shop assistants can immediately inform them whether they have it in the shop at that time.
- A record of customers has to be kept with the videos they have on hire so that overdue notices can be sent if required.
- The various pricing strategies have to be calculated so that special offers such as 'hire three get one free' and others can be applied.
- Letters can be sent to customers if a new film, which matches their particular preferences, comes into the shop.

Choose one or more of these aspects of the business when devising your solution. In order to gain high marks, at least two aspects of the business will need to be considered.

Your solution should include these aspects:

- Interviews with possible users of such a system.
- Documents and forms in use in the current system.
- Identification of the inputs, outputs and processing currently employed.

- Designs of the structure of databases/spreadsheets/word processing documents required.
- Design of the input screens and the output documents/screens of the new computerised system.
- Documentation of how the databases/spreadsheets/word processing documents and how the associated input screens and output documents/screens were created.
- The combination of the outputs from one piece of software into another.
- Evidence of testing.
- A User Guide showing how to use the new system.
- An evaluation of the final system compared with their original design.

You would be well advised to cover all the above aspects of the business. This will put you in an excellent position to get high marks for your work.

Below are the marks available together with an explanation of what you have to do to meet each requirement.

Remember, you have to meet the requirements for the mark above before you can get the next mark. This applies to every section.

Analysis – 12 marks

Identify a problem – 4 marks

- Provide evidence that you have identified a problem by writing a description of it. (If you are trying to produce an information system to solve the video shop problem, you have to show that other problems have been considered. The best way to do this is to include in your work, a list of problems set by your teacher and an indication of your choice.)
- Make a list of the problems, which might be being faced by the user of the current system. You might want to wait at this stage until you have spoken to the owner or manager of such a shop.
  For example, items on the list might be:
  - It is difficult to say whether a certain video is available or not.
  - It is difficult to find out what each borrower likes in the way of videos, etc.

If you get this far you will get 1 mark out of 4

- List the requirements of the user of the current system.
  For example, write down that the user needs a system.
  - Easily find out if a particular video is available.
  - Send out letters to borrowers if their videos are overdue etc.

If you get this far you will get 2 marks out of 4

- Add some detail to each item on the list of problems being faced by the user of the current system.
  Write about items on the list like this:
  - It is difficult to say whether a certain video is available or not. The reason being that the information is kept in folders in filing cabinets which are not kept in any particular order.

- It is difficult to find out what each borrower likes in the way of videos as it takes so long to write down their favourite types of film, their favourite actors or directors.

  etc.

- Describe the user's requirements.

  Now you have to add some detail to the list of the owner's requirements.

  For example, the owner needs a system which lets him easily find out if a particular video is available. When customers make enquiries about availability the owner will need to be able to give details such as type of film, actors in it, length of film, director, price etc., if it is in stock.

  If you get this far you will get 3 marks out of 4

- Write down at least two aspects of the problem. (These need to show that you are going to have to use at least two different types of software from Databases, Spreadsheets, Communicating software (i.e. word processors /DTP etc.), Measuring software and Control.)

If you write down all the aspects of the above problem you will be solving a complex problem. This is because:

Aspect 1 requires a record of all the videos to be kept so that if a customer comes in and make enquiries about a specific video, shop assistants can immediately inform them whether they have it in the shop at that time. This needs the use of a database.

Aspect 2 requires a record of customers to be kept with the videos they have on hire so that overdue notices can be sent if required. This requires the use of a database.

Aspect 3 – The various pricing strategies have to be calculated so that special offers such as 'hire three get one free' and others can be applied. This requires the use of a spreadsheet.

Aspect 4 – Letters can be sent to customers if a new film, which matches their particular preferences, comes into the shop. This requires the use of a word processor.

Describe the problems as you did for 3 marks. In addition you need to make sure that you have done this for **all** aspects of the problem.

If you get this far you will get 4 marks out of 4

Use methods of collecting information – 4 marks

- Provide evidence that you have used a method of collecting information from people who could use your system.

  (This might be to go and speak to the owner or manager of a video shop and ask them about the system they use. You will need to be well prepared. You will need to make an appointment to see the owner or manager. Don't just turn up! You will need to make a list of questions that you want to ask them. You will want to ask about how they currently store information about videos and customers. What information do they store about them? How do they contact customers? How do they add new information to their system? etc. The information you collect must relate to the current method used for dealing with aspects of the problem.)

- Include with your work one or all of the following:
  - transcripts of interviews;
  - completed questionnaires;
  - documents currently being used by the owner/manager.

    For a variety of reasons, it might be difficult to actually visit a shop. Another method might be to write letters to different shops. Again you must plan your letter so that you get the information that you need. You will start off by describing yourself and explaining why you need the information. You will ask for information about the shop and how they deal with specific problems. You will want to include questionnaires which you will ask the manager/owner/supervisor and their staff to complete.

    If you get this far you will get 1 mark out of 4

- Describe how you obtained the information. (For example, if you have sent letters to video shops, you will need to provide a copy of the letter sent together with the details of the shops that replied. If you interviewed the owner, you will need to provide a list of the questions you asked together with the replies you received to the questions.)

    If you get this far you will get 2 marks out of 4

- Describe alternative methods of collecting information. (If you sent letters to shop owners, as well as describing this you could describe the use of questionnaires. You will describe how it is possible to visit shops to interview owners and obtain copies of paperwork in use by the shop.)

    If you get this far you will get 3 marks out of 4

- Write down the advantages and disadvantages of the method you used.
- Write down the good points and the bad points of the alternative methods.
- Explain why you chose the method that you used.

    For example one of the reasons you might give is to describe how you considered visiting a shop and interviewing the owner. Unfortunately, the owner could not spare you very much time when you had free time to speak to them. When they had time to spare you would be at school. You felt that there would be an advantage in using questionnaires to obtain information as you could leave them at the shop and the owner could contact you when they were completed.

- Make comparisons of your method with each alternative method.

    If you get this far you will get 4 marks out of 4

Identify the inputs, outputs and processing required – 4 marks

- Make a list of the inputs to the current system.

    These are just going to be a list of details that might be input to the system.
    Usually these will be customer requests.
    For example:
    A comedy film less than or equal to £2.00 rental.
    A horror film starring Christopher Lee.
    A film directed by Steven Spielberg for £1.50 (or less) rental.
    etc.

- Make a list of the outputs.

  These will be a list of details that will need to be found out from the system.

  For example:

  The titles, types and prices of comedy films with a rental less than or equal to £2.00.

  The titles, types and starring actors of horror films starring Christopher Lee.

  The titles, directors and prices of films directed by Steven Spielberg with a rental equal to or less than £1.50.

- Make a list of the processing requirements of the current system.

  For example:

  The owner needs to be able to search through the documents and match all those videos which are comedy films. He then needs to look through only those details and find all the videos, which have a rental less than £2.00. He then writes down the titles of these films together with the rental price of each matching film. You do this for some of the input/output situations you have listed.

  If you get this far you will get 1 mark out of 4

- Add some details to what you have done so far. (It might be easier if you link all three items together.)

  For example you might describe a situation where a customer comes into the shop and wants to hire a comedy film but does not want to pay more than £2. The owner then has to search through his records for comedy films. He then searches through all these comedy films for those which are £2 or less to hire. Having found all the videos which match these conditions, he writes down the prices, titles and types of these videos. You must now sum this up by saying that the input data was the price and type of the video. The processing was the searching for the matching type and price. The output is the title and price of the matching films.

- Include other situations like the need for letters to go to customers. Other situations will involve the need for the calculation of total prices of videos and discounts where appropriate.

  If you get this far you will get 2 marks out of 4

- List the software which you intend using.

  You may mention the need for a database to store and process the customer records and videos records. You may also need some spreadsheet software to handle the pricing aspect. The other piece of software, which you may need, is a word processor to deal with the letters to customers. At this stage you will not need to state which particular software you intend using i.e. the brand names.

- List the hardware required for the solution. This will need to be written down in terms of:

  Type of processor.

  Internal memory (RAM).

  Hard disk capacity in gigabytes.

  Type of printer etc.

  If you get this far you will get 3 marks out of 4

- Compare the specification you have chosen with an alternative.
- Give reasons why your choice would be more appropriate for the problem that you need to solve.

> For example, you may feel that there is a choice between using a single piece of software and separate pieces of software. You might want to explain the possible limitations of using integrated software – if one thing goes wrong the whole system will fail. If you use different pieces of software for each aspect, everything else will work even when one part fails. At this stage you are not suggesting specific brands of software such as Microsoft Access, Microsoft Works, Pinpoint etc. You are only talking in general terms about databases, spreadsheets, word processors etc. It may be that your hardware system will depend on the software you have chosen. That is to say it will have to be of a specification which will allow it to run the software.

If you get this far you will get 4 marks out of 4

Design – 12 marks

Produce designs for the data structure – 3 marks

- Produce a file structure for your database. (If you are attempting other aspects of the problem you could produce a design of a spreadsheet which includes the formulae you intend to use. If you are using a word processor you could design a template of the letter incorporating the variables which will be used.)

> e.g. A design for the video database would be the field names, field types and field lengths for each field on your database. The requirement is for you to produce an **appropriate** structure. This means that it must contain the fields you mentioned in your input and output lists in your Analysis section. It also means that the field lengths and types must be sensible. In other words 10 characters for a rating (PG, 12, 18, U etc.) of a film would not be considered appropriate.

If you get this far you will get 1 mark out of 3

- Produce alternative designs. You will write about each design so that somebody else looking at them will understand what they represent.

> e.g. You will need to produce structures, which have a different number of fields. You will need to produce structures which have got different field lengths or field types for the same fields. The word appropriate means that these must be reasonable alternatives. You cannot just invent a new structure for the sake of it.

If you get this far you will get 2 marks out of 3

- Write down a list of the advantages and disadvantages of each structure and give reasons why your choice is best.

> e.g. One of the reasons you might give is that originally you were going to have a field for 'year of release'. However, after thinking about it you decided that most customers would not pick a film just because it was released in a particular year.

If you get this far you will get 3 marks out of 3

Produce designs for the user interface – 3 marks

- Produce a design of a database data entry screen. (or a design of a spreadsheet data entry screen or a design of a database query screen etc.).

For example, you could produce a hand drawn sketch of the video database data entry screen. This would be a sketch of the layout of the screen. You would indicate the names of the fields and their sizes. You might highlight certain important fields by using different colours. In order for it to be appropriate it will need to contain the fields that you used for the design of your database structure. This is also true if you have concentrated on producing a user interface for the spreadsheet.

If you get this far you will get 1 mark out of 3

- Produce alternative designs.
- Write about each design, describing it and what it consists of.

For example you can produce different designs of input screens. The differences between the designs will be the:

- position of the fields;
- colour of the field labels or contents;
- size of the fields;

etc.

If you get this far you will get 2 marks out of 3

- Write about each of your screen designs. Say what is good and what is not so good about each one.
- Give reasons why your choice is best.

If you get this far you will get 3 marks out of 3

Produce a design for the output formats – 3 marks

- Draw by hand the layouts of suitable printouts or output screens.
- Show the layouts, in terms of the fields that you expect for different searches, the order of the fields and position of the fields. (Appropriate means that you should not design a layout which includes all the fields on the database. Design a layout including just those which are considered to be relevant to the search.)

For example, one of the searches on the video database might be to find out which customers were overdue with their videos. The design of the output format would be a list of the required field names. The field names needed might be the name, phone number, address of the customer, the name of the video, and when it was due back. You would design the output format so that the most important fields such as customer's name and phone number were highlighted. You need to do this for more than one search.

If you get this far you will get 1 mark out of 3

- Produce alternative designs.

The information you are going to print out or display on the screen can take several forms. You may want to have a specific layout which highlights the key data as above.

An alternative is to printout the data in table format with headings.

Another alternative is to produce a list of the data you want with field names and contents printed out in one column. Design at least two alternatives. You must not just produce the designs and leave it at that. You will need to write about them in some detail.

If you get this far you will get 2 marks out of 3

- Compare the alternative designs.
- Write down all the good points and bad points for each design.
- Explain which is the best design.

  Let us use the overdue videos as an example. You might have a design using a separate form for each overdue video with the customer's phone number highlighted. This might make it easier to contact the customer as you can see the phone number straight away. An argument against this might be that if there are lots of overdue videos and you might waste time going through separate pieces of paper rather than just looking at a table or list on one piece of paper.

  If you get this far you will get 3 marks out of 3

Produce software and hardware requirements – 3 marks

- List the software and hardware which you feel is essential for the solution of the problem.

  Your list of the hardware, software and operating system required for the solution may include the following:

  - Type of processor.
  - Minimum speed of processor.
  - Internal memory (RAM).
  - Operating system (Windows 95/98/2000/RISCOS 3.6 etc).
  - Hard disk capacity in gigabytes.
  - Type of printer (laser, desk jet etc.).
  - The database software which you have chosen.
  - The spreadsheet software.
  - The word processing software.
    etc.

  At this point you can be specific and mention brand names.

  If you get this far you will get 1 mark out of 3

- Suggest possible alternatives.

  This may be other types of computer and software available to you in school or at home. You must write down sensible alternatives and not just write down any old thing. Most schools have some very old equipment stored away somewhere. It would not be sensible to describe such a system as an alternative. You will need to write down about how there could be an alternative system to the one you have chosen.

  If you get this far you will get 2 marks out of 3

- Justify the system you have chosen.

  There are two ways of approaching this and it is essential you do both. One is to be negative about the system you have not chosen. You can make the point that the alternative system does not have sufficient memory to cope with your proposed database. This is because you intend storing lots of scanned images such as the front covers of each video. The second approach is to be positive about your alternative but that the good points about your choice outweigh the bad points. For example, you might say that your choice of software is not as good at producing graphs as the alternative. However, you do not think you will need to produce many graphs but you will want several different types of output format. You will go on to say that your chosen software allows you to do this whereas the alternative can be difficult to do this.

- Give reasons for both your choice of hardware and your choice of software.

If you get this far you will get 3 marks out of 3

Implementation/development – 14 marks

Implement your data structure – 4 marks

- Write two or three brief statements about how you created your solution. For the database part of your solution, you will write down how you:
  - Loaded the software.
  - Went to the part of the software which lets you create a new file.
  - Typed in the field names, data types and lengths.
  - Saved the format.
    etc.

If you get this far you will get 1 mark out of 4

- Make quite a detailed description of how you created your solution. (This means that somebody else reading your description should be able to produce the same database structure. This is easy enough to prove. You can get a friend to follow what you've written and see if they can produce the same structure.)

If you get this far you will get 2 marks out of 4

- Write about the changes made whilst creating your structure.

  Somewhere along the line you are likely to come across a problem you had not thought about. You will need to change the structure of your database so that it is now different to your design. It might be that your chosen software is not as easy to use as you first thought. It might be very difficult to produce a multi-choice field. In these circumstances you might feel it necessary to change the field type back to text. You must do this for more than one change.

If you get this far you will get 3 marks out of 4

- To get this extra mark write down the reasons for the changes you made.
- Write a simple explanation of why you made the changes.

If you get this far you will get 4 marks out of 4

Implement your input and output formats – 4 marks

- Write a few sentences about how you created your user interface and your output formats.

  Most packages now have the facility for you to move the field names and data around the screen. You can highlight your fields in different colours. Write briefly about how you have done this. Write a few words about how you created your output formats. For example you will write about how you went to the part of the software which allows you to do this. You will say how you moved the fields around the screen (input) or how you told the computer to print the appropriate fields out.

If you get this far you will get 1 mark out of 4

- Write in more detail about how you created the formats.

- Test your description out on a friend. See if they can produce the same input screens and printouts after reading it.

If you get this far you will get 2 marks out of 4

- Describe how you have made changes to your formats when compared to your designs. It might be that you have suddenly discovered that the input format which you designed does not all fit on to the screen. You may have to alter the number of fields present on the screen at any one time or change the sizes.

If you get this far you will get 3 marks out of 4

- Give reasons for the changes you have made. For example you may argue that to change the number of screens may be too complicated for the user to cope with. You might propose to reduce the size of the fields in terms of their font size etc. (not the actual length of the fields) in order to have to get them all on the screen together.

If you get this far you will get 4 marks out of 4

Use features of software appropriately – 4 marks

This part of the work does not actually have to be written about. It will be marked by your teacher according to how well you have used the software. Your teacher will mark the evidence you have provided for the previous two sections. In addition, your teacher will look at your testing and user documentation sections.

- Provide evidence that you have used one feature of your software appropriately. For example, in your Analysis section you will have outlined some of the searches which need to be performed. It would be appropriate to carry out one of these searches in your testing section.

If you have done this you will get 1 mark out of 4

- Show that you have used more than three features appropriately. (You will need to show that you have implemented your designs and carried out the searches mentioned in your analysis section.) The features which you would be expected to have used are features such as the use of forms, searches, reports and producing graphs etc.

If you have done this you will get 2 marks out of 4

- Show that you have used another software package.
- Provide evidence that you have used more than three features of that package as well. If you have used a spreadsheet you will be expected to provide evidence of using features such as:
  - the use of formulae (you will have done this by getting a printout of your spreadsheet containing formulae);
  - replication (you will do this by including it in your User Guide and explaining how it is done – appropriately);
  - automatic recalculation (you will do this by showing printouts of the spreadsheet before and after you have changed some variables),
  - functions available within the package such as AVE, SUM, COUNT etc. (again you will show this by printing out your spreadsheet containing formulae) and so on.

If you done this you will get 3 marks out of 4

- Give reasons for each feature used.

    This is the only mark in this section where you have to write something in addition to the rest of your work. Your use of the features of the software will be present in your Implementation, Testing and User documentation. In those sections you will need to say why you have chosen to use the features which you have used. This is fairly straightforward as you can choose to compare the methods with alternative ways of doing this.

    For example, There are two ways of searching a database. One package might let you create a query which can be saved. The alternative might only allow you to search the database without saving your search conditions. With the first method, if you lose your printout of the results, you will still be able to get another copy without having to type in the search conditions all over again.

    You will need to give reasons for at least two features used.

    If you do this you will get 4 marks out of 4

Combine software features – 2 marks

As with the previous section, this part of your work will be in evidence in other sections of your documentation. You will be awarded this mark if you have moved data from one package and the purpose is appropriate.

For example, you may want to knock 10% off the prices of videos. The prices may be stored in a database and you may want to move them to a spreadsheet to do the calculation.

If you do this you will get 1 mark out of 2

You will be awarded 2 marks if you have moved data from one package to another on two occasions. This needs to be done for two different purposes. You may have moved data from a database to a spreadsheet for the purpose outlined above. In addition you may well have to produce a standard letter to customers who have overdue videos. The details of the video and the customer will be imported from the customer database to the word-processed standard letter.

If you do this you will get 2 marks out of 2

Testing – 7 marks

Describe your testing – 4 marks

- Print out the results of a test. (This can be a fairly straightforward search matching one of those that you outlined in your Analysis section. The search will need to be relevant and not just concocted for the purpose of performing a search.)
- Write a description of the test.

    If you get this far you will get 1 mark out of 4

- Print out the results of a minimum of two tests.
- Describe the tests and what you are trying to achieve.

    For example you may perform two of the searches which you wrote about in your design section. You will write about what you are trying to find as well as writing down the search conditions you are using. You will need to make sure that the two tests are different. There will need to be different conditions used and different data types which tested. It would seem sensible to perform comparison operations on numeric fields. It would also be appropriate to use conditions such as starts with, contains etc. with text fields.

If you get this far you will get 2 marks out of 4

- Perform searches on your database to prove that it works.
- Include validation routines to prove you have thoroughly tested your database or spreadsheet etc. (A simple validation check would be a range check on the rental price field. It will be necessary to change variables in your spreadsheet to test that. It will be necessary to use different formats of standard letters to test that aspect. You will provide written descriptions of each test together with expected results and actual results.)

If you get this far you will get 3 marks out of 4

- Get users to test your solution. (This can be done by the actual video shop manager or somebody acting the role of the video shop manager.)
- Get critical feedback from the user (otherwise you may not be awarded the mark. It is best to produce a response sheet, on which the users can put their comments down.)
- Ask about each aspect of your solution and how easy it was for the person to use.
- Include questions about whether or not the different aspects of the solution did actually work as intended.

If you get this far you will get 4 marks out of 4

Describe the results – 3 marks
For every search you have done on the database

- Write out what you expect the results to be
- Show printouts of the actual results.
- Do this for every test you performed on the database.

If you get this far you will get 1 mark out of 3

- Comment on the actual results when compared with the expected results.
  Quite often there will be very little comment as the actual results will be identical to the expected results. There will be occasions when this is not the case because:
  - the wrong comparison operator was used when searching a database, *or*
  - you made mistakes when entering the data *or*
  - the wrong formulae was typed into a spreadsheet *or*
  - the wrong variable names were used in a standard letter.
    etc.

If you get this far you will get 2 marks out of 3

- Explain your choice of data. (You will have typed data in to your database or spreadsheet etc. and now you have to explain why you chose it. If part of your testing involved the use of validation routines then you will need to have included some invalid data in with your ordinary data. You will need to explain how you included some data which would be printed out as a result of a particular test etc.)

If you get this far you will get 3 marks out of 3

User documentation – 7 marks

Show a potential user how to enter, amend and save data – 2 marks

- Produce a user guide which will allow somebody reading it to enter and save data (how to load your database, how to enter the details of a new video or how to load your spreadsheet and how to type in new prices).
- Produce a user guide which will allow somebody reading it to save data. (Describe how to save the work after data has been entered.)

If you get this far you will get 1 mark out of 2

- Produce a user guide which enables a competent user to add new records.
- Produce a user guide which will allow them to change data and then save the work.
- Cover each piece of software used.
- Use screen dumps to illustrate your work so that the user guide is easy to follow.

If you get this far you will get 2 marks out of 2

Show a potential user how to process and output data – 3 marks

- Provide a guide to a user showing them how to use your solution. (For this mark you need to show how to perform a search on the videos database or calculations on the prices spreadsheet. In addition, you need to show the user how to print out the results of the searches or calculations.)

If you get this far you will get 1 mark out of 3

- Produce descriptions of how to perform searches on the database, how to do calculations on your spreadsheet, and how to generate standard letters.
- Give easy to follow instructions on how to print out the results of the searches, calculations etc.
- Use an example of the processing you identified in your analysis section under the heading 'Identify the inputs, outputs and processing required'.
- Include screen dumps to illustrate the guide.

If you get this far you will get 2 marks out of 3

- Produce a user guide which, in addition to the above, covers other aspects of the solution.
- Show how to perform a variety of searches on the database. (If your solution includes several aspects of the problem, show how to perform calculations on the spreadsheet, how to produce different types of standard letter and how to produce different forms of output in terms of graphs and different layouts.)
- Show how to use all the output formats which you created in your implementation.

If you get this far you will get 3 marks out of 3

Show a potential user how to avoid problems – 2 marks

- Write down at least two errors that the user should avoid when using the system. (Do not copy out the trouble-shooting guide to the software or the hardware. This is meant to be advice to the user about **your system**.)

For example, one error you could mention is what happens if someone were to type in the wrong search conditions. They will need to be careful when typing in the search conditions. If they misspell the name of a customer or video they will get the wrong output.

If you get this far you will get 1 mark out of 2

- In addition to what you did for 1 mark, describe ways these errors can be corrected. (One of the simplest methods is verification. Before carrying out a query the user should be encouraged to read through what they have typed in. They should compare it to what they have written down. They should be encouraged to write down their queries before typing them in and then correcting them if mistakes are still noticed.)

If you get this far you will get 2 marks out of 2

Evaluation – 4 marks

Evaluate the solution – 4 marks

- Write down simple statements about what the solution can do. Write down such things as:
  - the videos database contains data about videos and allows you to search for information about all the videos directed by a particular director;
  - the customer database contains data about the customers and allows you to search for information about which customer has a particular video;
    etc.
- Make a list of all the things the solution can do.

If you get this far you will get 1 mark out of 4

- Compare what the solution can do with how the problem was outlined in the analysis section.
- Write about the user's requirements of the solution.
- Give examples of how you feel these requirements have been met.

  For example, one of the user's requirements might have been to have printouts of all the overdue videos. You will write this down and say that your testing shows that this has been achieved. You will need to point out where this test is written about e.g. 'the test on page 24 shows this'.

If you get this far you will get 2 marks out of 4

- List the features of your design and compare each feature with the solution you have produced.
  There will be parts of your design which have not worked out.
- Describe how you could improve your solution so these problems could be overcome.

  For example, the videos database might have produced incorrect results when searching for particular categories. This could be that different words might have been used for the same category e.g. 'light entertainment' and 'musical'. To overcome this problem a multichoice field or lookup list could be used.

If you get this far you will get 3 marks out of 4

- Include comments from users of the system.
- Describe how improvements might be made to the solution to allow for their comments.

> For example it might be that a user might find that they often have difficulty typing in the names of customers because they are not good typists. You may now suggest that it would be a good idea to give every customer a four-digit reference number. This should make it easier for the user to type.
>
> *If you get this far you will get 4 marks out of 4*

Section F

Exam preparation

This section will help you when the time comes to sit the exam. We will look at the type of questions you will be asked as well as some of the special words used. You might not realise that the word syllabus is no longer used. What used to be the syllabus is now called the *specification*.

Designing exam papers

The people who make up the examination papers have to follow a few basic rules. They have to

- cover a wide range of the specification but not every single item every year;
- avoid concentration on one particular area of the specification;
- meet the needs of the assessment objectives given in the specification;
- make sure everyone can read and understand what is being asked for;
- design questions that can be marked correctly and in the same way by the markers.

Questions often target a particular grade and usually the easy ones come first.

The examples given show a number of factors that must be taken into account when answering an examination question. The examples are often taken from real examination papers but in some cases have been changed to emphasise a specific point.

Revision

You may remember all you have been taught but may need a period before the examination to go over your work. Some of the work will be from notes you have written and some from a textbook. There are some general guidelines for revision.

1. You need to start your revision early – perhaps when the coursework has been handed in if not before.
2. Plan the revision by taking the number of weeks (less one maybe to account for a lost week and unforeseen events) and dividing the work into manageable segments. ICT will probably not be your only subject but make sure it gets an equal amount of time with the other subjects.
3. Make sure you have worked through all the past examination papers.
4. Make sure you have got the mark schemes for all the past examination papers.
5. Make sure you have written the answers in the way they are expected.

Examination technique

Mark schemes contain a list of acceptable answers. However, whilst the writers of the questions on the question paper and the answers in the mark scheme have to follow the rules provided by the specification (used to be called the syllabus) the answers you give may be outside what is in the specification.

EXAMPLE

E1 There are many reasons for using computer modelling. One reason is to reduce cost. State two other reasons.

Reason 1 _____

_____

Reason 2 _____

_____

(OCR GCSE June 2000)

A1 **Too time consuming to build many physical models.**

Too dangerous to build the real thing.

The mark scheme may have a list of acceptable answers. However you write down that 'Variables can be changed easily to see the effects of any change in output'. The answer you give is just as correct as those listed as acceptable answers and so your answer should be given the credit. However this is quite rare since the mark schemes cover all the correct answers.

Sometimes the question will tell you how many answers are required. You should not give more, or less, than the required number of answers.

EXAMPLE

E2 State two **reasons why it is better to use automatic data-logging equipment rather than recording the data manually.**

Reason 1 _____

_____

Reason 2 _____

_____

(OCR GCSE June 2000)

A2 **Two from:**

Not having to remember to take the readings.

More accurate readings.

Being able to plot a graph directly as the readings are taken.

Safer to do with remote data logging.

Accurate timing of data collection.

Accurate values being read from the experiment.

Can be left for a very long time without human intervention.

Can be set to time very short periods.

Can be set to start at a future time.

Can be set to record for a specific length of time.

Can be set to record one event when another event takes place.

Can record more than one event at once.

The mark scheme asks for any **two** of the answers.

Obviously if you state only a single reason then the mark for the second reason cannot be given. Also if you give more than two reasons then you have wasted your time since you can not gain more than two marks for the question.

Some questions will ask you to give a longer answer. You would be advised to look at the mark required by the question and to make at least that number of different points when answering the question.

EXAMPLE

E3 Discuss with conclusions the benefits and drawbacks of using electronic ankle tagging on people convicted of a crime.   **[5]**

(*OCR GCSE June 2000*)

The five marks given to the question points you to the number of different statements in the answer. You would be advised to make at least this number of statements in the answer.

Using source material

You may have to use a scenario created by the question in order to provide an answer.

Questions such as 'With reference to' or 'Relating your answers to ABC plc' give you specific instructions and answers to questions containing these phrases should be related to the scenario.

EXAMPLE

E4 A computer model of a bridge has been designed. Describe the stages of implementing and evaluating the computer model.

(*OCR GCSE June 2000*)

There might then follow a number of questions related to this scenario. The scenario may reflect a real situation or not as the case may be. Even if you have never come across the given scenario it should be used since this is a statement of how things are done at the present. Each question should be answered within the context of the scenario. General answers should not be given. In the above case all answers should be related to the model of the bridge.

Expressing an opinion

More difficult questions, where a large number of marks are available, expect you to express (and maybe justify) an opinion.

These are more open-ended questions and you need to think carefully about how to structure your answers to obtain all the marks available.

A simple structure might be to first look at how many marks are available for the question and then make sure that you make this many different points in your answer. Do not labour the same point. You may want to bullet or number the parts of your answer to emphasise all the different parts.

The use of examples and fully reasoned responses considering all aspects of the question asked is often essential if you are to convince the examiner that you understand the topic.

At no time will a question be asked such as 'What do you think...' This is because the answer must always be correct since it is your opinion!

What not to do when answering examination questions

There are a number of things which you should avoid when answering any examination question.

- Only give the number of answers asked for.
- Do not make the same point over and over again.
- Do not write a long list of answers and hope that one of them is correct. Often only the first member of a list is taken as the your answer.
- Do not waffle.

- Do not make a disadvantage the opposite of an advantage.
- If asked to ring the correct answers then ring only the number asked for. Ringing too many will only lose marks.
- If you do not know the answer to a question (where you are asked to ring the correct answer) then ring something. You might be correct. Marks are not deducted for wrong answers.
- Never leave out a question.
- Make sure you have answered all the questions. Go through the answer book to make sure every page has been answered.
- Do not give general answers that could apply to anything to a question relating to a specific topic.
- Try not to write more than can be written on the lines provided. Use the number of lines as a guide to how much is expected.
- Do not repeat what was provided in the question.
- Do not rewrite the question as the answer.
- If the question excludes something from the answer do not write about it.
- Do not use trade names in your answer. For example, talk about a 'word processor' and not the specific product.
- Read the question carefully and make sure you understand what is being asked of you, then answer the question. Do not give an answer that is not asked for just because you spotted a few key items that you know about. It wastes valuable time and does not gain you any marks.

The most important words in a question (the key words)

The beginning of a question tells you what you have to do to answer the question. Often certain Key Words are used to tell you what has to be done. These key words are state, give, describe, explain and discuss. Each of the words provides an indication of what is required of you.

Questions where you have to make a choice

Sometimes questions ask you to choose from a list of given answers.

EXAMPLE

E5 Name the objects A, B, C and D using words from the list.

A   B

C

D

CD-ROM	computer	disk drive	floppy disc
hard disc	keyboard	modem	mouse
printer	plotter	scanner	screen

A _____   B _____

C _____   D _____

(OCR GCSE June 1999)

You should not give an answer that is not in the list. No extra credit would be given if you make up your own answer.

State

You have to make a straightforward statement of fact. This is probably the only time a one-word answer would provide an acceptable answer.

● EXAMPLE

E6 State what type of printer the company would need to give a high quality graphics output.

_____

(OCR GCSE June 2000)

Correct answers you could state are a laser printer, ink-jet printer or a bubble jet printer. A single phrase like these in the list is all that is required. Other correct answers may be possible and you would gain marks from these.

Give

You have to provide the marker with more information than a mere single word statement.

● EXAMPLE

E7 The company decides to sell the game on a CD-ROM instead of many floppy discs. Give three reasons why it would do this.

Reason 1 _____

_____

Reason 2 _____

_____

Reason 3 _____

_____

(OCR GCSE June 2000)

A7 Three from:
   More difficult to copy.
   Larger video clips.

Easier to install from CD-ROM.

Sell better because people think only good programs come on CD-ROM.

Other companies do it.

Cheaper to produce than many floppy discs.

(Do not include capacity of store.)

Just writing the one word answer 'cheaper' or 'capacity' down would not gain any marks since you have not said what the 'cheaper' or 'capacity' is related to. The 'capacity' answer would only be correct if you stated that there was more stored in a smaller space. Other correct answers may be possible and you would gain marks from these.

Describe

You have to show the marker your ability to describe an answer that is appropriate to the question and the context within which the question is phrased.

EXAMPLE

E8 **State two features of a spreadsheet which are particularly suited to modelling.**

Feature 1 _____

_____

Feature 2 _____

_____

(OCR GCSE June 2000)

The answer should relate everything to the ability of the spreadsheet to perform modelling tasks. Features of a spreadsheet, such as rows and columns, are not relevant to the question. Modelling is related to trying to predict future events.

EXAMPLE

E9 **Two of the features of good software are that it is free of any bugs and has a good user manual. Describe what other features the user would expect to find in good software.**

_____

_____

_____

_____

_____

_____

(OCR GCSE June 2000)

You would be awarded marks for stating what the feature was e.g. on-line help and for describing what it was used for e.g. looking up explanations of techniques without having to look in a manual. Other correct answers may be possible and you would gain marks from these.

Explain

You have to write down both advantages and disadvantages to show both sides of an argument in the given situation. It must be clear what are considered to be the advantages and the disadvantages. The question is looking for reasoning from you.

EXAMPLE

E10 **Explain how the introduction of the new computer system will affect the staff and pupils.**

_____

_____

_____

_____

_____

_____

(OCR GCSE June 1999)

Your answers should include

Advantages:

- faster access to data
- giving students more access to computer hardware

Disadvantages:

- the expense in buying the hardware
- training of staff/pupils
- re-organisation of the timetable
- upheaval during installation

You should give an answer that will give the good and bad points of a situation.

Information provided as advantages should not be repeated as negative facts under disadvantages.

EXAMPLE

E11 Explain the advantages and disadvantages of digital and analogue watches. You might write:

Advantage: **The digital watch does not need winding up.**

Disadvantage: **The analogue watch needs winding up.**

Other correct answers may be possible and you would gain marks from these.

Discuss

A discussion is an extension of an explain-type answer but you also have to include a relevant conclusion.

EXAMPLE

E12 Discuss the relative advantages and disadvantages of electronic mail (e-mail) and fax to communicate information around the world.

(OCR GCSE June 1999)

The answers expected include a discussion of both the advantages and disadvantages. Themes for discussion are:

Email

Advantages

- Fast communication to anywhere in the world.
- Can send large electronic documents very quickly.
- Is very cheap – local telephone call rates.

Disadvantages

- User must connect to the computer to get the messages.
- Not everyone has electronic mail.
- Some people worried about security.

- Cannot send original material – documents.
- Viruses attached to e-mails.

Fax

Advantages

- More secure way of sending credit card details.
- Data not saved on intermediate computers.

Disadvantages

- Paper may not be in the receiving machine.
- Not everyone has a fax machine.
- Cannot send original material.

with a statement in conclusion which gives your view. This statement can be either in favour of the situation or against as long as it has a reasoned explanation. Other correct answers may be possible and you would gain marks from these.

Sitting the examination

There are a number of things you should do both before and during the examination.

1. Make sure you have all the correct equipment for the examination. You will not need a flowchart template or a calculator. However you will need a pen.
2. Check if you are required to wear any specific school uniform to the examination. You do not want to lose all those years of hard work simply because you are not dressed correctly.
3. Do not waste time during the examination by going to the toilet. The time you take will not be added on to the time for the examination. You will just have lost it. Go before the examination starts.
4. Do not take anything that could distract others into the examination room. An example might be mobile telephones or pagers.
5. There might be a clock at the front or back of the examination room. Use this to make sure you have left enough time to do all the questions. If there is no clock make sure you have a watch with you.
6. Remember that if you leave out the answer to a question you cannot gain any marks from it. You may get some marks even from a partial answer.
7. In some cases there will be lots of examinations going on at the same time. Make sure you have got the correct examination paper from the correct board. You can make sure of this by having your examination entry slip with you so that you can check the details.
8. When you are allowed to open the paper quickly skim through it to make sure there are the correct number of pages and no pages have been left blank (except those that are meant to be blank – usually at the end).
9. There is no set order in which you have to answer the questions so when you are reading the paper at the beginning put a mark by each question you know you know the answer to and do those first.
10. Look for the key words in the question (see above). These will tell you how much you have to do.

11. If you have run out of space to write your answer on the paper then ask for some more.

12. If you have more to write but there are no more lines then continue the answer at the back or on a new sheet of paper. Make sure you show where the answer is.

13. If you want to change an answer then cross out what you have written and write it again at the end.

14. If you finish the examination and there is still some time left then re-read all your answers to make sure they are as correct as possible. You can not leave the examination room so use your time usefully.

Index